Lecture Notes
in Business Information Proce:

T0237894

Series Editors

Wil van der Aalst
  Eindhoven Technical University, The Netherlands
John Mylopoulos
  University of Trento, Italy
Norman M. Sadeh
  Carnegie Mellon University, Pittsburgh, PA, USA
Michael J. Shaw
  University of Illinois, Urbana-Champaign, IL, USA
Clemens Szyperski
  Microsoft Research, Redmond, WA, USA

Christof Weinhardt   Stefan Luckner
Jochen Stößer (Eds.)

Designing E-Business Systems

Markets, Services, and Networks

7th Workshop on E-Business, WEB 2008
Paris, France, December 13, 2008
Revised Selected Papers

 Springer

Volume Editors

Christof Weinhardt
Stefan Luckner
Jochen Stößer
Universität Karlsruhe (TH)
Lehrstuhl für Informationsbetriebswirtschaftslehre
Englerstr. 14, 76131 Karlsruhe, Germany
E-mail: {weinhardt,luckner,stoesser}@iism.uni-karlsruhe.de

Library of Congress Control Number: 2009930312

ACM Computing Classification (1998): J.1, H.3.5, J.2, C.3

ISSN   1865-1348
ISBN-10   3-642-01255-8 Springer Berlin Heidelberg New York
ISBN-13   978-3-642-01255-6 Springer Berlin Heidelberg New York

springer.com

© Springer-Verlag Berlin Heidelberg 2009
Printed in Germany

Typesetting: Camera-ready by author, data conversion by Scientific Publishing Services, Chennai, India
Printed on acid-free paper   SPIN: 12661350   06/3180   5 4 3 2 1 0

Preface

The 7th Workshop on e-Business (WeB 2008) was held on December 13, 2008, in Paris. As a pre-ICIS workshop, it provided an open forum for e-business researchers and practitioners to share research findings, explore novel ideas, discuss success stories and lessons learned, and map out major challenges with regard to the design of e-business systems.

The workshop theme was "Designing e-Business Systems: Markets, Services and Networks." With WeB 2008 having been located in Europe, we wanted to highlight the increasing importance of the design science approach for information systems research, which has a long tradition in the European IS community.

We received a large number of submissions that addressed key issues specific to the workshop theme as well as e-business in general. Based on a rigorous review process, a total of 31 full papers and 30 research-in-progress papers were accepted for presentation at the workshop, covering a broad range of technical, empirical, managerial, and economic aspects of e-business. Of the 31 full papers, 17 selected papers are contained in this volume of *Lecture Notes in Business Information Processing*. We hope that you will find them an interesting read and that you will benefit from the authors' fine contributions.

We acknowledge the great contributions by the following individuals for organizing and managing 17 focused sessions at the workshop:

- Mu Xia: E-Business Standards
- Jan Krämer and Stefan Seifert: Economic Modeling of Telecommunication Markets and Services
- Ravi Sen and Chandra Subramaniam: Economics of E-Commerce
- Dirk Neumann and Omer F. Rana: Grid Economics
- Clemens van Dinther and Christoph Mayer: IS in eEnergy
- Gregory Kersten and Stefan Klein: Market and Service Engineering
- Tuure Tuunanen: Mobile Technologies
- Wolf Ketter and Jörg Müller: Multiagent-Based Business Process and Supply-Chain Management
- Victoria Y. Yoon, Rahul Singh and Stephen Russell: Multiagent System, Semantic Web, and Context-Aware Computing
- John Zhang: Organizational Implications of Electronic Markets
- Andreas Gräfe and Martin Spann: Prediction Markets
- Samuel Fosso Wamba and Ygal Bendavid: RFID and Supply Chain Management
- Raj Sharman and Daniel Zeng: Security Informatics
- Nanda Kumar: Social Networks
- Raquel Benbunan-Fich: Social Computing Applications
- Xiao Fang and Lin Lin: Web Intelligence
- Minder Chen and Dongsong Zhang: Web Services and Architectures

We would further like to acknowledge the contributions and support of the conference Co-chairs Ting-Peng Liang and Michael J. Shaw who gave us numerous comments, suggestions and support in preparing WeB 2008, keynote speakers Eric van Heck, Vikas Krishna and Andrew B. Whinston, Local Arrangements Chair Frank Goethals, International Liaison Chairs Steven Miller, Fethi Rabhi and Michael Chau, as well as all the Program Committee members and reviewers. We also thank our sponsors, the Karlsruhe Institute of Technology (KIT), Germany; AIS SIGeBIZ; Electronic Commerce Research Center, National Sun Yat-Sen University, Taiwan, R.O.C.; Center for IT and e-Business Management, University of Illinois, Urbana-Champaign; Institute of Information Systems and Management (IISM), Universität Karlsruhe (TH), Germany; IESEG School of Management, France.

March 2009   Christof Weinhardt
                                                                    Stefan Luckner
                                                                    Jochen Stößer

Organization

WeB 2008 was organized by the Institute of Information Systems and Management, Universität Karlsruhe (TH), in cooperation with AIS SIGeBIZ.

Organizing Committee

Conference Chairs	Ting-Peng Liang, National Sun Yat-Sen University
	Michael J. Shaw, University of Illinois at Urbana-Champaign
Program Chairs	Christof Weinhardt, Universität Karlsruhe (TH)
	Stefan Luckner, Universität Karlsruhe (TH)
Review and Publication Chair	Jochen Stößer, Universität Karlsruhe (TH)
Local Chair	Frank Goethals, IESEG School of Management
International Liaisons	Michael Chau, The University of Hong Kong
	Steven Miller, Singapore Management University
	Fethi Rabhi, The University of New South Wales

Program Committee

Raquel Benbunan-Fich	The City University of New York
Ygal Bendavid	Ecole Polytechnique de Montreal
Jamal Bentahar	Concordia University
Martin Bichler	Technische Universität München
Minder Chen	California State University Channel Islands
Kenny Cheng	University of Florida
Tsang-Hsiang Cheng	Southern Taiwan University of Technology
Clemens van Dinther	Forschungszentrum Informatik Karlsruhe
Torsten Eymann	Universität Bayreuth
Ming Fan	University of Washington
Xiao Fang	Toledo University
Judith Gebauer	University of Illinois, Urbana-Champaign
Andreas Gräfe	Forschungszentrum Karlsruhe
Paul Hu	University of Utah
San-Yih Hwang	National Sun Yat-sen University
Patrick C. K. Hung	University of Ontario Institute of Technology
Gregory Kersten	Concordia University
Wolf Ketter	Erasmus University Rotterdam
Stefan Klein	Westfälische Wilhelms-Universität Münster
Jan Krämer	Universität Karlsruhe (TH)
Nanda Kumar	The City University of New York

Hsiangchu Lai	National Sun Yat-sen University
Steffen Lamparter	Universität Karlsruhe (TH)
Karl Reiner Lang	The City University of New York
Divakaran Liginlal	University of Wisconsin-Madison
Fu-ren Lin	National Tsing Hua University
Lin Lin	Lehigh University
Christoph Mayer	OFFIS Oldenburg
Jrg Mller	TU Clausthal
Matt Nelson	Illinois State University
Dirk Neumann	Universität Freiburg
Manoj Parameswaran	Santa Clara University
Selwyn Piramuthu	University of Florida
Omer F. Rana	Cardiff University
Stephen Russell	George Washington University
Gerhard Satzger	Universität Karlsruhe (TH)
Stefan Seifert	Universität Karlsruhe (TH)
Ravi Sen	Texas A&M University
Raj Sharman	University of Buffalo, SUNY
Olivia Sheng	University of Utah
Rahul Singh	University of North Carolina at Greensboro
Martin Spann	Universität Passau
Chandra Subramaniam	University of North Carolina, Charlotte
Vijay Sugumaran	Oakland University
Stefan Tai	Universität Karlsruhe (TH)
Tuure Tuunanen	Auckland University
Daniel Veit	Universität Mannheim
Samuel Fosso Wamba	The Ecole Polytechnique de Montreal
Chih-Ping Wei	National Sun Yat-sen University
Andrew B. Whinston	University of Texas at Austin
Mu Xia	University of Illinois, Urbana-Champaign
Victoria Y. Yoon	University of Maryland, Baltimore County
Daniel Zeng	University of Arizona
Dongsong Zhang	University of Maryland
Han Zhang	Georgia Tech
John Zhang	University of Connecticut
Xianfeng Zhang	Xi'an Jiaotong University
Leon Zhao	University of Arizona

Focused Session Chairs

- **E-Business Standards**
  Mu Xia (University of Illinois at Urbana-Champaign)
- **Economic Modeling of Telecommunication Markets and Services**
  Jan Krämer (Universität Karlsruhe (TH))
  Stefan Seifert (Universität Karlsruhe (TH))

- **Economics of E-Commerce**
  Ravi Sen (Texas A&M University)
  Chandra Subramaniam (University of North Carolina at Charlotte)
- **Grid Economics**
  Dirk Neumann (Albert-Ludwigs-Universität Freiburg)
  Omer F. Rana (Cardiff University)
- **IS in eEnergy**
  Clemens van Dinther (Forschungszentrum Informatik Karlsruhe)
  Christoph Mayer (OFFIS Oldenburg)
- **Market and Service Engineering**
  Gregory Kersten (Concordia University)
  Stefan Klein (Universität Münster)
- **Mobile Technologies**
  Tuure Tuunanen (Auckland University)
- **Multiagent-Based Business Process and Supply Chain Management**
  Wolf Ketter (Erasmus University)
  Jörg Müller (Technische Universität Clausthal)
- **Multiagent System, Semantic Web, and Context-Aware Computing**
  Victoria Y. Yoon (University of Maryland Baltimore County)
  Rahul Singh (University of North Carolina at Greensboro)
  Stephen Russell (George Washington University)
- **Organizational Implications of Electronic Markets**
  John Zhang (University of Connecticut)
- **Prediction Markets**
  Andreas Gräfe (Forschungszentrum Karlsruhe)
  Martin Spann (Universität Passau)
- **RFID and Supply Chain Management**
  Samuel Fosso Wamba (Ecole Polytechnique de Montreal)
  Ygal Bendavid (Ecole Polytechnique de Montreal)
- **Security Informatics**
  Raj Sharman (University at Buffalo, SUNY)
  Daniel Zeng (University of Arizona)
- **Social Networks**
  Nanda Kumar (The City University of New York)
- **Social Computing Applications**
  Raquel Benbunan-Fich (The City University of New York)
- **Web Intelligence**
  Xiao Fang (Toledo University)
  Lin Lin (Lehigh University)
- **Web Services and Architectures**
  Minder Chen (California State University Channel Islands)
  Dongsong Zhang (University of Maryland Baltimore County)

Sponsoring Institutions

The Organizing Committee gratefully acknowledges the sponsoring of the following insitutions:

- Karlsruhe Institute of Technology (KIT)
- AIS SIGeBIZ
- National Sun Yat-Sen University
- Center for IT and e-Business Management, University of Illinois at Urbana-Champaign
- Institute of Information Systems and Management (IISM), Universität Karlsruhe (TH)
- IESEG School of Management

Table of Contents

Virtual Communities

Web Intelligence

IDEM: A Prediction Market for Idea Management

Efthimios Bothos[1], Dimitris Apostolou[2], and Gregoris Mentzas[1]

[1] Institute of Communication and Computer Systems, National Technical University of Athens,
Iroon Polytechniou 9 Zografou Athens Greece 157 80
`mpthim@mail.ntua.gr, gmentzas@mail.ntua.gr`
[2] University of Piraeus, Karaoli & Dimitriou St. 80 Piraeus Greece 185 34
`dapost@mail.ntua.gr`

Abstract. Collaborative systems and methods are used within corporate environments to support innovation and management of new ideas. The aggregation of innovation-related information from a community of users is a non-trivial task that requires the use of specialized collaborative systems and methods. In this paper we explore the use of Prediction Markets for community-based idea management and present IDEM, a software system that is used for generating and evaluating new ideas utilizing the concept of Prediction Markets. In addition to trading, IDEM supports users submit new ideas, rate and comment on them. Academic experiments and industrial pilots reveal the perceived usefulness of the system.

Keywords: prediction markets, community innovation, idea management.

1 Introduction

Contemporary research on innovation stresses the importance of collaboration of diverse stakeholders (see e.g. [1] and [2]). Moreover, the need to ensure the participation of many employees in the innovation processes of an organization has been also emphasized in the literature [3,] [4]. It has been shown that the use of cross-functional teams with diverse occupational and intellectual backgrounds increases the likelihood of combining knowledge in novel ways [5]. In such teams, the amount and variety of information available to members is increased, enabling the creation and consequent evaluation of different ideas from a number of different perspectives [6].

Adamides and Karacapilidis [7] provide an overview of information technology tools for collaboration in the innovation process. They distinguish between tools that aim to facilitate and to increase the productivity of exchange of ideas through shared workspaces [8], [9], systems for the controlled execution of routine sequences of work tasks associated to idea development projects [10] and Group Decision Support Systems that take into account explicitly the processes of idea creation, decision-making, negotiation and argumentation. However, existing tools either aim to increase the productivity of communication among the actors involved without implementing a strategy for achieving shared understanding about the innovation process or rely on heavy use of modeling formalisms for representing and enacting collaboration routines and decision rationales that are time-consuming to implement and cumbersome for non-experienced users to take advantage of.

C. Weinhardt, S. Luckner, and J. Stößer (Eds.): WEB 2008, LNBIP 22, pp. 1–13, 2009.
© Springer-Verlag Berlin Heidelberg 2009

The global build-up of the World Wide Web has made possible that anyone with a computer and Internet access may explore, join, and contribute to any Web community at any time. This new web computing paradigm is often attributed to the "Web 2.0 era" of services and applications that let users easily share opinions and resources [11]. An exemplary form of this new trend is "collective intelligence". According to Malone and Klein [12] collective intelligence is the synergistic and cumulative channeling of the vast human and technical resources now available over the internet, while Kapetanios [13] defines collective intelligence as "human–computer systems in which machines enable the collection and harvesting of large amounts of human-generated knowledge, while enabling emergent knowledge, i.e., computation and inference over the collected information, leading to answers, discoveries, or other results that are not found in the human contributions".

In this paper we focus on a typical example of collective intelligence, internet-based Prediction Markets (PMs). These are virtual stock markets whose purpose is to collect, aggregate and evaluate information [14], [15], [16]. Participants trade on contracts that represent future events, and upon market closure an index, the price of these virtual stocks, incorporates the available information with respect to that event.

PMs can be used in the innovation process for harnessing the collective intelligence of employees inside organizations. As reviewed in this paper however, although several tools exist for deploying PMs, none of them corresponds to the particularities of the idea management process. First they do not fully support user feedback, and in most cases user participation is limited to trading. Second they are configured to aggregate information regarding well defined future events. When PMs are utilized for idea management, the underlying contracts are correlated to the potential of success of the ideas. This situation creates uncertainty since some ideas may never be realized and the future event may never happen. The third issue is the limited information they provide as output. Besides market price, analysis of other data such as transactions and user participation may reveal useful information.

These limitations urged us to develop a web–based software tool named IDEM, which is designed to facilitate the use of PMs within companies in the idea management process. When designing it, we took into consideration that such a tool should allow the generation of new ideas and should be able to record feedback from the market participants. Furthermore it should be flexible enough in its configuration options to allow the formation of various usage scenarios, adapted to the needs of different companies.

The rest of the paper proceeds as follows. Section 2 reviews the use of PMs in the context of idea management and outlines the use of IDEM in this process. In section 3 we describe the functionalities our tool supports in the context of a trial carried out to test IDEM. We continue with a report on the results of our trial. In section 5 we focus on the idea evaluation process and discuss how important methods, including PMs, address its particularities. This paper concludes with a discussion of future research directions for enhancing our tool and for further studying its use empirically.

2 Prediction Markets for Idea Management

PMs are being used by many companies to support decisions by gathering disperse information. Examples range from identifying product launch dates to determining future amount of sales [15], [16]. The majority of the cases have provided useful results. This success triggered researchers to apply them in the context of innovation management. Early results are promising as they show that PMs conform well to the restrictions of the idea evaluation process whereas with the proper design they can support the idea generation phase of idea management as well [17], [18]. Past research has provided evidence that the quality of new ideas is influenced positively by the participation of many employees. It has been shown that the use of cross-functional teams with diverse occupational and intellectual backgrounds increases the likelihood of combining knowledge in novel ways [5]. In such teams, the amount and variety of information available to members is increased, enabling the creation and consequent evaluation of different ideas from a number of different perspectives [6].

At least two large experiments with PMs in the context of innovation management have been conducted in large corporations: one in General Electric [18] and another in a large German B2B company [17]. Both were successful and showed encouraging results. In both experiments PMs managed to attract a fairly high number of participants across several departments, which resulted in the incorporation of the opinion of the many in the final result. It is important that the evaluation results were compared with existing methods and in both cases a similar outcome was observed. Meanwhile, several platforms supporting the use of PMs in an innovation management context have emerged. Platforms from Spigit (www.spigit.com), InnovateUs (www.innovateus.net), VirtualVentures (www.virtualventures.com) provide, in ASP mode, the means for employees to participate through intranets or the Internet in stock markets of ideas.

As part of our research we have created IDEM, a PM platform for idea management. The architecture of our system is depicted in Figure 1. We were motivated by the fact that innovation management poses specific challenges to prediction markets that are not fully addressed by existing platforms. First, they are configured to aggregate information regarding well defined future events. When PMs are utilized for idea management, the underlying contracts are correlated to the potential of success of the ideas. This situation creates uncertainty since some ideas may never be realized and the future event may never happen. Second, they have not been specifically designed to support different usage scenarios besides idea evaluation while in most cases user participation is limited to trading. The third issue is the limited information they provide as output. Besides market price, analysis of other data such as transactions and user participation may reveal useful information.

PMs initial context of application was for predicting well defined events (e.g. who will be the winner in the next political elections?) that resolve at some point in time. In the aforementioned applications participants are compensated based on the outcome of the underlying events. Such conditions cannot be achieved when evaluating ideas since some ideas may never be realized and the future event may never happen. Since such an exogenous event cannot be used to evaluate ideas at market closure and rank them accordingly, in IDEM we rank ideas based on the Volume Weighted Average Price value (VWAP) [19] which helps to obtain an accurate view of the traders' preferences by taking into consideration not only the price but also the volume of the trading actions. Furthermore we compensate participants using an external valuation

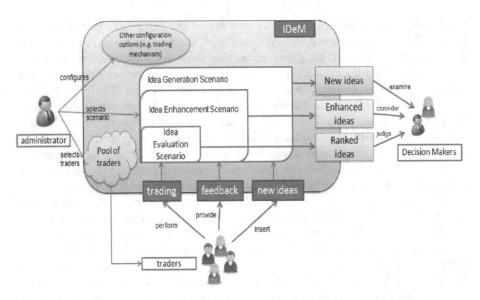

Fig. 1. Representative Idea Management Scenarios and IDeM Support

methodology. The final valuation of each idea derives from the average of the opinion of a set of experts and this valuation is used to calculate the value of the participants' portfolios. The winner is declared the one that has the highest portfolio.

IDEM was designed to be able to support several usage scenarios within the idea management process. The following three scenarios are representative of major innovation management processes:

- Idea generation. The purpose of this scenario is the generation of new ideas. The game like process of the PMs impels users to propose their ideas which are entered in the market. Trading occurs for all ideas, newly proposed and old. Participants are compensated not only according to their stock portfolio but also for their idea contributions.

- Idea enhancement. The purpose of this scenario is to enhance the ideas in the market. Market participants can invest on an idea and then contribute to it by e.g. questioning some aspects of the idea, suggesting idea improvements or changes according to their personal view. We have also implemented a variation of this scenario where ideas are posts in an 'idea evaluation blog'. Traders submit their proposals for enhancing/ extending ideas as 'comments' and all enhancement suggestions become tradable assets that participants may buy or sell. In this way decision makers benefit by collecting different views on enhancing existing ideas and by obtaining a ranked list of the proposed enhancements.

- Idea evaluation. The purpose of this scenario is the evaluation of new ideas. A market is setup with a number of new ideas and traders act as evaluators. They trade idea stocks in an effort to increase the value of their stock portfolio. Transactions are used to identify the most promising ideas. Explicit traders' feedback can be requested as well.

3 Trial Overview and System Walkthrough

In order to test the perceived usefulness and IDEM's ability to support collaborative idea management, we implemented a trial. The trial involved 31 post graduate students enrolled in a course on Group Decision Support Systems. During the course, subjects were introduced to the concepts and tools of group decision making. They were then asked to assume that they are employees of a venture capital firm and that they are about to collaboratively decide on an investment on one out of various alternative web 2.0 technologies and applications. Our subjects were not familiar with the concept of PMs although most had a basic knowledge of how stock exchanges operate. We conducted an introductory session for two hours where the main concepts of PMs and the functionalities of the software were explained.

Since we expected low liquidity of the market, we chose a Continuous Double Auction with Market Maker (CDAwMM) trading algorithm. In our case the system takes over the role of the Market Maker (MM) and is always ready to accept buy and sell orders at a certain price acting as an "always there" buyer and seller. A price function inspired from the Zocalo open source tool (http://sourceforge.net/ projects/zocalo) is utilized to simulate real life supply and demand conditions. The function follows a logarithmic rule that increases the MM's price when many are buying (high demand) and decreases it when many are selling. The original algorithm utilized a span of prices between 0 and 1 so we scaled it from 0 to 100 in order to make trading more intuitive. Moreover we configured the system so that one market contains many market makers, one for each idea-contract since in the Zocalo implementation each contract constitutes a separate market and therefore only one market maker was provided for each market.

To alleviate possible evaluation apprehension effects, participant contribution was anonymous. The market was open continuously for 3 weeks and each trader was initially allocated 10,000 imaginary monetary units. In addition to trading, subjects were also allowed to introduce new ideas from other sources (e.g. from Internet searches). The introduction of new ideas in the market was controlled by two appointed judges. The latter selected the most relevant to the problem space of the trial. The ideas that passed this test were introduced in the market as new ones. The starting trading price of all new ideas was set at 50 imaginary monetary units and the traders' portfolios were updated with 50 shares of each one. In the following we provide a short system walkthrough aiming to demonstrate how IDEM supports the three generic scenarios outlined in section 2, while the evaluation results of the trial are reported in the next section.

Before presenting the walkthrough from the trader's perspective, let us see which are the steps required by the administrator to set up the market environment. The Market Administrator logs in and sets up a new market and assigns traders. S/he selects the configuration options (i.e. trading mechanism), whether idea submissions by traders are allowed and the type of feedback traders can provide besides their market transactions. In our trial we selected the CDAwMM to be the trading mechanism, as mentioned above, and activated the option of adding new ideas. Furthermore we allowed the submission of comments to the ideas. The market was initially populated with 6 ideas (the Yahoo Answers - answers.yahoo.com -, the LinkedIn - www.linkedin.com -, the Feeds2 - www.feeds2.com -, the MyFilmz - myfilmz.net -, the Ta-Da Lists - www.tadalist.com - and the ToEat.com - www.toeat.com -) acting as an initial seed so that our subjects could understand the kind of ideas relevant to the problem space.

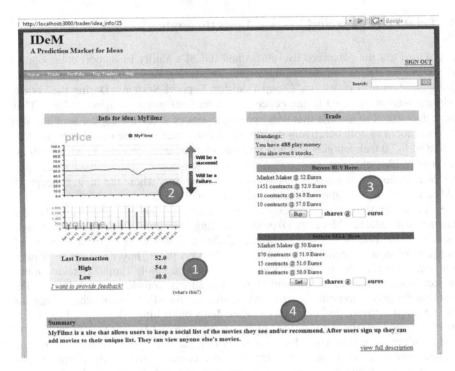

Fig. 2. Trading screen

From this step onwards traders log in and place their orders. Assume that a trader enters the system and selects the "MyFilmz" idea. The trading screen appears which displays various information as depicted in Fig. 2. The high, low and last trade prices are presented in section (1) of the screen. Graphs are used for the volume and price history, see section (2). Furthermore the trader can view the best four orders of the market book and enter her/his offers in section (3). In section (4) the description of the idea stock is given. Once having reviewed the available information our trader can buy stocks of the idea if s/he believes will be successful or sell stocks of the idea if s/he believes it will fail. New idea submission was allowed in our trial, hence a link to a relevant form was activated (screen 1 of Fig. 5). We chose to limit the mandatory information for a new idea in order to ease the submission so the mandatory information included a title, an abstract and a category which was selected from a predefined list.

Since the feedback option was activated, a hyperlink was provided leading traders to the feedback page through which they could submit comments. Traders occasionally accessed their portfolio where a list of the idea-contracts they own is presented. Traders can view their pending buy/sell offers and have the possibility to cancel them. During market operation the administrator monitors the course of the market, views newly proposed ideas and adds those that are considered adequate in the market. Upon market closure, s/he accesses a ranked list of the ideas in the market based on the VWAP. Further, s/he can view comments on ideas provided by traders.

4   Trial Results

An expert committee consisting of five professionals valuated all the idea contracts of our trial on a scale of 1 to 100 upon market closure. The mean price of the above valuations was the final value of the contracts and that price was used in the payoff function which produced the final portfolio value of each trader. The payoff function took into consideration the ideas that traders proposed. Those who proposed new ideas received a bonus of 10 extra shares of their ideas. The trader with the highest portfolio received a prize. A total of 1572 trading actions were recorded in the 3 weeks time frame and a total of 34 ideas were proposed. 26 were judged as adequate and were inserted in the market as new but not all of them were traded.

We evaluated our trial in terms of the ability of PMs as a method to support the generation of new ideas and their evaluation at the same time, and the ability of IDEM as a software to support the same tasks. The evaluation was performed with the use of questionnaires given to participants and the expert committee. A total of 15 questions were addressed to our traders and 5 questions to our experts. The participants' questionnaire gathered information regarding previous involvement of the subjects in innovation processes, their assessment of the PM methodology, the usability of our system and how the characteristics of our trial (e.g. anonymity) affected their behavior. As depicted in Fig. 3, participants found the game fairly interesting (65%) on a 5 point Likert scale while most of them (68%) would be willing to take part in a similar game in the future. With respect to the perceived usefulness of PMs in the business environment 80% of the participants agreed or highly agreed that PMs are useful. It is also important to mention that participation was found to be not time consuming. Regarding IDEM, the process of trading was found to be quite understandable (37% agreed, although 50% didn't have a strong opinion) and transitions between the

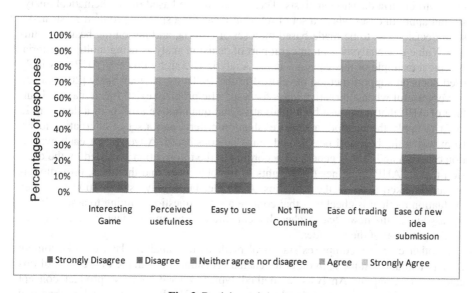

Fig. 3. Participants' Answers

various screens easy enough (80% provided positive feedback). Moreover the new idea submission procedure was considered easy to follow (74,1%).

The same experts who valuated the idea contracts were asked to review all the proposed ideas and assess whether their quality and number was adequate. In addition they evaluated the market outcome (ranked list of ideas) and provided feedback regarding the perceived usefulness of the method. The proposed ideas were found quite interesting (80% agreed) and yielded a positive answer when asked of the method's usefulness (80%). Furthermore a positive answer was provided when questioned about the possibility of using PMs in their business.

5 Discussion

In this section we provide a comparison of prominent methods for idea evaluation including PMs with respect to five different criteria. We focus only on idea evaluation since the primary use of PMs is to forecast the outcome of future events, in our case the potential of success of ideas. We present information regarding the type of ideas that each method can support and how each one behaves when the number of the ideas for evaluation increases. Moreover, we analyze the reasons that motivate and impel evaluators into participating in the process and we identify the number of evaluators contributing to the process. We also examine the type of feedback provided by each method to the innovator. A comparison of the idea evaluation methods examined is summarized in Table 1.

5.1 Idea Evaluation Methods

An important category of methods for new idea evaluation comprises methods that use multi-criteria decision analysis. These methods are based on mathematical analysis and apply in cases where a set of relevant ideas for a specific problem exists and a solid decision has to be made based on a set of criteria, and not on the basis of intuition. Value tree analysis is an integral part of decision analysis using multiple-criteria. A typical example of this category is the Analytic Hierarchy Process (AHP), a widely used decision support method developed in the 1980s by Thomas Saaty [20] and can be very useful when alternative ideas for a specific problem exist. It is a major advantage of AHP that it can use both qualitative and quantitative aspects of a decision. In order to apply the method, a set of evaluation criteria and a set of alternative ideas, from which the best will be selected, must be considered. A weight for each evaluation criterion and idea is generated according to the information provided by the decision maker. AHP combines the weights of the objectives and the ideas, providing as output a ranked order of the scenarios. A simpler but highly used multi-criteria idea evaluation method is checklists that contain a set of questions aiming to assess different aspects of the new idea. A checklist constitutes a means of identifying at the outset the potential of the new idea.

Another category comprises statistical methods that analyze data, usually coming from potential consumers, in order to reach a decision. An example of methods of this category is Conjoint Analysis, a method typically used for new product concept screening in the new product development process [21]. It is a statistical method that takes into consideration consumer opinion. Respondents provide overall evaluations of product variations presented to them as combinations of attributes. These evaluations are then used to infer the importance of the individual attributes comprising the products and finally define the optimal combination of features. Data are collected using various means such as telephone and online surveys. Data gathered when conducting such surveys can be statistically analyzed in order to derive conclusions regarding the marketability of the new idea.

Besides the above analytical methods, there exist methods that exploit qualitative information gathered from prospective consumers of the new product or service. In this category, Focus Groups and Applied Ethnography are methods widely used for idea evaluation. Applied Ethnography refers to observational research in the field, watching how customers utilize a company's products. Ethnography can be used in the discovery of new product or services opportunities, during the design of new products or services when the new product or service idea is conceptualized and designed, and in the evaluation of a new product or service in terms of usability and market acceptance [22]. A Focus Group involves a moderator leading a group of participants, usually ranging from 5 to 12 people, through a set of questions on a particular topic. Interactions among group participants can generate a number of insights and queries [23]. Taking into consideration these insights and addressing the questions raised, new ideas are criticized and improved, thus maximizing their potential for success.

Advances in software and hardware development technologies have paved the way for Rapid Prototype Development, a new idea evaluation method based on the rapid implementation of new product ideas using special materials or tools. Having developed a prototype, product tests and assessments can be performed. The software industry uses its own version of rapid prototyping under the name of "agile programming", a conceptual framework for undertaking software engineering projects. There are a number of agile programming methods, such as those espoused by the Agile Alliance (http://www.agilealliance.org/). Most agile methods attempt to minimize risk by developing software in short timeframes (iterations), which typically last one to four weeks. Each iteration resembles a miniature software project and includes all the tasks necessary to release the mini-increment of new functionality: planning, requirements analysis, design, coding, testing, and documentation.

Another widely used idea evaluation method is the conduction of a Feasibility Study. This is a preliminary study undertaken before the real work of a project is initiated, in order to ascertain the likelihood of the project's success. It is an analysis of all possible solutions to a problem and a recommendation on the best solution to use, involving an evaluation of how the project will fit into the whole organization. A Feasibility Study is the first time in a project development process that all pieces are assembled to see if they perform together to create a technical and economically feasible concept. An idea's feasibility is typically considered from economic, ecological, technical and organizational viewpoints. At this point, we should mention that the economic viewpoint is used for commercial ideas and treats the screening decision as a conventional investment decision. Such studies use computational approaches like payback period, return-on-investment and discounted cash flow methods [4]. Moreover, a Feasibility Study also shows the sensitivity of the business to changes in these basic assumptions.

Collective Intelligence Systems establish a whole new family of technologies and methods for collaborative work, effective social communication and decision-making in very large groups of users. Collective Intelligence Systems strive to rise the "wisdom of the crowd" in order to support collaborative decision making and in consequence assist the idea evaluation process. A well-known example is PMs, which are used primarily for forecasting purposes. PMs were put in practice for the first time in the 1980s at the University of Iowa, with the aim of forecasting the outcomes of elections. As mentioned in section 2 PMs have begun to establish their position among other idea evaluation methods.

5.2 Comparison

PMs are based on software-implemented virtual stock markets and can easily support large numbers of ideas. Adding more ideas in the market implies that evaluators simply have to go through their description and decide whether they wish to buy the corresponding stocks or not. On the other hand for the majority of the methods examined scalability is an issue because evaluators have to consider and evaluate each and every idea in detail (e.g. according to specific criteria), a process which is both time consuming and error-prone when it is performed for many ideas.

The native-market based character of PMs renders them capable of supporting the participation of an unlimited number of users, with the only restriction posed by the underlying software and hardware infrastructure. However the number of participants is limited in the majority of the other methods examined. Most methods involve a team of experts or one person only who typically is the innovator himself. Focus Groups and Applied Ethnography usually involve small groups of people. On the other hand, survey methods are highly scalable as participants may be added at will; in fact high participation is needed for allowing statistical analysis of results. Nevertheless, in the case of survey methods, it is the cost that augments rapidly with the involvement of more evaluators, rendering the methods unpractical.

A major advantage of PMs against other methods is the fact that they can support the evaluation of every type of idea. In this sense, it is possible to enter into PMs not only ideas that are well structured and described but also those that are at a much earlier stage, with just a basic description earlier stage,. Most of the other methods we researched need well-defined ideas as input (AHP, Conjoint Analysis, Focus Groups, Applied Ethnography, Telephone and Online Surveys, Feasibility Studies, Rapid Prototype Development). This is because they involve experts and/or potential customers who need to fully understand the new idea in order to efficiently evaluate and express their opinion on it. Regarding economic feasibility studies and commercial ideas, a considerable amount of financial data is required as input while at the early stages of a new idea relatively little is known. AHP and Conjoint Analysis are based on the definition of criteria that can only be derived and determined for well-understood ideas. For those that are at an early stage of their conception, the task of defining such criteria is very difficult, if not impossible. Moreover, well-defined ideas are required in methods belonging to the categories of qualitative and quantitative research since they are aimed at consumers.

Table 1. Comparison of idea evaluation methods

Criteria / Methods	Number of Ideas	Number of evaluators	Type of Ideas	Type of Feedback	Motivation of Evaluators
Multi-criteria methods	◐	◐	◐	●	◐
Statistical methods	◐	●	◐	●	◐
Qualitative research methods	◐	◐	◐	●	◐
Rapid Prototype Development	○	◐	○	●	◐
Feasibility Studies	○	◐	○	●	◐
Prediction Markets	●	●	●	◐	●

Checklists can be applied to all kinds of new ideas and range from those that support technical analysis in order to find out whether an innovative product matches the company's capabilities to ones that gather the marketing and information requirements in order to understand if they match the company's capabilities.

Regarding the type of feedback, most methods provide concrete justification as feedback. AHP and Conjoint Analysis, besides ranking ideas, illustrate the degree to which ideas fulfill the defined criteria. A different approach is the one applied in PMs. In this case, the output is a graphical presentation of the course of the stocks that basically represents how well is the idea perceived by the market participants. When concrete justification is required for the selection of new ideas such type of feedback is a limitation since it only provides the aggregated opinion of the participants but no information on how the idea conforms to specific business, or other, indices. With IDEM, we try to overcome this issue by requesting explicit feedback from the participants.

Finally, as far as the motivation of the stakeholders is concerned, in the majority of the presented methods (Checklists, AHP, Conjoint Analysis, Forecasting Methods, Feasibility Studies, Rapid Prototype Development) motivation is linked to the professionalism of the evaluators, who are experts employed specifically for the purpose of evaluating new ideas. In the cases of qualitative and quantitative methods, the participants are rewarded (usually financially) for their participation. PMs offer a game-like process that is able to motivate the evaluators even more. In this way, PMs stimulate them to participate more actively, providing a more credible input to the evaluation process.

6 Conclusions

We have described the use of PMs for idea management and presented IDEM, a software system that aids decision makers in the idea management process to collect, enhance and evaluate ideas by involving a broad range of participants, aggregating their opinions through the mechanism of PMs. Specifically, IDEM 1) supports user feedback in terms of new idea-contracts submission, rating of the idea-contracts already in the system and commenting, 2) confronts the uncertainty of the underlying event by offering the option to enter an expert based valuation of the contracts and 3) ranks ideas based on the Volume Weighted Average Price of the idea-contracts, a measure that takes into account both price and transaction volume of ideas.

Although the use of PMs in the idea management process is new, existing research including our own inaugural trial shows encouraging results but points out several issues that need to be further researched. First, we confronted the issue of the large number of ideas. At the market's closing point, 31 ideas were available. In a realistic corporate environment this number can be significantly higher. It is important for traders to be able to navigate among them in an efficient way, such that it lets them identify those that best match their interests. To this direction, support for automatically categorizing and clustering of similar ideas as well visualization and personalization techniques can help users quickly comprehend the available ideas.

Another issue worthy of research is the role of the facilitator in the idea generation scenarios. In our trial we used a "dictatorial" method for introducing new ideas to the market i.e. appointed judges decided which ideas were to be entered. However this process may be democratized by allowing participants themselves decide on which ideas should be inserted in the market. This would mean to hold Initial Public Offerings (IPOs) and decide based on trader's interest during them. Another solution could be to allow total anarchy in the system and publish every proposed idea in the market without any filtering. In this variant the market itself rejects low quality ideas through the ranking mechanism. An enhancement to this anarchist scenario is to use wiki-like markets in which new ideas are freely modified or extended by their investors. Towards the testing and evaluation of the above issues we have planned a series of experiments among which one, testing PMs for the evaluation of new ideas, will take place in a large automotive company. In conclusion our first results are encouraging showing that the use of PMs is a promising method able to reduce time and cost since it can combine idea generation and evaluation at the same time.

References

1. Miles, R.E., Miles, G., Snow, C.: Collaborative Entrepreneurship: How Communities of Networked Firms Use Continuous Innovation to Create Economic Wealth. Stanford University Press, Stanford (2005)
2. Shin, D.G.: Distributed inter-organizational systems and innovation processes. Internet Research 16(5), 553–572 (2006)
3. Diehl, M., Stroebe, W.: Productivity Loss in Brainstorming Groups. Journal of Personality and Social Psychology 53, 497–509 (1987)
4. Griffiths-Hemans, J., Grover, R.: Setting the Stage for Creative New Products: Investigating the Idea Fruition Process. Journal of the Academy of Marketing Science 34, 27–39 (2006)
5. Nonaka, I., Takeuchi, H.: The Knowledge-Creating Company. Oxford University Press, Oxford (1995)

6. Brown, S.L., Eisenhardt, K.M.: Product development: past research; present findings, and future directions. Academy of Management Review 20(3), 343–378 (1995)
7. Adamides, E.D., Karacapilidis, N.: Information Technology Support for the Knowledge and Social Processes of Innovation Management. Technovation 26, 50–59 (2006)
8. Christensen, C., Magnusson, M.G., Zetherstrom, M.B.: Implementation and Use of Collaborative Product Development Systems—Observations from Swedish Manufacturing Firms, working paper 2003:1, Chalmers University of Technology, Department of Innovation Engineering and Management (2003)
9. Sethi, R., Pant, S., Sethi, A.: Web-based product development systems integration and new product outcomes: a conceptual framework. J. of Product Innovation Management 20, 37–56 (2003)
10. Bose, R.: Group support systems: technologies and products selection. Industrial Management and Data Systems 103(9), 649–656 (2003)
11. Lin, K.J.: Building Web 2.0. IEEE Computer 40, 101–102 (2007)
12. Malone, T.W., Klein, M.: Harnessing Collective Intelligence to Address Global Climate Change, Innovations: Technology, Governance, Globalization, vol. 2(3), pp. 15–26. MIT Press, Cambridge (2007)
13. Kapetanios, E.: Quo Vadis computer science: From Turing to personal computer, personal content and collective intelligence. In: Data & Knowledge. Engineering Press (2008) (forthcoming)
14. Spann, M., Skiera, B.: Internet-Based Virtual Stock Markets for Business Forecasting. Management Science 49, 1310–1326 (2003)
15. Skiera, B., Spann, M.: Opportunities of Virtual Stock Markets to Support New Product Development, pp. 227–242. Verlag Gabler Wiesbaden (2004)
16. Chen, K.Y., Plott, C.: Information Aggregation Mechanisms: Concept, Design and Implementation for a Sales Forecasting Problem, working paper 1131, California Institute of Technology, Social Science (2002)
17. Soukhoroukova, A., Spann, M., Skiera, B.: Creating and Evaluating New Product Ideas with Idea Markets, The Wharton School of the University of Pennsylvania, Marketing Department Colloquia (2007)
18. LaComb, C., Barnett, A.J., Pan, Q.: The imagination market. Information System Frontiers 9, 245–256 (2006)
19. Lim, M., Coggins, R.J.: Optimal trade execution: an evolutionary approach. The 2005 IEEE Congress on Evolutionary Computation 2, 1045–1052 (2005)
20. Saaty, T.: The Analytic Hierarchy Process. McGraw-Hill, New York (1980)
21. Lakshmikantha, K.S., Shridhar, T.N., Sridhara, B.K., Sreekanta Gupta, B.P.: Application of Conjoint Analysis in New Product Development. In: National Conference on Product Development with Mechatronic Systems for Global Quality, India-Madurai, pp. 33–37 (2005)
22. Sanders, E.: How applied ethnography can improve your NPD research process, Product Development and Management Association (2002),
http://www.pdma.org/visions/apr02/applied.html
23. Nielsen, J.: The use and misuse of focus groups. Software 14(1), 94–95 (1997)

Understanding Dynamic Competitive Technology Diffusion in Electronic Markets

Cheng Zhang[1], Peijian Song[1], Yunjie Xu[2], and Ling Xue[3]

[1] School of Management, Fudan University, Shanghai, China
[2] Department of Information System, National University of Singapore, Singapore
[3] Kania School of Management, University of Scranton, Pennsylvania, United States
{zhangche, 061025018}@fudan.edu.cn, xuyj@comp.nus.edu.sg,
xue12@scranton.edu

Abstract. The extant literature on information technology (IT) diffusion has largely treated technology diffusion as a generic and independent process. This study, in contrast, examines the diffusion of different IT products with brand differentiation and competition. Drawing upon existing theories of product diffusion, we propose a research model to capture the dynamics of the competitive diffusion of web-based IT products and validate it with longitudinal field data of e-business platforms. Our findings suggest that IT product diffusion can be better predicted by a competitive model than by an independent-diffusion-process model. This research extends IT research to the context of competitive diffusion and provides practitioners an effective model to predict the dissemination of their products. The research also suggests the existence of asymmetric interactions among competing products, prompting scholars and practitioners to pay attention to the influence of competing products when making forecast of their product market.

Keywords: Technology Diffusion, Competing Products, Asymmetric Interactions.

1 Introduction

Online businesses are highly competitive in various markets due to low entry barriers, easy imitation of product/service offerings, and convenient customer search for information. It is, therefore, hard for incumbent online companies to sustain their technological advantage when facing fierce competition from new players [1]. For example, after Google's success in the search engine market, Microsoft launched online search engine services with similar functions. In the e-mail service market, Yahoo, Microsoft and Google provide similar services with comparable mailbox sizes. The competition in electronic markets is also global: When eBay entered the Chinese consumer-to-consumer (C2C) market, it faced intensive competition from Taobao.com, a local C2C platform providing almost identical services. When Google entered the Chinese search engine market, it was confronted by the local search provider Baidu.com. The competition between eBay (China)[1] and Taobao.com is illustrative. In 2003, eBay (China) had

---

[1] In the Chinese market, it is called eBay Eachnet.

C. Weinhardt, S. Luckner, and J. Stößer (Eds.): WEB 2008, LNBIP 22, pp. 14–24, 2009.
© Springer-Verlag Berlin Heidelberg 2009

72.4% of the Chinese C2C market after acquiring the top Chinese C2C vendor, Eachnet.com. However, in 2007, eBay(China)'s market share dropped to 7.7% due to the competition from Taobao.com, whereas Taobao.com's market share increased from 7.8% in 2003 to 84.9% in 2007 [2, 3]. Table 1 provides more examples of online competition. All of these cases pose a critical question: how can we assess the impact of competition on online technology diffusion?

Table 1. Examples of Competition in Online Markets

Segmented Markets	Provider 1	Provider 2
Web Browser	Internet Explorer (IE)	Firefox
Instant Messenger	MSN	Skype
Online Social Networking	Myspace	Facebook
Music Downloading	ITune	Real
Instant Messenger (China)	MSN	QQ
Search Engines (China)	Google (China)	Baidu
C2C (China)	eBay (China)	Taobao

Understanding the dynamics of competitive technology diffusion in electronic markets is important for both scholars and practitioners. Forecasting product sales with competitive diffusion has long been a challenge in marketing. Many early models of forecasting tried to incorporate of the competition of product diffusion at the category level [4]. The existing literature also suggests that due to the coexistence of market expansion effect (i.e., new entrants may create additional demand for a product) and the competitive effect (i.e., the new entrants' stealing of market shares from the incumbents), the competitive diffusion can be complex and challenging for forecasting [5]. Similarly, the consideration of the competitive effect in technology diffusion is importance in IS discipline and to IT product managers since, as we illustrate in this paper, the competitive diffusion model can yields more accurate forecasts of market growth and help better allocate firms' R&D and marketing resources.

To illustrate the forecasting issue, Figure 1 depicts the annual growth of the entire Chinese C2C market and that of individual C2C platform providers. As shown in the figure, the market, measured by transaction volume, has increased over the past seven years from 0.06 billion USD[2] in 2001 to 7.40 billion USD in 2007. Before 2003, the market's growth followed a smooth linear trend with eBay (China) capturing almost 90% of the market. In 2003, Taobao entered the market. It was also this year that the Chinese C2C market experienced an exponential increase in transaction volume. While the graph shows a clear expansion of the C2C market, individual firms, such as eBay (China) can still suffer from the competitive effect in this diffusion process.

---

[2] The exchange rate of USD to RMB was estimated as 1:7 at the time of this study.

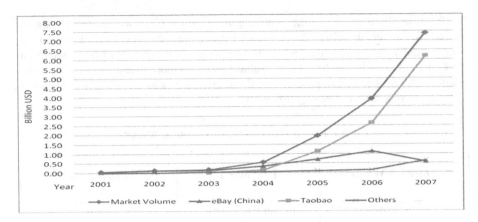

Fig. 1. Diffusion of the C2C electronic market in China

Therefore, it is imperative to build forecasting models that can capture this dynamic impact of competition in the diffusion of technology.

In this paper, we extend the standard Bass-type diffusion model to incorporate the dynamic competitive diffusion of two competing products. This model captures the dynamics of cross-product competition in market expansion. It is worth noticing that although competitive product diffusion has long been examined in marketing and economic literature, scant research have been conducted in examining the competitive diffusion of new technology in online markets. Therefore, this attempt to model and test the competitive online diffusion generates important theoretical as well as managerial implications.

2   Literature Review

Compared with the single-product diffusion models, multi-product diffusion models have received relatively less attention [5]. Rogers [6] argues that people should not view innovation in isolation. Instead, innovation can be considered as a bundle of interrelated new ideas and technologies which he called a technology cluster. The diffusion of the cluster depends on the presence of related technologies that enhance its value. However, the nature of this diffusion has rarely been investigated [6]. A careful analysis of IT technology diffusion literature reveals that most IT diffusion models treat a technology in isolation and as generic. They often ignore the interactions among multiple competing technologies in the same market. More specifically, prior studies have focused on the adoption or diffusion of a single product at different stages [7, 8], in different contexts of user tasks [9, 10], and with diverse user characteristics [11, 12]. In contrast, there were few empirical studies on the diffusion of competing IT products. Consequently, IT disciplines are calling for more multi-technology diffusion research.

In marketing discipline, after Bass' classical product growth model [13], an increasing body of literature focused on multi-product growth models has emerged [5, 14, 15]. Research attention has been paid especially to the complementary effect and the competitive effect between existing incumbent products and new products. With complementary effect, the increasing adoption of one product by consumers enhances the adoption of the related products[3]. With competitive effect, the adoption of one product undermines the adoption of the competing products[4]. The interaction between the incumbent product and the new product can involve both of these effects. First, the entry of a new competitor may lead to a market expansion due to increased promotions, product variety, and customer awareness. Second, the new product may also negatively affect the market share of the incumbent products due to substitutability [4, 16]. Although several marketing studies have explored multi-product diffusion across product generations [17] and product categories [18], studies on multi-product diffusion in a competitive and dynamically growing electronic market are rare. The current study, therefore, complements the existing literature by examining, both theoretically and empirically, competitive diffusion in an online context.

3 Model Development

Our study focuses on the integration of both dynamic market growth and competitive effect in an IT diffusion model. Consider a duopoly case with two competing technology products, denoted by the subscript $i = 1, 2$. To keep the model general, we begin by extending the Bass model, which stipulates that the market's adoption rate of technology product i in a dynamic market can be modeled by the discrete analogue expression:

$$f_i(t) = \left[a_i + b_i \frac{F_i(t-1)}{M_i(t-1)} \right] [M_i(t-1) - F_i(t-1)], \tag{1}$$

where, for product i, $f_i(t)$ denotes the adoption of i during the time period t, $F_i(t-1)$ denotes the cumulative adoption of i at the beginning of t, $M_i(t-1)$ denotes the potential market size, a_i denotes the coefficient of external influence intended to create consumer awareness of product i (e.g., advertising, media coverage), and b_i denotes the coefficient of network influences on product i through consumer word-of-mouth and various network contacts [13].

Then we consider the competitive effect of product one on product two and vice-versa during their diffusion in the same market. It is clear that the diffusion of one product can negatively affect the adoption of the competing product. For example, in a C2C market, loyal users who have established a preference for a particular service vendor will stick to that vendor's website for transactions, at least as their first choice. The more other people use the preferred service, the less they will use a competing service. When users of one product interact with users from other product, they might

---

[3] More specifically, the complementary effect can be one-way (e.g., increasing the adoption of the Internet by increasing the sales of personal computer modems, but not vice versa), or two-way (e.g., the sales of personal computers and application software increase simultaneously).
[4] The competitive effect may appear in successive product generations (e.g., different versions of office software), on competitive technologies (e.g., desktop and laptop personal computers) and on competitive products (e.g., different brands of instant photography).

draw other users to their product or vice-versa. This is the competitive effect between products. Because the two products compete in the same market, they have the same potential market at a given time point, i.e., $M_1(t) = M_2(t)$. Therefore, factoring the competitive effect between products, the diffusion rate of product i in the electronic market, given the effects of competition and market growth, can be expressed as

$$f_1(t) = \left[a_1 + b_1 \frac{F_1(t-1)}{M(t-1)} - c_1 \frac{F_2(t-1)}{M(t-1)} \right] [M(t-1) - F_1(t-1)] \tag{2}$$

$$f_2(t) = \left[a_2 + b_2 \frac{F_2(t-1)}{M(t-1)} - c_2 \frac{F_1(t-1)}{M(t-1)} \right] [M(t-1) - F_2(t-1)] \tag{3}$$

respectively, where $c_1 (c_2)$ denotes the coefficient of the competitive effect of product one (two) on product two (one). The larger the value of c, the greater the tendency for the product to slow down the diffusion of its competitor. The technology diffusion rate, therefore, can be represented by a regression equation consisting of three independent variables: $F_1(t-1)$, $F_2(t-1)$ and $M(t-1)$.

4 Data Collection and Model Estimation

We chose eBay (China) and Taobao.com as a context for our study for three reasons. First, the total market share (measured by the dollars of market transactions) of these two companies in China was 80% in 2003 and 95% in 2006. Therefore, the competition between these two companies in the Chinese C2C market can be best characterized as a duopoly. Second, when Taobao.com first entered the market in 2003, eBay (China) dominated the Chinese C2C market with a share of 72.4%. However, eBay's share dropped to 36.4% in 2006 due to the competition from Taobao.com. This dramatic turn-around provides a good opportunity to study the diffusion of two competing products. Third, the online C2C market is characterized by an intensive network effect. The wide adoption of online communities and instant messages provide numerous opportunities to spread the online word-of-mouth for certain C2C platform service.

Our diffusion data were collected from Alexa.com, one of the largest third-party data companies tracking online traffic. Alexa provides reach information of numerous websites. The reach of a website is the amount of unique internet protocol (IP) addresses accessing the websites. The data provides a good estimation of the adopted user base of websites' e-service. Because eBay (China) has two domain names, each-net.com and eBay.com.cn before 2008, we combined the data from the two websites to represent eBay (China). We obtained from Alexa.com consumers' monthly reach usage of the two companies' products, i.e. C2C platform service, between January 2002 and December 2006.

The dependent variable is diffusion rate of the e-service, measured by the monthly change in the reach of the websites. The independent variables are (a) the adoption of the e-service, measured by the monthly reach of the websites and (b) potential market size measured by internet users provided by Internet World Stats which is an organization to provide world-wide Internet usage, population statistics and Internet market research data. A similar design has been used by Krishnan et al. [4] to study service products. Because the model is polynomial only in independent variables, ordinary least squares (OLS) is still a valid choice to verify the model and estimate its parameters. We assume eBay (China) provides IT product one and Taobao provides IT product two. In order to measure the effectiveness of our proposed model, we used Bass' classical model of single product diffusion [13] as a base model and benchmark.

Table 2. Regression analysis of the competitive diffusion of e-platforms

Un-standardized Coefficients	eBay (China)		Taobao	
	Base Model	Competitive Model	Base Model	Competitive Model
(Constant)	-6.318	-10.878 **	-28.995***	28.204***
a	0.016	0.018 **	0.052***	-0.054***
b	0.013	0.179***	0.066***	-0.149***
c	n.a.	0.103***	n.a.	-0.344***
Variance Explained (R^2)	0.250	0.744	0.665	0.878
Significance	p<0.001	p<0.001	p<0.001	p<0.001

***: $p < 0.01$, **: $p < 0.05$, *: $p < 0.1$.

The results, as shown in Table 2, show that our model to assess competitive technology diffusion is better than the traditional diffusion model with a superior explanatory power. Compared with the traditional model, our competitive technology diffusion model produces higher R^2 values for both eBay and Taobao.com (by 0.494 and 0.213, respectively). Note that overall R^2 values obtained from this empirical test are lower than those in the existing literature employing Bass model to examine product diffusion. In the few studies that have addressed multi-product diffusion, R^2 was found to vary between 0.532 and 0.932 when multi-product interactions and market expansion were incorporated into the model [4]. Figure 2 shows how the estimated trend for C2C e-platform diffusion fits the real growth of the market between 2002 and 2006.

The results also show a two-way interaction between the diffusion of eBay and Taobao.com, i.e., each product had a significant influence (*c*) on the other during the period. Furthermore, the interaction was asymmetric: whereas the diffusion of Taobao.com significantly slowed down that of eBay ($c_1=0.103***$), the diffusion of eBay significantly increased diffusion of Taobao ($c_2= -0.344***$). This two-way asymmetric effect has been found in previous diffusion studies across different generations of products [17], for example, pagers and cellular phones, and across different product categories [18], for example, universal product codes (UPCs) and scanners. However, this is the first time the result has been found between products offered by competing firms. For this reason, the findings should draw the attention of scholars and practitioners who seek to estimate and forecast multi-product diffusion.

The results further reveal that our model to assess competition may capture firms' strategic influence on diffusion better than the traditional diffusion model. Compared with the traditional model, the coefficients of external influence on consumer awareness and coefficient of network influences are negative in the new model. The outcomes fit what happens in the industry well: between 2003 and 2005, eBay used both

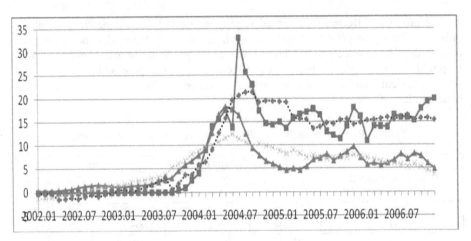

Fig. 2. Diffusion estimation of Taobao.com and eBay (China)'s e-platform
Line with squares: Taobao.com's monthly reach. Line with triangles: eBay (China)'s monthly reach. Dotted line with diamonds: estimation of Taobao.com's monthly adoption. Dotted line with crosses: estimation of eBay (China)'s monthly adoption. Monthly adoption is measured by millions of monthly access to the website.

traditional channel like national TV channels and Internet heavily to promote their service and signed exclusive advertisement contracts with almost every portal website in China to force out other C2C vendors. On the other hand, Taobao.com was a late entrant with low reputation to consumers. It experienced difficulties in its marketing since many websites refused to carry its advertisements due to exclusive contracting agreements with eBay. As shown in the results, when considering the growth of eBay's adoption into Tabao.com's diffusion process, the coefficients of Taobao's external and network influence changed to negative. Taobao, however, chose not to be a copy-cat of eBay. Besides similar core platform of transaction, Taboao differentiated itself from eBay by providing complementary services like user communication tools and, more importantly, provided a free-charge trial service for customers in first five years and only charged value-added service after trial period expired. This differentiation and pricing strategy achieves a great success in Chinese price-sensitive and experience-seeking C2C market [19]. As shown in the result, eBay's adoption positively accelerates Taobao's diffusion process.

5 Forecasting Analysis

Although the competitive technology diffusion model confirms the theoretical importance to factor in competition in explaining diffusion and it provides a good fit with empirical data of e-platforms, it is still necessary to validate its usefulness as a tool for forecasting, because brand managers and IT development managers are interested in gauging how well their IT products diffuse in relation to competing products. We tested the forecasting performance of the proposed model in two-stage experiments. In each experiment, the data set was split into a training set and a validation set. In every first stage of experiment, we used the training set to estimate the parameters of the diffusion model. Then in the second stage, we predicted the future diffusion trend using these parameters and compared these predicted values with the data observed in the validation set. To check the reliability of the predictions, we tested the model in three rounds of experiments. In the first round, we used 95% of the data set to estimate parameters and the remaining 5% to forecast; in the second round, we used 90% to estimate and 10% to forecast; in the third round we used 80% to estimate and 20% to forecast. Using the 5-year monthly data records in the total dataset, in the first round the model forecasted the market for competitive technology in the next quarter (3 months), in the second round for the next half year (6 months), and in the third round for the next year (12 months). Again, we used Bass' classical model of single product diffusion [13] as a base model for benchmarking.

The root mean-squared error (RMSE) and the mean absolute percent error (MAPE) were used as indicators of forecasting efficiency. RMSE measures the square root of the variance representing the differences between each forecast and the corresponding observation and MAPE measures the average forecast error by the absolute percentage difference between each forecast and the corresponding observation. Suppose $\hat{y}$ represents the predicted series and y represents the observed series. Then,

$$RMSE\left(\hat{y}\right) = \sqrt{\frac{1}{n}\sum_{i=1}^{n}\left(\hat{y}_i - y_i\right)^2} \tag{4}$$

$$MAPE\left(\hat{y}\right) = \frac{1}{n}\sum_{i=1}^{n}\frac{\left|\hat{y}_i - y_i\right|}{y_i} \tag{5}$$

In essence, both RMSE and MAPE measure the error in forecasting. In both cases, a smaller value indicates less error. Table 3 shows that the competitive model evidently gives better forecasts than the base model. By factoring in the effect of substitution, the proposed model provides more accurate forecasting and better estimates of the empirical data than does the base model.

Table 3. RMSE and MAPE of the forecast error for e-platform diffusion*

Competitive Technology	Model Type	RMSE			MAPE		
		R1	R2	R3	R1	R2	R3
eBay(China)	Base Model	5.5677	3.7395	1.4585	1.6220	1.3750	0.7818
	Competitive Model	1.0588	1.3962	0.8892	0.2807	0.4925	0.3892
Taobao	Base Model	2.2835	1.1483	1.3489	0.1853	0.1209	0.2851
	Competitive Model	1.6413	0.9825	0.7614	0.1347	0.1015	0.1302

* R1/R2/R3: first / second / third round of experiment.

6 Discussion

Previous research on multi-product interactions involving competitive technologies has been rare. Moreover, the literature on IT product diffusion is usually limited to the diffusion of a single product. To extend the current research, this study modeled IT product diffusion in a competitive context. Drawing upon the existing theories of innovation diffusion, network effect, and product growth models, we proposed a predictive model and validated it with longitudinal data of e-commerce platforms. Our findings suggest that product diffusion can be predicted better by a model that incorporates competition in a dynamic market than by one that treats a product in isolation. The research also provides evidence for the existence of two-way asymmetric interactions between competing products in a diffusion process.

The proposed model has several managerial implications. First, it can be used to monitor the diffusion of competing IT products and evaluate their interactions in the process of diffusion. The implications of the model and its findings can be generalized to the diffusion of other types of web-based IT products in a category. For example, similar approaches can be used to study the competition among music downloading services such as iTune and Real, as well as instant communication technologies such as MSN messenger and Skype. Compared with previous models, our model has more implications for management because it incorporates two important strategic variables: competition and dynamic market growth, into diffusion. That is, product managers may use the model's estimates of diffusion to understand the market structure. Managers can then use this market information to guide pricing strategies and product differentiation strategy in view of existing products that provide similar customer utility. Our model, based on the market response of the competitors, can also help managers predict possible outcomes of their strategies and, armed with this information, response to market conditions to their benefit. In addition, by understanding the possible competitive effects of their products on other firms' technological products, managers may choose a better timing for their products to enter the market.

This study also suggests an alternative strategy for online information product vendors, especially if they are new to the market. Because of the fierce competition online, newcomers need to differentiate their own products to decrease substitution effects. For example, as a newcomer to social network sites, Facebook first had to focus on college students to decrease the substitution effects between itself and Myspace. Furthermore, our research explains some important phenomenon pertaining to the C2C market in China. For example, although eBay (China) and Taobao.com have similar platforms, Taboao.com differentiated itself from eBay (China) by focusing more on additional functions and services, such as communication tools, friendly interfaces, better community service, and an integrated payment system, and provided these services for free when it entered the market.

This study is not without limitations, however, and it could be expanded in several ways. First, we could model the network effect in more detail, for example, by treating market growth as an endogenous variable. Currently, it is treated as exogenous, which means that network effect does not fit into the model well. A new model that further explores the dynamics of online, cross-brand, word-of-mouth network externality [20] may better explain a real situation, provide more insight into competitive diffusion, and better predict IT diffusion in electronic markets. Furthermore, we should consider non-linear regression techniques to estimate the parameters in a future model. As ours is one of only a few models that address competitive technology diffusion and can be expressed as a simple polynomial, we chose OLS, a technique that is robust in many regression situations, to verify the model and to estimate its parameters. However, we believe the precision of the model's parameters can be improved by applying different regression techniques. Furthermore, it would be desirable to integrate the two-sided market effect into the diffusion model, because many, if not most, electronic markets with network externalities are now two-sided [21, 22]. Modeling a two-sided market effect into our diffusion model would provide a more comprehensive understanding of competitive diffusion across brands and markets, and it would shed light on many recent strategies IT firms are using to develop cross-market product development and social network platform promotion.

References

1. Porter, M.E.: Strategy and the Internet. Harvard Business Review 79(3), 62–79 (2001)
2. iResearch. China C2C E-Commerce Research Report 2005, iResearch Consulting Group, Shanghai, China (2006)
3. iResearch. China Online Shopping Research Report: 2007-2008, iResearch Consulting Group, Shanghai, China (2008)
4. Krishnan, T.V., Bass, F.M., Kumar, V.: Impact of a Late Entrant on the Diffusion of a New Product/Service. Journal of Marketing Research 37(2), 269–278 (2000)
5. Chandrasekaran, D., Tellis, G.J.: A Critical Review of Marketing Research on Diffusion of New Products. In: Review of Marketing Research, ME Sharpe, pp. 39–80 (2007)
6. Rogers, E.M.: Diffusion of Innovations. The Free Press, New York (2003)
7. Kim, S.S., Malhotra, N.K.: A Longitudinal Model of Continued IS Use: An Integrative View of Four Mechanisms Underlying Postadoption Phenomena. Management Science 51(5), 741–755 (2005)
8. Venkatesh, V., Morris, M.G., Ackerman, P.L.: A Longitudinal Field Investigation of Gender Differences in Individual Technology Adoption Decision-Making Processes. Organizational Behavior and Human Decision Processes 83(1), 33–60 (2000)
9. Ahuja, M.K., Thatcher, J.B.: Moving Beyond Intentions and Toward the Theory of Trying: Effects of Work Environment and Gender on Post-Adoption Information Technology Use. MIS Quarterly 29(3), 427–459 (2005)
10. Wang, W., Hsieh, J.P.: Beyond Routine: Symbolic Adoption, Extended Use, and Emergent Use of Complex Information Systems in the Mandatory Organizational Context. In: Proceedings of Twenty-Seventh International Conference on Information Systems, Milwaukee, pp. 733–749 (2006)
11. Au, Y.A., Kauffman, R.J.: Should We Wait? Network Externalities, Compatibility, and Electronic Billing Adoption. Journal of Management Information Systems 18(2), 47–63 (2001)
12. Li, D., Chau, P.Y.K., Lou, H.: Understanding Individual Adoption of Instant Messaging: An Empirical Investigation. Journal of the Association for Information Systems 6(4), 102–129 (2005)
13. Bass, F.M.: A New Product Growth for Model Consumer Durables. Management Science 15(5), 215–227 (1969)

14. Bayus, B.L., Kim, N., Shocker, A.D.: Growth Models for Multiproduct Interactions: Current Status and New Directions. In: Vijay Mahajan, E.M., Wind, Y. (eds.) New-Product Diffusion Models, pp. 141–163. Kluwer Academic Publishers, Boston (2000)
15. Mahajan, V., Muller, E., Bass, F.M.: New Product Diffusion Models in Marketing: A Review and Directions for Research. Journal of Marketing 54(1), 1–26 (1990)
16. Mahajan, V., Sharma, S., Buzzell, R.D.: Assessing the Impact of Competitive Entry on Market Expansion and Incumbent Sales. Journal of Marketing 57(3), 39–52 (1993)
17. Kim, N., Chang, D.R., Shocker, A.D.: Modeling Intercategory and Generational Dynamics for A Growing Information Technology Industry. Management Science 46(4), 496–512 (2000)
18. Bucklin, L.P., Sengupta, S.: The Co-Diffusion of Complementary Innovations: Supermarket Scanners and UPC Symbols. Journal of Product Innovation Management 10(2), 148–160 (1993)
19. Chen, J., Zhang, C., Yuan, Y., Huang, L.H.: Understanding the Emerging C2C Electronic Market in China: An Experience-Seeking Social Marketplace. Electronic Markets 17(2), 86–100 (2007)
20. Libai, B., Muller, E., Peres, R.: The Effect of Within-Brand and Cross-Brand Word of Mouth on Competitive Growth, The University of Texas at Dallas (2007)
21. Parker, G., Van Alstyne, M.: Two-Sided Network Effects: A Theory of Information Product Design. Management Science 51(10), 1494–1504 (2005)
22. Rochet, J.C., Tirole, J.: Platform Competition in Two-Sided Markets. Journal of the European Economic Association 1(4), 990–1029 (2003)

Examining Agencies' Satisfaction with Electronic Record Management Systems in e-Government: A Large-Scale Survey Study

Fang-Ming Hsu[1], Paul Jen-Hwa Hu[2], Hsinchun Chen[3], and Han-fen Hu[2]

[1] Department of Information Management
National Dong Hwa University, Taiwan
fmhsu@mail.ndhu.edu.tw
[2] Department of Information Systems and Operations Management,
David Eccles School of Business, University of Utah, USA
{actph,han-fen.hu}@business.utah.edu
[3] Department of Management Information Systems
Eller School of Management, University of Arizona, USA
hchen@eller.arizona.edu

Abstract. While e-government is propelling and maturing steadily, advanced technological capabilities alone cannot guarantee agencies' realizing the full benefits of the enabling computer-based systems. This study analyzes information systems in e-government settings by examining agencies' satisfaction with an electronic record management system (ERMS). Specifically, we investigate key satisfaction determinants that include regulatory compliance, job relevance, and satisfaction with support services for using the ERMS. We test our model and the hypotheses in it, using a large-scale survey that involves a total of 1,652 government agencies in Taiwan. Our results show significant effects of regulatory compliance on job relevance and satisfaction with support services, which in turn determine government agencies' satisfaction with an ERMS. Our data exhibit a reasonably good fit to our model, which can explain a significant portion of the variance in agencies' satisfaction with an ERMS. Our findings have several important implications to research and practice, which are also discussed.

Keywords: e-government, electronic record management systems, user satisfaction, regulatory compliance, job relevance.

1 Introduction

Governments need extensive information support in their services or operations, thus making the use of advanced computer-based systems essential [15]. Government agencies usually possess notable characteristics in structure or process that distinguish them from ordinary business organizations; e.g., environmental factors, legal constraints, political influences, accountability requirements, and internal structures or processes [19], [25]. These characteristics, in turn, demand reexaminations of important issues surrounding the use of advanced computer-based systems in government

C. Weinhardt, S. Luckner, and J. Stößer (Eds.): WEB 2008, LNBIP 22, pp. 25–36, 2009.
© Springer-Verlag Berlin Heidelberg 2009

contexts, in addition to the challenges common to private firms [19]. Examples include the mandatory relationships among agencies and the stringent reporting structure stipulated for administration and accountability purposes. Regulatory requirements represent an additional characteristic distinctive of government agencies [9], [25]. These characteristics, crucial and deserving properly considerations when examining the use or success of computer-based systems implemented in government agencies, however has received little attention in previous research [3].

Considerable previous information systems (IS) research has studied issues pertaining to system implementation, use, or success. Voluntary acceptance or use by target users seems to be a common focus, toward which "intention to use" is often used to measure initial user acceptance or adoption. However, initial user acceptance, measured by individuals' intentions, may play a smaller role in scenarios in which the adoption of a computer-based system is somewhat mandatory administratively [9]. In these situations, as in government settings, other factors that manifest system success become increasingly critical. In this connection, satisfaction is essential and has been identified as a crucial systems success factor in various organizational settings [5], [6], [8].

A handful of studies have examined satisfactions in e-government contexts, predominantly concentrating on citizens' satisfactions with novel e-government services; e.g., [30]. In parallel, user satisfaction has been studied substantially by IS researchers who often focus on individuals' satisfactions with a system newly deployed in their organization; e.g. [6], [32]. Some studies examine satisfaction at an organizational level, mostly in business organization contexts; e.g. [10], [23], [26]. Our review of the extant literature suggests the importance and desirability of bridging the user satisfaction research stream in IS and the significance of agencies' satisfaction with advanced e-government systems, as it expands the applicability and generalizability of prior IS research results and, at the same time, addresses the burgeoning need in the emerging e-government.

To address this backdrop, we study agencies' satisfaction with an electronic record management system (ERMS), a crucial type of information systems supporting electronic archival, transmittal, dissemination, and sharing of records/documents by various government agencies. Specifically, we propose a factor model for explaining an agency's satisfaction with an ERMS and test this model using data collected from a large-scale survey study that involves a total of 1,652 government agencies in Taiwan. In our model, we explicitly distinguish the agency's satisfaction with an ERMS and its satisfaction with the support services by designated call centers funded by the central government. Overall, the proposed model suggests that an agency's satisfaction with an ERMS can be jointly explained by regulatory compliance, relevance to the agency's operations and services, and satisfaction with the support services. According to our analyses, the data show a reasonably good fit to the model and support all of the hypotheses it suggests.

2 Literature Review

The deployment of advanced computer-based systems has grown at an increasing pace among government agencies, leading to the emergence of e-government that generally refers to the use of information and telecommunication technology to enhance information access and service delivery within existing government systems [15]. According to the target service recipients, an e-government service can be classified as government-to-government (G-to-G), government-to-business (G-to-B), or government-to-citizen (G-to-C) [18]. Among them, G-to-G represents a crucial dimension of e-government, entailing electronic data or document gathering, transmittal, organization, archive, dissemination, and sharing by government agencies within the incumbent administrative hierarchy [18]. The core benefits of e-government demand seamless integrations of information support extending above and beyond the existing agency boundaries. Evidently, this reveals the criticality of G-to-G e-government, which is worthy of our investigative attention. However, issues pertaining to G-to-G e-government have received relatively less research attention than those pertinent G-to-B or G-to-C e-government [18].

Fundamental to G-to-G e-government, electronic record management systems generally refer to the computer-based systems that provide efficient and systematic controls over the creation, archive, access, use and disposition of records or documents in an electronic format [22]. According to [27], the scope of an ERMS "must encompass the use of technology to handle paper documents or their electronic equivalent." (p. 31). The collective results from several studies show the use of ERMS can improve government agencies' effectiveness or performance; e.g., [22], [20].

The success of an e-government system, measured by the extent to which an adopting agency can realize the system's full benefits, requires appropriate system assessments and management attention, particularly at an organizational level. According to our literature review, most ERMS research tends to focus on technical challenges or follows a qualitative approach (e.g. [16], [33], [21]), thus offering limited empirical evaluations of an ERMS at the agency level. Of particular importance is satisfaction, which represents a crucial systems success measure in adopting organizations [10], [5], [6].

At an individual level, satisfaction is usually measured by the sum of an individual's feelings or attitude toward a system, taken into account a variety of factors affecting his or her feelings or attitude [5]. Although prior studies have defined user satisfaction with subtle differences, a review of the prevalent definitions shows a commonality reflecting a user's evaluation of the system under examination. Several related but distinct conceptualizations of satisfaction have prevailed: one targeting the system and another entailing crucial organizational support for using the system [10]. This signifies the importance of the support services facilitating or assisting the use of a computer-based system in an organization. Such support services are particularly important in e-government settings because an adopting agency likely will encounter difficulty or problems when using a newly implemented computer-based system [15].

In general, information systems can be assessed at an individual or an organizational level [14]. When an e-government system is deployed in an agency, assessments of the system need to extend beyond the individual level. As Melone [17] comments, the use of satisfaction to measure a system's effectiveness or success requires a perspective at the organization level; i.e., a social unit. Hence, examining satisfaction at the agency level is critical, partly because of the conceivable conflicts between individuals' interests and the agency's goals [1]. An individual satisfaction with an ERMS cannot automatically approximate the satisfaction at the agency level, which is crucial for the ultimate success of an e-government system in adopting agencies. Larsen [14] issues a call for empirical examinations of important success factors for organizational or inter-organizational information systems. In our context, this underscores the need of examining agencies' satisfaction with the implemented ERMS. Therefore, we propose and empirically test a factor model for explaining agencies' satisfaction with an ERMS.

3 Research Model and Hypotheses

Figure 1 depicts our research model. Regulatory compliance refers to the extent to which an agency's operations and use of an ERMS is compliant with the existing policies, regulations, rules, or procedures. Government agencies are often regulated by substantial bureaucratic red tape, a consideration that may not be heavily weighted by private organizations [24], [3]. In e-government, agencies must comply with the defined regulations concerning system choice, implementation, operations, security, or audit. Preferred or best practices are often incorporated in the regulatory requirements to foster standards or to ensure effective information archives or sharing by agencies. By following the specifications stipulated in the existing regulatory requirements, agencies are likely to improve their information sharing, coordination, planning, service delivery, and ultimately performance [3].

Job relevance also can affect an agency's satisfaction with an ERMS. Consistent with the analysis by Venkatesh and Davis [29], job relevance, in this study, refers to an agency's assessment of the degree to which an ERMS system is applicable to and supportive of its work tasks or services. The role of job relevance is prominent in work contexts and has been identified as an important predictor of systems success. In our case, job relevance can affect an agency's assessment of an ERMS.

The use of an advanced computer-based system may require appropriate support [4]. Accordingly, we distinguish between an agency's satisfaction with an ERMS system and its satisfaction with the support services for effective use of the system.

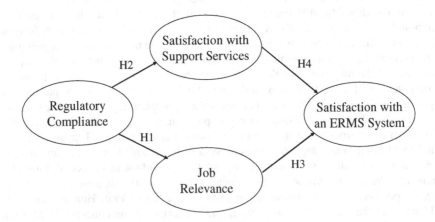

Fig. 1. Research Model

To ensure adopting agencies' effective utilization of an ERMS, the Taiwanese central government has established designated call centers to provide detailed instructions and timely trouble-shooting to agencies, in response to their questions, inquiries, or problems. Specifically, we define an agency's satisfaction with support services as the extent to which the agency is satisfied with the support services by the designated call center. Our decision to explicitly differentiate an agency's satisfaction with an ERMS and that with the support services is congruent with that by [13], who suggest that satisfaction should be assessed with respect to specific services or support, as a part of the overall system evaluation. Our model suggests several hypotheses, discussed as follow.

Regulations are created to guide government agencies' operations procedures or requirements for satisfactory compliance [24]. Such regulations specify essential record management activities by each agency. When implementing an ERMS, agencies can benefit more from the system for achieving their objectives by closely observing the relevant regulatory requirements. As a result, agencies are likely to perceive the relevance of an ERMS if it is chosen and implemented in accordance with the associated regulations or guidelines. In addition, agencies use an ERMS to streamline processes, improve performance, or reduce costs. By integrating ERMS and its management process, an agency can provide increased transparency to service recipients, internal or external, and at the same time creates auditable trails for control purposes [28]. Such integrations allow agencies to adjust their operations and workflows to better meet the concerning regulations; as a result, agencies likely will consider an ERMS relevant to their tasks and services. Furthermore, if an agency greatly relies on an ERMS to accomplish its objectives, the agency has to ensure the design of the ERMS satisfactorily meet all the regulatory requirements specified by the central government, in order to streamline or improve its data exchange process and the associated operations in an effective and efficient way. When implementing an ERMS, agencies motivated to comply with the incumbent regulations are more likely to perceive an ERMS to be relevant than otherwise. Thus, we test the following hypothesis:

H1: Regulatory compliance is positively associated with job relevance.

To foster effective use of an ERMS by adopting agencies, the central government provides support services through designated call centers, including specific instructions about detailed system operations and timely trouble-shooting. A call center establishes the working relationship with agencies by delivering essential information and problem-solving support in a timely manner [7]. When implementing an ERMS, agencies that have higher levels of regulatory compliance likely will exhibit greater reliance on the information processes specified by the central government and thus demand timely information updates and effective, swift support of system implementation through the designated call centers. That is, agencies highly compliant with the regulatory requirements tend to utilize the call centers' support more than otherwise, and are likely to show a higher satisfaction with the support services that include system details, specification updates, administration support, and new functionalities or features. Agencies with higher regulatory compliance are more likely to maintain close working relationships with call centers; such close interactions and participations by agencies in turn can positively affect their satisfactions with the support services. Hence, we test the following hypothesis:

H2: Regulatory compliance is positively associated with satisfaction with support service provided by call center

Job relevance denotes to an assessment of whether a system is relevant to target job
functions [29]. People know about their job situations and usually evaluate a new
system deployed in the work environment according to its relevance to their work
roles or tasks [2]. When a new system is perceived by an individual as relevant to his
or her work tasks, its value can be recognized easily [11]. In our case, the use of an
ERMS by an agency is somewhat administratively mandatory; its staff members
likely will scrutinize the system to assess whether it is relevant to their work performance, thus forming perceptions of its utilities [2] that ultimately determine the satisfaction. The implementation of an ERMS can involve business process redesigns. For
example, the design of an ERMS may incorporate some best practices in the record
management process or offers functionalities that ensure standard record management
operations. When an ERMS is highly relevant to an agency's operations or services,
its personnel would have a better understanding of the system's functionalities and
utilities. In turn, the increased understanding propels further explorations of an ERMS
by agencies that can benefit more from the system and thus become more satisfied
with the system. Hence, we test the following hypothesis:

H3: Job relevance is positively associated with user satisfaction with the
system.

A review of the growing academic research and practice guidelines suggests that
investments in technology by themselves cannot warrant the success in e-government.
Agencies must invest in processes and human capital, including training [4]. The
success of an ERMS in adopting agencies demands substantial efforts by agencies to
ensure desired system utilization or service enhancement. In our case, the call center
funded by the central government can help the agencies make better use of an ERMS,
enabling them to gain more understanding and familiarity with the system. As Ives et
al. [10] note, user involvement is likely to increase with appropriate assistance, and
thus resulting in a higher satisfaction with the system. Furthermore, the long-term
success of an ERMS requires resources and agencies' actual use of the system [4].
Agencies that receive great support from the call centers can better utilize their time
and resource for effective and efficient use of the system. As a result, agencies likely
will continuously devote to the ERMS implemented when they work closely with the
call center and make good use of the support services [12]. That is, agencies satisfied
with the support services are likely to exhibit a higher satisfaction with an ERMS than
otherwise. Therefore, we test the following hypothesis:

H4: Satisfaction with support service provided by call center is positively associated with user satisfaction with the system.

4 Study Design and Data Collection

We conducted a large-scale survey study to test the proposed model and the hypotheses in it. In this section, we detail our study design and data collection.

Measures: We use multiple items to measure each construct, on the basis of a seven-point Likert scale with 1 being "strongly disagree" and 7 being "strongly agree." Specifically, we operationalize regulatory compliance according to an analysis previous research in public administration [8], [3], [24] and our interviews with several domain experts. We use items from Venkatesh and Davis [29] to measure the relevance of an ERMS perceived by an agency with respect to its operations or services. We assess an agency's satisfaction with the support services using items from Feinberg et al. [7]. Finally, an agency's satisfaction with an ERMS, our dependent variable, is derived from the conceptualization of system satisfaction by Bhattacherjee [2].[1]

Target Agencies: Nearly all agencies in Taiwan are required to implement an ERMS to fulfill the requirements specified in the Archives Act that establishes the legal foundation and technology standards for managing government records and archives electronically. Each agency is responsible for managing its records electronically and provides the necessary accessibility and security. When issuing or receiving an official document, an agency must create the required electronic records or transform important records to archives. The National Archives Administration (NAA) is the supreme governing entity charged with the education, promotion, and advancements of using an ERMS by government agencies at all levels. To foster the use of electronic records or archives by agencies, the NAA has enacted a rule for digitalized record management, hereby establishing a necessary regulatory baseline for implementing an ERMS by agencies. In addition, NAA directly funds designated call centers to provide detailed instructions and timely trouble-shooting to agencies. For complete coverage, we target all the government agencies in Taiwan, each referring to an entity within the governing body that has an annual budget from the central government and is autonomous in its resource allocation decision making.

Pilot Study: A panel of domain experts reviewed a preliminary questionnaire and provided their evaluative feedback. These experts include IS managers from different government agencies who in general are knowledgeable about current electronic record management practices. Compliant with their assessments and suggestions, we made several wording choice changes and fine-tuned the language to better reach the targeted agencies. We then conducted a pilot study with key personnel from 10 agencies. Results from the pilot study suggest adequate validity of our instrument, which we therefore use in our formal study.

Data Collections: We take a key informant approach by targeting the principal officer in charge of the records management in each participating agency, primarily because of his or her overall understanding of the implementation and use of the ERMS in the agency. We send, via postal mail, the agencies with an ERMS the questionnaire packet consisted of a cover letter describing our objectives and data management plan, a support letter from the National Archives Administration (i.e., the governing central administrative agency), and the questionnaire. Each agency has 2 weeks to complete and return the survey. We offer an additional 2-week response time for those that did not return the completed survey within the initial response window. Through the official reporting channel, we collected completed questionnaires and the signature of the chief officer in participating agency.

---

[1] Detail items used in this research is available upon request.

We sent the survey packet to 8,029; among them, 1,652 completed and returned the survey, showing an effective response rate of 20.57%. Our sample includes agencies that provide various services; e.g., general administration, commerce, and education. Among the responding agencies, 82.02% of them are local government while the remaining 17.98% are central government. Agencies in our sample are highly representative of the targeted agency pool in terms of the portion of central versus local agencies, the administrative hierarchy, number of staff, and agency specialization or purpose.

5 Data Analyses and Results

We reexamine our survey instrument in terms of reliability and convergent and discriminant validity, and then test the hypothesized model.

Reliability and Validity: We assessed the reliability of our survey instrument on the basis of the Cronbach's alpha of each construct. According to our result, the Cronbach's alpha ranges between 0.69 and 0.93, close to or exceeding the common threshold of 0.7 and thus suggesting adequate reliability. We assessed our instrument's convergent and discriminant validity by performing a confirmatory factor analysis, using a 4-factor structure. The loadings are all significant (p-value < 0.05) and the variance extracted (AVE) for the investigated constructs ranges between 0.71 and 0.88, exceeding the common threshold of 0.5. Our results show the instrument's exhibiting adequate convergent validity. In addition, we assessed the instrument's discriminant validity of by comparing the square root of AVE for each construct with the correlations between that construct and other constructs. According to our results, the square root of AVE for each construct exceeds the correlations between that construct and other constructs, ranging from 0.60 to 0.12. Hence, our instrument shows satisfactory discriminant validity.

Model Testing: After establishing the validity and reliability of the measurement model, we examine the structure model using LISREL with the maximum-likelihood estimation procedure and the covariance matrix. Figure 2 depicts our model testing results. We also assessed the model's overall fit to the data, on the basis of common model goodness-of-fit measures. According to our results, our model has a good fit to the data, as suggested by a satisfactory model fit index in relation with the respective thresholds; i.e., GFI = 0.95, AGFI = 0.93, NFI = 0.97, NNFI = 0.97, CFI = 0.98, RMSEA = 0.067, and SRMR = 0.042.

We evaluated the model's explanatory power by examining the portion of the variances of the agency's satisfaction with an ERMS it explains. As shown in Figure 2, our model accounts for a significant portion of the variances in agencies' satisfaction with an ERMS; i.e., $R^2 = 0.39$. The model can explain 24% of the variables in job relevance but offers marginal explanatory power toward an agency's satisfaction of the support services; i.e., $R^2 = 0.03$.[2]

Hypothesis Testing Results: We tested our hypotheses by assessing the causal path corresponding to each hypothesis. We evaluate each path in terms of the statistical

---

[2] Detailed data analysis results are available upon request.

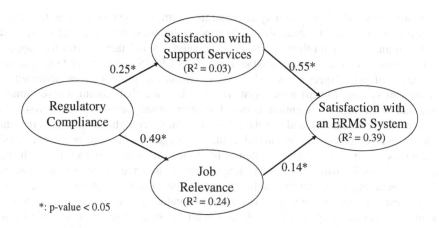

Fig. 2. Model Testing Results

significance and strength of its standardized path coefficient. As shown in Figure 2, the path coefficients are all significant at the 0.05 level, in support of all the hypotheses. According to our analyses, regulatory compliance affects job relevance (i.e., path coefficient = 0.49; *p-value* < 0.05), and the agency's satisfaction with the support service (i.e., path coefficient = 0.25; *p-value* < 0.05). Job relevance influences the agency's satisfaction with an ERMS (i.e.; path coefficient = 0.14; *p-value* < 0.05). In addition, the agency's satisfaction with the support service also impacts its satisfaction with an ERMS (i.e., path coefficient = 0.55; *p-value* < 0.05).

6 Discussion and Conclusion

We study government agencies' satisfaction with an ERMS, fundamental but critical to the digitalization of their internal operations and workflows, and document/record dissemination and sharing. We distinguish an agency's satisfaction with an ERMS and its satisfaction with the support services for effective use of the system. According to our model, an agency's satisfaction with an ERMS can be jointly explained by regulatory compliance, job relevance, and satisfaction with the support services. We test the proposed model and the hypotheses in it, using the survey data collected from a total of 1,652 government agencies in Taiwan. According to our analysis, our model accounts for 39% of the variance in agencies' satisfaction with an ERMS. The data exhibit a reasonably good fit to our model and support all the hypotheses we test, at the 0.05 significance level. Our results show regulatory compliance positively affecting an agency's perception of the relevance of an ERMS and its satisfaction with the support services. Furthermore, an agency's satisfaction with the support services and its perception of an ERMS's relevance have significant, positive influences on its satisfaction with the system.

Our study results provide several important insights. First, although prior research has shown the importance of user satisfaction for systems success [5], this research extends the literature by examining the satisfaction at an agency level as well as separating the satisfaction with a system and that with the support services for effective use of the system. Our analysis results support that these two construct are related but discriminant to each other; specifically, an agency's satisfaction with the support services positively affecting its satisfaction with an ERMS. Second, we highlight the importance of using agencies' satisfactions to assess the success of an advanced e-government system, toward which system usage is somewhat administratively mandated and hence makes "intention to use" less appropriate for assessing the system's success. Third, we analyze and test the role of regulatory compliance in e-government systems and generate some empirical evidence suggesting its effects on agencies' perceptions of an e-government system's relevance and their satisfactions with the support services for using the system. Regulatory compliance deserves more investigations, including its direct and indirect impacts on system adoption or success in government settings. According to our results, regulatory compliance only explains 3% of the variance in agencies' satisfaction with the support services. One plausible explanation is that the influence of regulatory compliance on agencies' satisfaction with the support services may be moderated by other factors. Further investigations are needed to assess such moderating effects as well as additional key satisfaction determinants.

Our findings also have several implications for practitioners. First, an agency's satisfaction with the support services is closely related to its satisfaction with an advanced computer-based system. This finding suggests the importance of a system's functionalities and the support necessary for using the system, which need to be deliberate together. That is, the implementation of a system by itself cannot result in a desirable success that requires adequate support services for advancing users' understanding of the system and facilitating their effective use of the system, hereby leading to increased satisfactions. Second, government agencies that vary in the regulatory compliance requirements may perceive the relevance of an ERMS differently. Agencies may choose an IS strategy less compliant with the incumbent regulatory requirements to achieve other objectives; e.g., cost reductions or time efficiency. These agencies normally have less reliance on computer-based systems for their workflows, operations, or services. Knowing this, regulators should consider diverse IS strategies that offer increased flexibility or adaptability to different agencies. Furthermore, our findings reveals that increased perceived job relevance of a system can promote agencies' satisfaction with the system. User resistance represents one common barrier in system implementation; such resistance may result from users' not able to recognize a system's benefits in relation to their work roles or job tasks. Our finding suggests the importance of connecting a system's functionality or utilities to target users' routine tasks when introducing the system in work contexts.

This study has several limitations that must be considered when interpreting our results. First, Taiwan is well regarded for e-government developments, which are categorized as grade 3 and 2 in 2007 and 2008, respectively in the global e-government report [31]. Thus, our findings may not be equally applicable to countries with less e-government maturity. Second, we focus on agencies' satisfaction with an ERMS, a specific type of e-government systems that conceivably differ from other important e-government systems, such as financial and auditing systems. Third, we obtain our data from a key informant from each participating agency and thus cannot rule out plausible self-selection or self-reporting biases. Forth, our model consists of several key determinants of agencies' satisfaction with an ERMS; there may be other important satisfaction antecedents that are not examined. For example, software vendor is not considered by model and may have significant effects on agencies' satisfactions with an ERMS. Last but not least, support services in this study refer to those services by the designated call centers by NAA, which might differ from the general notion of support services examined by prior research.

Several future research directions are worthy of explorations, including examinations of agencies' satisfactions with essential computer-based systems in countries characterized as less e-government developments. Continued investigations are needed to examine other important e-government systems as well as considering additional factors likely to affect agencies' satisfactions. The relationship between regulatory compliance and agencies' satisfaction with an e-government system also warrants our attention, in conjunction with probable moderating factors. Finally, agencies' satisfactions with the support service also need further examinations, preferably in different research or administrative contexts.

Acknowledgments. This research is partially funded by the National Archives Administration, Taiwan, the Republic of China.

References

1. Argyris, C.: Personality and Organization: The Conflict between System and the Individual. Harper & Row, New York (1957)
2. Bhattacherjee, A.: Understanding Information Systems Continuance: An Expectation-Confirmation Model. MIS Quart. 25(3), 51–370 (2001)
3. Caudle, S.L., Gorr, W.L., Newcomer, K.E.: Key Information Systems Management Issues for the Public Sector. MIS Quart. 15(2), 171–188 (1991)
4. Chircu, A.M., Kauffman, R.J.: Limits to Value in Electronic Commerce-Related Information Technology Investments. J. Manage. Inform. Syst. 17(2), 61–82 (2000)
5. DeLone, W.H., McLean, E.R.: Information Systems Success: The Quest for the Dependent Variable. Inform. Syst. Res. 3(1), 60–95 (1992)
6. DeLone, W.H., McLean, E.R.: The DeLone and McLean Model of Information Systems Success: A Ten-Year Update. Inform. Syst. Res. 19(4), 9–30 (2003)
7. Feinberg, R.A., Hokama, L., Kadam, R., Kim, I.: Operational Determinants of Caller Satisfaction in Banking/Financial Service Call Center. Int. J. Bank Marketing 20(4), 174–180 (2002)
8. Gil-Garcia, J.R., Chengalur-Smith, I., Duchessi, P.: Collaborative e-Government: Impediments and Benefits of Information-Sharing Projects in the Public Sector. Eur. J. Inform. Syst. 16(2), 121–133 (2007)
9. Hartwick, J., Barki, H.: Explaining the Role of User Participation in Information System Use. Manage. Sci. 40(4), 440–465 (1994)
10. Ives, B., Olson, M., Baroudi, J.J.: The Measurement of User Satisfaction with the Information Services Function. Commun. ACM 26(10), 785–793 (1983)
11. Kamis, A., Koufaris, M., Stern, T.: Using an Attribute-Based Decision Support System for User-Customized Products Online: An Experimental Investigation. MIS Quart. 32(1), 159–177 (2008)
12. Kearns, G.S., Lederer, A.L.: A Resource-Based View of Strategic IT Alignment: How Knowledge Sharing Creates Competitive Advantage. Decision Sci. 34(1), 1–29 (2003)

13. Kettinger, W.J., Lee, C.C.: Perceived Service Quality and User Satisfaction with the Information Services Function. Decision Sci. 25(5-6), 737–766 (1994)
14. Larsen, K.R.T.: A Taxonomy of Antecedents of Information Systems Success: Variable Analysis Studies. J. Manage. Inform. Syst. 20(2), 169–246 (2003)
15. Layne, K., Lee, J.: Developing Fully Functional e-Government: A Four Stage Model. Gov. Inform. Q. 18(2), 122–136 (2001)
16. Meijer, A.: Electronic Records Management and Public Accountability: Beyond an Instrumental Approach. Inform. Soc. 17(4), 259–270 (2001)
17. Melone, N.P.: A Theoretical Assessment of the User Satisfaction Construct in Information Systems Research. Manage. Sci. 36(1), 76–91 (1990)
18. Metaxiotis, K., Psarras, J.: E-Government: New Concept, Big Challenge, Success Stories. Electro. Gov. 1(2), 141–151 (2004)
19. Newcomer, K.E., Caudle, S.L.: Evaluating Public Sector Information Systems: More Than Meets the Eye. Pub. Admin. Rev. 51(5), 377–384 (1991)
20. Norris, D.F., Moon, M.J.: Advancing e-government at the Grassroots: Tortoise or Hare? Pub. Admin. Rev. 65(1), 64–75 (2005)
21. Parrish Jr., J.L., Courtney, J.F.: Electronic Records Management in Local Government Agencies: The Case of the Clerk of Courts Office in Lake County Florida. Inform. Syst. Manage. 24(3), 223–229 (2007)
22. Patterson, G., Sprehe, J.T.: Principal Challenges Facing Electronic Records Management in Federal Agencies Today. Gov. Inform. Q. 19(3), 307–316 (2002)
23. Paul, S., Samarah, I.M., Seetharaman, P., Mykytyn Jr., P.P.: An Empirical Investigation of Collaborative Conflict Management Style in Group Support System-Based Global Virtual Teams. J. Manage. Inform. Syst. 21(3), 185–222 (2006)
24. Relyea, H.C.: Paperwork Reduction Act Reauthorization and Government Information Management Issues. Gov. Inform. Q. 17(4), 367–393 (2000)
25. Rocheleau, B., Wu, L.: Public Versus Private Information Systems: Do They Differ in Important Ways? A Review and Empirical Test. Am. Rev. Pub. Admin. 32(4), 379–397 (2002)
26. Sabherwal, R., Jeyaraj, A., Chowa, C.: Information System Success: Individual and Organizational Determinants. Manage. Sci. 52(12), 1849–1864 (2006)
27. Sprague Jr., R.H.: Electronic Document Management: Challenges and Opportunities for Information Systems Managers. MIS Quart. 19(1), 29–49 (1995)
28. Thurston, A.: Records Management as a Public Sector Accountability Function. Int. J Gov. Auditing 24, 7–9 (1997)
29. Venkatesh, V., Davis, F.D.: A Theoretical Extension of the Technology Acceptance Model: Four Longitudinal Field Studies. Manage. Sci. 46(2), 186–204 (2000)
30. Welch, E.W., Hinnant, C.C., Moon, M.J.: Linking Citizen Satisfaction with e-Government and Trust in Government. J. Pub. Admin. Res. Theory 15(3), 371–391 (2005)
31. West, D.M.: Improving Technology Utilization in Electronic Government around the World (2008), http://www.brookings.edu/~/media/Files/rc/reports/2008/0817_egovernment_west/0817_egovernment_west.pdf
32. Wixom, B., Todd, P.A.: A Theoretical Integration of User Satisfaction and Technology Acceptance. Inform. Syst. Res. 16(1), 85–102 (2005)
33. Young, J.: Electronic Records Management on a Shoestring: Three Case Studies. Inform. Manage. J. 39(1), 58–60 (2005)

Practical Security of Large-Scale Elections: An Exploratory Case Study of Internet Voting in Estonia

Guido Schryen

International Computer Science Institute, Berkeley CA 94704, USA
schryen@gmx.net
http://www.icsi.berkeley.edu/~schryen/

Abstract. The Estonian parliamentary election in 2007 is regarded as a success story of large-scale Internet elections. I use this election in a single case study on practical security to show that low quality of security and its management does not necessarily prevent large-scale Internet elections from being conducted. I also provide research propositions with regard to future challenges for large-scale Internet elections.

Keywords: Internet voting, large-scale election, Estonian parliamentary election, security, security management.

1 Introduction

In the course of the recent development of electronic democracy, electronic voting has drawn remarkable attention. Beyond direct recording electronic (DRE) voting machines in designated polling places, remote electronic voting (Internet voting) has come into consideration, and it even reached for governmental elections on the national level in Estonia first [23]. With that event, Internet voting has finally reached the stage of international attention even though experts warned three years earlier in the SERVE report that the Internet is not ready for elections yet [17]. According to Krimmer [19], *"[...] most other nations are still in the phase of experimentation, while most trials do not follow classical experimental setups [2] and are embedded in their national context [32], which makes it hard for comparison and learning from others."* An overview of more than 100 elections with remote e-voting option [19] shows that while remote e-voting has arrived at the regional level, at the national level it is a very rare phenomenon.

Internet voting has turned out to be challenging for two different reasons: First, in the presence of threats due to denial-of-service (DoS) attacks, malware distribution and botnets, tools and infrastructures for large-scale attacks against Internet voting systems are available. Second, procedures related to traditional e-Commerce are limited in their applicability on Internet voting because of their very different nature [17]:

C. Weinhardt, S. Luckner, and J. Stößer (Eds.): WEB 2008, LNBIP 22, pp. 37–50, 2009.

- Elections are inseparably linked to democracy and malfunctioning election processes can directly and decisively influence it. Democracy relies on broad confidence in the integrity of elections. Thus, Internet voting requires a higher security level than e-Commerce does.
- It is not a security failure if your spouse uses your credit card with your consent, but the right to vote is usually not transferable.
- A DoS attack might occur and prevent consumers from performing e-Commerce transactions. However, generally there is a broad time window and once DoS attacks have been detected and mitigated, business can be transacted. In the context of Internet elections, a DoS attack can result in irreversible voter disenfranchisement and the legitimacy of the entire election might be compromised.
- Business transactions require authentication by sending passwords, PINs, or biometric data. In the context of Internet voting, however, authentication procedures shall only be applied to voter registration and voter authorization. The transaction (vote polling) itself requires anonymity. This duality leads to the requirement of implementing much more complex security procedures, be they organizational or technologic.
- People can detect errors in their e-Commerce transactions as they have audit trails: they can check bills and receipts and when a problem appears recovery is possible through refunds, insurance, or legal action. Vote receipts (showing the vote decision) must not be made out, as otherwise votes can be paid and extortion might occur.

Apparently, security issues are a main concern of researchers, practitioners and politicians. But although numerous security procedures for Internet voting have been proposed, there is only a few documents (e.g. [20,24]) that analyze security of real, large-scale Internet elections. In compliance with the objectives of the Web 2008 workshop - to discuss success stories and lessons learned and to map out major challenges - the overall goals of this work are to explore how election security has been practically considered in the past and to deduce implications for the prospective implementation of secure large-scale Internet elections. This leads to the following research questions:

1. What was the role of IT security and its management in large-scale Internet elections?
2. What are future challenges for secure large-scale Internet elections?

The type of these research questions methodologically calls for an exploratory case study analysis, with the large-scale governmental election in Estonia being considered as case.

I present my single case study following a linear-analytic structure, as proposed by Yin [36, pp. 151ff]: In Section 2, I provide the theoretical background of my work, including a brief literature review. Section 3 substantiates single-case study as an appropriate research methodology and presents a precise description of my methodology. Section 4 contains the exploration of the Estonian case. In Section 5, I provide an analysis of the case aiming at answering the research questions and at generalizing to theoretical propositions for the prospective consideration of security issues in large-scale elections. I conclude my work in Section 6 with an outlook on the role of security in prospective large-scale Internet elections.

2   Theoretical Background

As the description and the analysis of the Estonian case study is guided by a theoretical framework, I briefly provide the theoretical background of the different parts of this framework. These parts refer to (core) security and the security related issues of usability, transparency, quality and the electoral process.

2.1   Security

Security issues are considered most relevant in the discussion of electronic voting in general and Internet voting in particular. Based on characteristics of systems described in the literature, Cranor [7] formulates desirable characteristics for Internet elections, the directly security-related ones being as follows: a) accuracy: votes must not be altered or eliminated, invalid votes must not be counted, and the vote tally must be correct, b) democracy: eligible voters can vote, but only once, c) privacy: a link between cast and voter must be impossible, and the voter must not be capable of proving that s/he voted in a particular way, d) verifiability: anyone can independently verify the correctness of the vote tally. Schryen [29] proposes a theoretical framework, in which security requirements are derived from other, non-technological requirements, such as legal, economic and ergonomic ones.

Many technological voting protocols have been proposed, most of which are based on cryptography. One of the earliest protocols that rely on two agencies, an electronic validator and a tallier, was proposed by Nurmi et al. [21]. Based on blind signatures [5] is the two agency protocol [13], which was expanded in the Sensus system [8], that introduces a pollster, a third agency acting as a voters' agent. Protocols that address (the first part of) privacy by means of a "mix net" [6] are proposed by Jakobsson et al. [16] and Juels et al. [18]. Approaches that focus the second part of privacy, being designed to make voting receipt-free, are proposed by Benaloh and Tuinstra [3], Sako and Kilian [28], Okamoto [22], and Hirt and Sako [15].

Another critical part of the overall voting infrastructure is the users' end devices. The importance of the protection of such devices is stressed in the SERVE report, where Jefferson et al. [17, p. 3] argue that an *"[...] Internet- and PC-based system [...] has numerous other fundamental security problems that leave it vulnerable to a variety of well-known cyber attacks (insider attacks, denial of service attacks, spoofing, automated vote buying, viral attacks on voter PCs, etc.), any one of which could be catastrophic."* The following methods have been proposed to overcome the challenge of insecure voting devices [33]: voter manual regarding security measures, voting operating system, trusted computing elements, and code sheets.

2.2   Further Security Related Issues

The following issues seem to be relevant to security:

- *Usability*: The voter needs some kind of software and hardware to communicate with the server and to run the voting protocol. The most accessible
  implementation requires only a web browser, with either only SSL being
  enabled or, additionally, Java being enabled; further advanced approaches
  provide specific voting software, which needs to be installed. Depending on
  the authentication technique in place, in addition to software also hardware,
  such as a card reader, might be required to be available to the voter.
- *Transparency*: As the Internet voting system as a whole is probably not
  understood by most voters, it is necessary to implement procedures that
  increase transparency. This can be done by providing verifiability and open
  access to all information about the election and its procedures. According to
  Pieters [25], the following types of verifiability can be distinguished: *individual verifiability* allows voters to verify whether their votes have been counted,
  and *universal verifiability* allows anyone to verify the overall correctness of
  the tally. During the development of the election system and the election
  itself many documents including the source code and procedural documents
  are generated. The access to these documents can be generally permitted,
  allowed for particular groups, such as evaluators and observers, allowed for
  everyone (at a particular place after having signed a non-disclosure agree-
  ment), or allowed for everyone by making this documents public (e.g. on the
  Internet).
- *Quality Management*: There exist several options to ensure the quality of the
  technologic election system and the processes. The most popular ones are
  test elections (the voter can practice and get used to it), system evaluations
  (either by a security experts or according to a security standard like the
  Common Criteria), audits of the election procedures, or observations made
  by independent authorities.
- *Electoral Process*: The electoral process consists of two mandatory phases,
  complemented by an optional, third phase:
  1. Registration phase: In order to electronically check the user's eligibility
     to cast a ballot, an electronic version of the electoral register is required.
     This register can either be generated in the registration phase, in which
     those voters who want to cast their vote electronically apply and are
     thus added to the register, or by integrating the existing registers into a
     single one.
  2. Voting Phase: Voting is either enabled only before the election day, only
     on the election day, or during both periods.
  3. Vote Updating: An Internet voting system can support vote updating:
     for different implementation options see [34]. Thus a voter who casts his
     vote but is coerced, distrust her device, or changes his mind can update
     her vote later again, either using the same or a different electronic device,
     or even paper.

3   Methodology

I approach methodology in two parts. The first part describes why I choose to select case study as research strategy. The second part explains how I apply case study research in order to answer the research questions.

3.1   Research Strategy

As my approach is to choose research methodology problem-driven, I need to match the research questions with the characteristics of different research methodologies. The research questions, stated in the introduction and aiming at identifying (a) the role of IT security in large-scale Internet elections (b) future challenges for secure large-scale Internet elections, are of multidisciplinary nature and embedded in a multi-faceted social context. In order to appropriately consider the multi-facets of this context, I explored research methodology of the social sciences and considered as relevant research strategies the "experiment", "survey", "archival analysis", "history" and "case study". With regard to the latter research strategy, an early, conventional view was that a case study is not a valuable research methodology, as a case study cannot provide reliable information about the broader class [1,4]. However, during past years the acceptance of case study methodology as a necessary and sufficient method for many important research tasks has increased [27,31,35,36]. More precisely, I follow the arguments of Flyvbjerg [12], who shows in his literature synthesis that (1) general, theoretical (context-independent) knowledge is not necessarily more valuable than concrete, practical (context-dependent) knowledge, (2) one can generalize even on the basis of individual cases so that the case study can contribute to scientific development and (3) it is often not difficult to summarize and develop general propositions and theories on the basis of specific case studies.

Adopting the case study definition of Yin's [36, p. 13f] seminal work (see Definition 1), we find a good match between what is studied (large-scale Internet elections) and what can be investigated by using a case study, thereby identifying case study research as one candidate for methodology. However, we also need to consider the appropriateness of other research strategies. Thereto, I apply the methodological framework proposed by the COSMOS corporation and elaborated by Yin [36, Chapter 1], according to which the appropriateness of a research strategy depends on the "values" of three attributes: (1) the form of research question, (2) the control of behavioral events, and (3) the focus on contemporary events. As our research (1) poses what and how questions, (2) does not allow for controlling or manipulating behavioral events (elections) and (3) focuses on contemporary elections, in accordance with this framework, I choose to select case study as research methodology.

Definition 1. *"Case study is an empirical inquiry that investigates a contemporary phenomenon within its real-life context, especially when the boundaries between phenomenon and context are not clearly evident. [...] The case study inquiry copes with the technically distinctive situation in which there will be many more variables of interest than data points. [...]"*

Having identified the case study as appropriate research method, now the case study design has to be specified.

3.2   Case Study Design

The design of the case study is based on the suggestion of Yin ([35, Chapter 1] and [36, Chapter 2]), who regards the following components as important:

- Determination of the specific type of case study
- Definition of the study's questions
- Development of a theoretical framework
- Case selection
- Providing criteria for interpreting the findings

Type of Case Study. According to Yin [35,36], the type of case study is determined by three decisions:

1. Is the research exploratory, explanatory, or descriptive?
2. Does the research cover a single case or several cases (multiple case study)?
3. Does the study follow an embedded or holistic design?

I now briefly answer these questions with regard to this research: (1) While a descriptive case study presents a complete description of a phenomenon within its context and an explanatory case study presents data bearing a cause-effect relationship, an exploratory case study mainly focuses what questions and is aimed at developing pertinent hypotheses and propositions for further inquiry. In accordance with the research questions, I therefore apply an exploratory case study. (2) To explore practical election security in detail, it is advisable to choose cases, which are embedded in an innovative environment, which implement comprehensive security procedures, and for which sufficient data is available. To my best knowledge, this set of conditions is met only by the Estonian parliamentary election, which took place in 2007. Consequently, I select to consider only this case, resulting to a single case study. (3) If we need to address several units of analysis in the same context, the case study is denoted as embedded. Otherwise, the case study is holistic. As we have only on unit of analysis (one election), my case study is holistic.

Research Questions. The study's research questions are

1. What was the role of IT security and its management in large-scale Internet elections?
2. What are future challenges for secure large-scale Internet elections?

Theoretical Framework. In an exploratory case study, the theoretical framework should specify what is being explored, thereby guiding the description and analysis of the case. The framework provides a level at which empirical results of the case study are compared and at which the generalization of the case study results will occur. In order to address the research questions, the case is being explored with regard to security, quality, usability and transparency of the electoral process.Overall, for the Estonian case I explore

- what electoral environment was present,
- how the holistic electoral process was conducted with particular regard to the integration of anonymity and identification, which are core concepts of governmental elections,
- how technical and organizational security measures were implemented,
- what audits, tests and evaluations were conducted to assure quality,
- how usability (for voters) was determined through the usage of hardware and software, and
- how transparency in terms of verifiability and accessibility was assured.

Case Selection. The selection of cases in case study methodology does not focus on statistical sampling but much rather on theoretical sampling. This term was introduced by Glaser and Strauss [14] where they aim to gain a deeper understanding of analyzed objects in contrast to studying all possible variations of an object. This can be seen as a collection of independent pieces of information to get a better understanding of a thing that is only known in part [26].

For my case selection, I need to cope with the fact that the number of uses of Internet voting in large-scale Internet elections to date is limited [19]. As already mentioned above, the Estonian parliamentary election is the only one of these, for which sufficient data is available. Estonia is the first (and only) country worldwide to introduce legally-binding, nation-wide Internet voting without any preconditions.

Interpreting the Findings. The interpretation of the findings is intended to answer the research questions. This analysis will be done by investigating to what extent the technologic state-of-the-art in terms of security was implemented, to what extent security management was implemented, and how election security was perceived by different stakeholders.

4   The Case: Parliamentary Elections in Estonia

This case study refers to the 3 March 2007 parliamentary (Riigikogu) elections in Estonia, which was the first parliamentary election in the OSCE area in which voting by Internet was available (but not obligatory) to all eligible voters in order to increase voter turnout. The exploration of this election is based on publicly available reports of the OSCE Office for Democratic Institutions and Human Rights (ODIHR) [23], the European Union Democracy Observatory [11] and the Estonian National Electoral Committee [9,10]. For a brief overview of political issues see [30].

4.1   Electoral Environment

In the Estonian electoral system, the country is divided into 12 multi-mandate electoral districts. Political parties compete for the 101 parliamentary mandates distributed in an electoral district by registering with the National Election Committee (NEC) the lists of candidates for each electoral district contested. To cast a ballot, voters write the registration number of the candidate of their choice on the ballot when voting by ballot paper or mark the name of the preferred candidate when voting by Internet. Voters were offered different options to use advance paper ballot voting, voters could cast their ballot in polling station at the day of election, and voters could cast their ballot in advance through the Internet (due to an amendment of the Riigikogu Election Act). The law permitted voters to change their votes during the advance voting period, either by voting again through the Internet or by casting a ballot paper at a polling station. The voter could change his/her vote an unlimited number of times electronically, with the last ballot cast being the only one counted, but a vote cast by paper is final and annuls all Internet votes cast by the voter. Voters who casted a vote by Internet were not allowed to cast a vote on election day itself.

4.2   Usability

The technical cornerstone of the Internet voting system in Estonia is the use of a personal identification document (ID card), which is already legally accepted for identification via the Internet and to sign documents digitally. The computer used by the voter must have a smart card reader installed in order to process the digitally-enabled ID card, as well as two PIN codes associated with the ID card. Installation software must be downloaded. With regard to the user's Voting Application, voters using Microsoft Windows (98.9%) use a web browser, while for voters who use Mac OS (0.75%) or Linux (0.42%) the voting interface is a stand alone program. The voting interface itself is only available in the Estonian language.

4.3   Electoral Process

In the course of general voter registration, the distribution of designated voting cards, PIN codes, keys or certificates for Internet voting was not necessary, because the already deployed Estonian ID card contains a user-specific certificate and a private key on an embedded chip. Together with two PIN codes, the card allows the holder to authenticate and digitally sign during the Internet voting process. This voting process is displayed in Figure 1 and involves the following steps:

1. The *Voter Application* requests data from the voter's ID card. To proceed, the voter types a personal code (PIN1) to identify her/himself. Through an SSL connection between the *Internet Server* and the voter's computer, the *Voter Application* checks whether the voter is on the voter list.
2. The voter chooses one candidate by clicking on the name of the candidate and then confirming the choice. Unlike the paper balloting, the system does not allow voters to cast a blank ballot or to spoil their ballot.
3. The vote is encrypted with the public key of the *Counting Server*. In order to cast the vote, the voter must type in a second personal code (PIN2). This

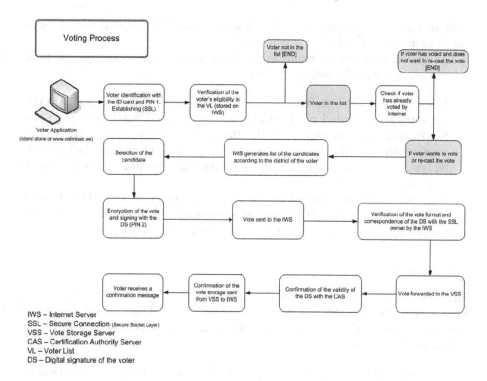

Fig. 1. Internet voting process in Estonia's 2007 parliamentary elections; source: [23, Annex 2]

code is the confirmation that it is the voter him/herself who is voting. The PIN2 enables the card to sign the encrypted vote.

4. The encrypted vote is then sent to the *Internet Server* which checks whether the digital signature corresponds to the session owner.
5. The Internet Server then forwards the encrypted vote to the *Vote Storage Server*, which requests a check of the validity of the voter's certificate from the *Certification (Authority) Server*. If valid, the *Internet Server verifies* the digital signature using the voter's public key from the voter's certificate.
6. At the end of the voting process, the voter receives an on-screen confirmation that the vote has been cast. The encrypted vote remains on the *Vote Storage Server* until counting and tabulation is performed on election day.

As voters could select advance ballot voting in addition to Internet voting, a consolidation of votes needed to be conducted: After receiving lists from polling stations regarding any voters who cast a paper ballot during advance voting and who also cast a vote by internet, NEC staff mark the corresponding electronic votes on the *Vote Storage Server* as "not to be counted". The process of canceling votes is logged. The advance paper ballot is counted in the normal counting process. Finally, the NEC staff burns a CD from the *Vote Storage Server* that contains the last electronic vote of each voter. This CD is sealed and given to the Chairman of the NEC.

The counting of the electronic votes takes place on election day, one hour before the closing of the polling stations:

1. The encrypted votes are transferred to the *Counting Server* by a CD-ROM. All entries transferred to the *Counting Server* are logged. The *Counting Server* decrypts the votes using the *Hardware Security Module (HSM)* and counts them. In order to enable the *HSM*, six physical keys must be inserted. By law, at least half of the NEC members must be present in order to decrypt and count the votes.
2. After the votes are counted on the *Counting Server*, a new CD is burned with the results. The CD is taken to a personal computer where the results are processed so that they can be viewed in a spreadsheet.

4.4   Security

The core security architecture of the Internet voting system is based on the separation of the *Vote Storage Server* connected to the Internet and the offline *Counting Server*. With regard to specific security prerequisites, the following provisions were taken:

– The installed voting software was checked to ensure that it was identical to the software received.
– There is a firewall between the *Internet Server* and the *Vote Storage Server*.
– Traffic to the *Internet Server* was monitored by system operators to attempt to identify any abnormalities or external attacks.
– The *Internet Server* and the *Vote Storage Server* were located in a locked room which was guarded by a policeman and continuously filmed. In addition, these servers were sealed.
– To ensure the availability of the election results in the event of failure of the *HSM*, there was a backup of the private key which was kept secret by one of the members of the NEC.
– To limit the likelihood of attacks to voters' computers, the NEC advised voters to type in the correct IP web address, published the server certificate and provided information to the voter to verify whether he/she has the proper voting application.

4.5   Quality

There was no obligation to certify or test the system, the Internet voting system was not officially certified by an independent body and no full end-to-end logic and accuracy test were performed on the system. The auditing was conducted by an external auditing company, which monitored and checked the activities of the NEC against written documentation, which describes the necessary steps and procedures. In addition to the formal auditing, all of the above steps were videotaped. However, the final report is not public, and the external auditing company was not requested to conduct any post-election audits. It is not clear to what extent the voting software was formally audited after being received from the company.

4.6 Transparency

Main characteristics of the Estonian Internet voting system are that (1) no "Voter Verified Paper Audit Trail" as an independent verification system was implemented so that the voter receives no proof that his/her vote has been counted (correctly) and (2) the separation of voter's decision and identity is realized at organizational level, not providing the voters any option to monitor this separation.

The NEC stated that all political parties and accredited observers were invited to observe the administration of Internet voting in every phase of the process, including the opportunity to review the documentation of the system, the source code of the software, and all of the setup procedures in the process. However, overall, there appeared to be no oversight of the Internet voting process by political parties or civil society.

5 Analysis

In this section the Estonian election is analyzed with regard to the extent the technologic state-of-the-art in terms of security was implemented, to the extent security management was implemented, and how election security was perceived by different stakeholders.

For authentication and confidentiality, strong cryptographic solutions based on digital signatures and a public key infrastructure were used. However, voters used their PCs with card readers attached, and possible threats against these PCs were neglected. For example, web side spoofing and malware, which makes the card reader sign other data than displayed on the screen, were not seriously addressed or even not considered. Anonymity was established in the post-election period (the encrypted votes are linkable to voters) at organizational level: links were removed before decrypting the votes. No designated e-voting protocols were applied. Even worse, the voters got no proof of the separation of their decision and their identity. As no voter verified paper audit trail was implemented, voters did not know whether their vote had been correctly counted. Summing up, the Estonian election did not implement or seriously consider designated protocols provided in the e-voting literature.

Although some general IT security provisions were taken, these were kind of ad-hoc approaches, as the Riigikogu Election Act does not contain specifications of the Internet voting system, does not foresee the responsibility of any institution, and does not provide for sanctions in case of failure of the system. Main concerns about the security quality of the Internet voting system are raised in the report of the OSCE/ODIHR Election Assessment Mission team [23]. For example, if the *Certification Server* were to fail or be unavailable, voting by Internet would not function. Furthermore, there did not appear to be a formal plan to monitor network traffic and to deal with the risk of DoS attacks against the *Internet Server*.

According to [23], there was no obligation to certify or test the system. The Internet voting system was also not officially certified by an independent body and no full end-to-end logic and accuracy test was performed on the system. Although some auditing was conducted by an external auditing company, the final report is not public. Even worse, the external auditing company was not requested to conduct any post-election audits. Overall, the security management was at a poor level. Taking this essential weakness into consideration, the fact that no security incidents have been reported does not mean that none occurred.

Although the overall level of security (management) was quite poor, no severe complaints were reported. The election and its security (management) seem to have been broadly accepted by voters, politicians, and election officials. This might be due to the fact that this Internet voting project was a milestone project.

Having addressed the first research question, I now formulate the research propositions, which are intended to be a starting point for further research:

1. Low quality of security (management) does not necessarily prevent authorities to conduct Internet elections for the sake of technologic leadership.
2. The propagation of carelessness with regard to security would attract serious large-scale attacks against Internet elections, once the voter turnout increases.
3. The diffusion and adoption of large-scale Internet elections will fail, unless profound knowledge about the implementation of sophisticated e-voting protocols and infrastructures as well as comprehensive and transparent security management is available.

6 Conclusions and Outlook

The Estonian election analyzed in this paper shows that the implementation of secure large-scale Internet elections is still a hard task, even in a highly innovative environment. It remains a future challenge to bridge the gap between what has been proposed in the literature and what is implemented in practice. In addition to conducting research along the propositions of this paper, the implementation of further pilot projects and comprehensive testing seem preconditions for any further adoption of Internet voting. Although the Estonian case is regarded as a success story in the press, serious security (management) concerns raise the question whether such elections are useful for the prospective adoption of Internet voting.

Acknowledgments. This work was supported by a fellowship within the Postdoc-Programme of the German Academic Exchange Service (DAAD).

References

1. Abercrombie, N., Hill, S., Turner, B.S.: Dictionary of sociology. Penguin, Harmondsworth (1984)
2. Alvarez, R.M., Hall, T.: Point, Click, & Vote. Brookings Institution Press, Washington (2004)
3. Benaloh, J., Tuinstra, D.: Receipt-free secret-ballot elections. In: STOC 1994, pp. 544–553 (1994)
4. Campbell, D.T., Stanley, J.C.: Experimental and quasi-experimental designs for research. Rand McNally, Chicago (1966)
5. Chaum, D.: Blind signatures for untraceable payments. In: Chaum, D., Rivest, R.L., Sherman, A.T. (eds.) Crypto 1982, pp. 199–203 (1983)
6. Chaum, D.: Untraceable Electronic Mail, Return Addresses and Digital Pseudonyms. CACM 24(2), 84–88 (1981)
7. Cranor, L.F.: Electronic Voting: Computerized polls may save money, protect privacy. ACM Crossroads Student Magazine 2(4) (1996)
8. Cranor, L.F., Cytron, R.K.: Sensus: A Security-Conscious Electronic Polling System for the Internet. In: HICSS 1997, pp. 561–570 (1997)
9. Estonian National Electoral Committee: Main Statistics of E-Voting (2007), http://www.vvk.ee/english/Ivotingcomparison2005_2007.pdf
10. Estonian National Electoral Committee: Parliamentary elections 2007: Statistics of e-voting (2007), http://www.vvk.ee/english/Ivoting_stat_eng.pdf
11. European Union Democracy Observatory: Report for the Council of Europe: Internet Voting in the March 2007 Parliamentary Elections in Estonia (2007), http://www.vvk.ee/english/CoEandNEC_ReportE-Voting2007.pdf
12. Flyvbjerg, B.: Five Misunderstandings About Case Study Research. Qualitative Inquiry 12(2), 219–245 (2006)
13. Fujioka, A., Okamoto, T., Ohta, K.: A Practical Secret Voting Scheme for Large Scale Elections. In: Seberry, J., Zheng, Y. (eds.) AUSCRYPT 1992. LNCS, vol. 718, pp. 244–251. Springer, Heidelberg (1993)
14. Glaser, B., Strauss, A.: The discovery of grounded theory: Strategies for Qualitative Research. Aldine, New York (1967)
15. Hirt, M., Sako, K.: Efficient receipt-free voting based on homomorphic encryption. In: Preneel, B. (ed.) EUROCRYPT 2000. LNCS, vol. 1807, pp. 539–556. Springer, Heidelberg (2000)
16. Jakobsson, M., Juels, A., Rivest, R.L.: Making mix nets robust for electronic voting by randomized partial checking. In: USENIX Security Symposium 2002, pp. 339–353 (2002)
17. Jefferson, D., Rubin, A.D., Simons, B., Wagner, D.: A Security Analysis of the Secure Electronic Registration and Voting Experiment (SERVE) (2004), http://www.servesecurityreport.org
18. Juels, A., Catalano, D., Jakobsson, M.: Coercion-Resistant Electronic Elections. In: De Capitani di Vimercati, S., Dingledine, R. (eds.) WPES 2005, pp. 61–70. ACM Press, New York (2005)
19. Krimmer, R., Triessnig, S., Volkamer, M.: The Development of Remote E-Voting Around the World: A Review of Roads and Directions. In: Alkassar, A., Volkamer, M. (eds.) VOTE-ID 2007. LNCS, vol. 4896, pp. 1–15. Springer, Heidelberg (2007)
20. Mohen, J., Glidden, J.: The Case for Internet Voting. CACM 44(1), 72–85 (2001)
21. Nurmi, H., Salomaa, A., Santean, L.: Secret ballot elections in computer networks. Computers and Security 36(10), 553–560 (1991)

22. Okamoto, T.: Receipt-free electronic voting schemes for large scale elections. In: Christianson, B., Crispo, B., Mark, T., Lomas, A., Roe, M. (eds.) Security Protocols 1997. LNCS, vol. 1361, pp. 25–35. Springer, Heidelberg (1997)
23. OSCE: OSCE/ODIHR Election Assessment Mission Report in the 2007 parliamentary elections in Estonia (2007),
    http://www.vvk.ee/english/OSCEreport_EST_2007.pdf
24. Philips, D.M., von Spankovsky, H.A.: Gauging the Risks of Internet Elections. CACM 44(1), 73–85 (2001)
25. Pieters, W.: What proof do we prefer? Variants of verifiability in voting. In: Ryan, P. (ed.) Proceedings of the Workshop on Electronic Voting and e-Government in the U.K. (2006), http://www.cs.ru.nl/~wolterp/Verifiability.pdf
26. Punch, K.F.: Introduction to Social Research: Quantitative and Qualitative Approaches. Sage Publishing, London (2005)
27. Ragib, C.C., Becker, H.S. (eds.): What is a case? Exploring the foundations of social inquiry. Cambridge University Press, Cambridge (1992)
28. Sako, K., Kilian, J.: Receipt-free Mix-type Voting Scheme. In: Guillou, L., Quisquater, J.-J. (eds.) EUROCRYPT 1995. LNCS, vol. 921, pp. 393–403. Springer, Heidelberg (1995)
29. Schryen, G.: Security Aspects of Internet Voting. In: HICSS 2004 (2004)
30. Solvak, M., Pettai, V.: The parliamentary elections in Estonia, March 2007. Notes on Recent Elections/Electoral Studies 27(3), 547–577 (2008)
31. Stake, R.E.: The art of case study research. Sage Publications, Thousand Oaks (1995)
32. Svensson, J., Leenes, R.: E-Voting in Europe: Divergent democratic practice. Information Polity 8(1-2), 3–15 (2003)
33. Volkamer, M., Alkassar, A., Sadeghi, A.-R., Schultz, S.: Enabling the Application of Open Systems like PCs for Online Voting. In: FEE 2006 (2006),
    http://fee.iavoss.org/2006/papers/fee-2006-iavoss-Enabling_
    the_application_of_open_systems_like-PCs_for_Online_Voting.pdf
34. Volkamer, M., Grimm, R.: Multiple Cast in Online Voting – Analyzing Chances. In: Krimmer, R. (ed.) Electronic Voting 2006. LNI, vol. 86, pp. 97–106. Springer, Heidelberg (2006)
35. Yin, R.K.: Applications of case study research, 2nd edn. Sage Publications, Thousand Oaks (2003)
36. Yin, R.K.: Case study research: design and methods, 3rd edn. Sage Publications, Thousand Oaks (2003)

Situational Effects on the Usage Intention of Mobile Games

Ting-Peng Liang and Yi-Hsuan Yeh

Department of Information Management, National Sun Yat-sen University,
Kaohsiung, Taiwan
tpliang@mail.nsysu.edu.tw, celeste.epaper@m2k.com.tw

Abstract. As value-added services on mobile devices are developing rapidly, text messaging, multi-media messaging, music, video, games, GPS navigation, RFID, and mobile TV are all accessible from a single device. Mobile games that combine mobile communication with computer games are an emerging industry. The purpose of this research is to explore what situation factors may affect the intention to play mobile game. We propose a research model to fit the nature of mobile games and conducted an online survey to examine the effect of situational factors. The model integrates constructs in TAM and TRA. The findings are as follows. First, Subjective norm affects a user's intention in using mobile games when a user has no other task. Second, perceived playfulness affects a user's intention to use mobile games when the user has another task.

Keywords: Mobile games, Situation influences, Technology Acceptance Model, Theory of Reasoned Action.

1 Introduction

As mobile devices become more and more popular, value-added mobile services develop rapidly. Text and multi-media messaging, music, video, games, GPS navigation, RFID, mobile TV, and many innovative applications are available on mobile devices. An application that has gained much attention in entertainment is mobile games that allow the user to play games on their mobile devices. A recent survey by Informa Telecoms & Media (2007) shows that the global revenue of mobile games in 2006 was more than $2.5 billion, and that will exceed $7.5 billion in 2011, tripled in five years. Many experts forecast that cell phones will play a pivotal role in meeting personal demands in a variety of environments in the near future.

As a major characteristic of mobile games its availability in different places, situation is considered a critical factor in affecting consumer's intention to play. Previous literature has indicated that consumer decisions are frequently affected by situational factors, such as particular occasions, time restrictions, or task characteristics [9]. A major advantage of mobile technology is its ability to provide users with instant, new and useful information at appropriate time and in a variety of places. If mobile technology is not able to satisfy user needs instantly, m-commerce will lose its important economic value. Therefore, when we investigate issues related to mobile commerce, situational factors must be considered.

C. Weinhardt, S. Luckner, and J. Stößer (Eds.): WEB 2008, LNBIP 22, pp. 51–59, 2009.

With the above rationale, this study targets at the following two questions:

1.   What factors affect a user's intention to use mobile games; and
2.   Do situational factors have moderating effects on a user's intention to use mobile games?

The remainder of the paper is organized as follows. Section 2 reviews related literature. Section 3 describes our research framework that is based on an integration of TAM and TRA model and augmented with situational factors. Section 4 outlines research method and instruments. Section 5 describes research findings. Finally, Section 6 concludes the paper and discusses potential implications.

2   Background and Literature Review

2.1   Mobile Commerce and Mobile Games

The convergence of the Internet and mobile technology has resulted in the development of electronic commerce via mobile devices—m-commerce. M-commerce can be defined as any direct or indirect transaction performed using a mobile device such as a cell phone or personal digital assistant (PDA). As a new channel of electronic commerce, m-commerce has received much attention in both academic and trade journals (e.g., [6], [8], [10], [12], and [14]). M-commerce has been viewed as the next big wave of technology evolution, and revenues created from transactions conducted through mobile devices are estimated to reach more than $554 billion in 2008 [20].

Among various value-added applications, mobile entertainment is considered to have a great potential. The introduction of 3G broadband capabilities provides a fast platform for transmitting videos, which is expected to have a considerable effect on mobile entertainment consumption. At present, mobile games, broadly defined as games played on mobile devices, are one of the primary entertainment services. Mobile games gain popularity in some countries recently and are expected to grow rapidly in coming years.

The adoption of mobile services is a research direction that gains popularity recently. For example, Ngai et al. [17] used a case study to examine RFID applications in m-commerce. The results show that RFID can benefit the operators of a container depot. Mallat [15] presented a qualitative study on consumer adoption of mobile payment technology and found that the relative advantage of mobile payments is different from that specified in adoption theories.

These prior studies indicate that the adoption of mobile services must have some additional factors as compared to the adoption of other technology. Since a unique feature of mobile commerce is its sensitivity to time and location, a potential direction for investigation is the factor related to the situation in which a mobile service is used.

2.2   Situational Effects

Situation is viewed as a critical mediating factor in consumer behavior research. Consumers making decisions often encounter many situational factors, such as occasion, time limitation, or tasks [18]. For instance, Hansen [7] proposed three situational characteristics in the decision making process: consumption situation, purchase situation, and communication situation. Belk [1] classified situational variables into five categories: physical surroundings, social surroundings, temporal perspective, task definition, and antecedent states.

Some prior research has studied the effect of situation variables. For examples, Topi et al. [21] investigated the relationship between task complexity and time availability in database query. The results show that time availability does not have any effect on task performance whilst task complexity has a strong influence on performance. Schmitt and Shultz [19] studied the influence of situational variables (such as the purchasing situation and the purchasing target) on consumer preferences toward the image product of men's fragrances.

In m-commerce research, some scholars suggest that the design of m-commerce customer interfaces should take into account the particular mobile setting. Researchers used three characteristics to describe the mobile setting: spatiality, temporality, and contextuality. Spatiality refers to users being able to carry their mobile device anywhere they go. Temporality refers to users being able to access the Internet instantly. Contextuality is concerns with the dynamic environments in which mobile devices are used [11]. Mallat [15] pointed out that the adoption of mobile payments is dynamic, depending on certain situational factors such as a lack of other payment methods or urgency.

3 Research Model and Hypothesis

In this section, we present a research model that is based on the Theory of Reasoned Action (TRA) and Technology Acceptance Model (TAM), and augmented with situational factors.

3.1 TRA and TAM

TRA and TAM are two models that have been used to interpret and predict the intention of technology use in the information systems area. TRA was derived from social psychology and proposed by Ajzen and Fishbein [5]. It has three major constructs: behavioral intention, attitude, and subjective norm. Attitude is affected by beliefs. Attitude, combined with subjective norm, determines behavioral intention. This theory has been applied to study many information technology applications and is certainly appropriate for investigating the intention to use mobile games. However, a shortcoming of TRA is that it does not have a clearly definition of what precedents may affect attitude.

Another popular theory in predicting technology adoption is the technology acceptance model (TAM) [3]. Its two main tenets are perceived usefulness and perceived ease of use (EOU). Perceived usefulness refers to the degree to which a person believes that using a particular system would enhance his/her job performance. Perceived EOU refers to the degree to which a person believes that using a particular system would be free from effort. Perceived usefulness and perceived EOU are also influenced by external factors. TAM proposed that perceived usefulness and perceived EOU will affect the usage attitude, and further affect user behavior. Perceived EOU will enhance the perceived usefulness of technology and further influence the attitude toward using IT. TAM is usually used to measure user cognition of IT applications and behavioral attitude [3] and [4].

A shortcoming of TAM is its assumption that user attitude is the sole factor that determines user intention and tends to ignore the influences of reference groups and other contextual factors. Therefore, it seems that the integration of these two models can provide a better predictive power.

Integration of TAM with other models is not new in information systems research. For example, López-Nicolás et al. [13] combined TAM and innovations diffusion theory (IDT) models to explore the usage behavior of mobile services. Yi et al. [23] integrated TAM, IDT, and the theory of planned behavior (TPB), and measured the adoption of PDAs in medical treatment. However, most of these works did not include the situational factors in their combined models.

3.2 Perceived Playfulness for Games

Another issue related to using TAM for mobile games is that the perceived usefulness may be different for mobile games than for other business applications. We replace it with perceived playfulness, which is well-supported by existing literature. For instance, Moon and Kim [16] used an extended TAM in different task contexts (entertainment-purpose vs. work-purpose). They found that perceived playfulness is an important factor for entertainment-oriented tasks and perceived usefulness is an important factor for work-oriented tasks. Van der Heijden [22] argued the hedonic nature of an information system is an important boundary condition to the validity of TAM. The result showed that perceived enjoyment and perceived EOU are stronger determinants of intention to use than perceived usefulness. Thus, perceived usefulness loses its dominant predictive value in hedonic domains. Mobile gaming is obviously a pleasure-oriented use of information technology. Therefore, TAM is revised by replacing usefulness with playfulness. We posit the following hypothesis:

Hypothesis 1: *Attitude toward playing mobile games is affected by the perceived playfulness and perceived ease of use of the game.*

3.3 Subjective Norm

Subjective norm (SN) refers to the social pressure exerted on an individual to perform or not perform a particular behavior [5]. Consequently, the social pressure causes the relevant behavior to become the individual's normative beliefs with which he/she would comply. Motivation to comply refers to his/her wanting or being willing to comply with these beliefs. That is, a user may exhibit different motivations for complying with the opinions of relevant people on the adoption of mobile technology. In TRA, subjective norm is a major factor that can influence attitude. Hence, we posit the following hypothesis:

Hypothesis 2: *Intention to play mobile games is affected by perceived playfulness, perceived ease of use, the attitude toward playing the game, and the subjective norm of the user with respect to playing the game.*

3.4 Situational Factors

As many decisions may be affected by certain situational factors, we augment our research model with a major situational factor related to mobile games: it is a psychological factor of whether the user has another task on hand. This situational factor makes two different usage situations for examining their effects. The following hypotheses can be posited:

Hypothesis 3: *The combined TRA and TAM model is moderated by situational factors.*

Hypothesis 3-1: *Different situations will affect the relationship between perceived playfulness and intention to use a mobile game.*

Hypothesis 3-2: *Different situations will affect the relationship between perceived ease of use and intention to use a mobile game.*

Hypothesis 3-3: *Different situations will affect the relationship between attitude toward a mobile game and intention to use.*

Hypothesis 4: *Different situations will affect the relationship between the SN and intention to use a mobile game.*

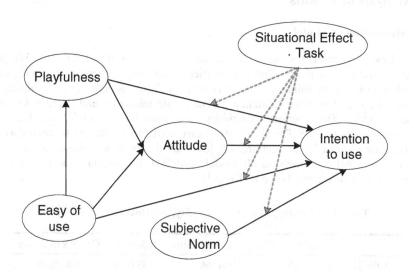

Fig. 1. Theoretical Framework

Based on the above description, we can put together a research model based on the integration of TRA and TAM, with the augmentation of situational factors. Figure 1 shows the schematic illustration of the model.

4 Instrument Development and Research Methodology

4.1 Instrument Development

A cross-sectional survey was conducted to evaluate the proposed research model. Validated items were used to measure perceived playfulness [2], perceived EOU [3], attitude [3], SN [5], and intention to use [3]. We chose task as our situational variable (have task vs. no task) for study. Likert scales (ranging from 1 to 5) with anchors ranging from "strongly disagree" to "strongly agree" were used for all questions. After pretesting the measures, these items were modified to fit the mobile game context.

4.2 Measure and Data Collection

Voluntary mobile game users were recruited to participate in the online survey. Each person was randomly assigned three situations when completing the questionnaire. There were three versions of the questionnaire for different situations. Each version had 78 respondents. There were 234 usable responses and the overall response rate was 95.12%. Respondents ranged from 20 to 30 years of age. The ratio of male to female was 53.8% to 46.2%, and student to non-student was 46.2% to 53.8%. Of all the respondents, 89.8% have at least a college degree.

5   Analysis of Results

5.1 Measurement Model

Partial Least Squares (PLS) were used to analyze the measurement model. We proceeded to evaluate the psychometric properties of the measurement model in terms of reliability, convergent validity, and discriminant validity. Reliability and convergent validity of the factors were estimated by composite reliability and average variance extracted (AVE). The composite reliability value must be above 0.70, and the AVE value must be above 0.05. Discriminant validity verifies whether the squared correlation between a pair of latent variables is less than the average variable extracted for each variable. All constructs in all models satisfied the criteria, thus requiring no changes to the constructs (shown in Table 1).

Table 1. Reliability, Convergent Validity, and Discriminant Validity

	AVE	Composite Reliability	R Square	Cronbachs Alpha
Attitude	0.760517	0.904966	0.381940	0.842805
EOU	0.772038	0.910202		0.851067
Intension	0.854324	0.946201	0.648250	0.914610
Playfulness	0.581126	0.917012	0.142316	0.896536
SN	0.817764	0.930850		0.889096

5.2 Structural Model

Figure 2 presents a graphical depiction of the PLS results. This is the original model without any situational influence. Most of paths are significant with the model accounting for 14.2% of the variance in playfulness, 38.2% of the variance in attitude, and 64.8% of the variance in intention. The results reported that perceived EOU has significant influence on perceived playfulness and intention to use mobile games, but

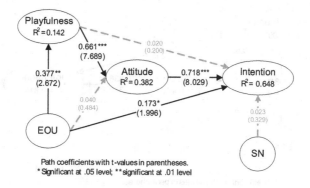

Fig. 2. Path analysis of mobile games

not on users' attitude toward using mobile games; Perceived playfulness has a strong significant effect on users' attitude toward using mobile games, but not on the intention of mobile games; SN has no significant effects on the intention to use mobile games. Therefore, hypotheses 1 and 2 are partially supported. That is, TRA and TAM can help predict the intention to play mobile games.

5.3 Situational Factor

Given the base model being reasonably supported, we further analyze the moderating effect of situational factor by analyzing the model in two different situations.

We found that different situations have moderating effects in our model. SN has a positive significant effect on intention while a user has no task, but does not have any effect on intention while a user has a task. It implies that a user's perception of peer attitude has a different effect on intention in different situations. Perceived playfulness has a positive significant effect on intention when a user has another task; on the contrary, it has no effect on intention when a user has no other task. It seems that when a user is busy, he/she may be distracted by a mobile game because, for example, there is a need to lift his/her mood or to relax for a while (Shown in Figure 3 and 4).

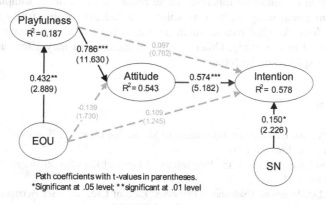

Fig. 3. No Task

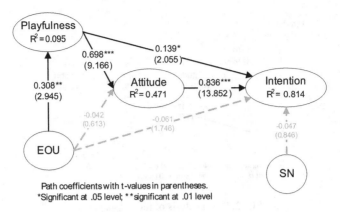

Fig. 4. Having a Task

6 Conclusion

This paper aims to shed light on consumer adoption of mobile games using an inte-grated TRA and TAM model. In the theoretical model, we examined the moderating effects of alternative situations on the relationship between playfulness and intention, attitude and intention, EOU and intention, and SN and intention. The findings are as follows. First, SN affects a user's intention in using mobile games only when a user has no other task. A user's perception of peer attitude has a different effect on inten-tion in different situations. Secondly, perceived playfulness affects a user's intention to use mobile games when he/she has a task. When a user is in that situation, the play-fulness of mobile games can stimulate a user's intention to use mobile games.

The contributions of this study are as follows. This paper has proposed a hybrid in-tension model to explore the moderating effects of certain situations on a user's inten-tion to use mobile games. This is the first study that considers situational influences in the hedonic information systems context. The findings provide critical information for marketers and advertisers. Situational factors should be taken into consideration when new mobile services are marketed.

One potential limitation of this research surrounds the size of the sample collected. Also, the convenient sampling used to solicit respondents for the survey may not be perfectly random. Another measurement limitation is that only one contextual effect was investigated in this study. Other situational factors that may affect users' inten-tions may be explored in the future.

References

1. Belk, R.W.: An Exploratory Assessment of Situational Effects in Buyer Behavior. J. Mar-keting Res. 11, 156–163 (1974)
2. Csikzentmihalyi, M.: Flow, the Psychology of Optimal Experience. Harper & Row, New York (1990)
3. Davis, F.D.: Perceived Usefulness, Perceived Ease of Use, and User Acceptance of Infor-mation Technology. MIS Quart. 13(3), 319–340 (1989)

4. Davis, F.D., Bagozzi, R.P., Warshaw, P.R.: User Acceptance of Computer Technology: A Comparison of Two Theoretical Models. Manage. Sci. 35(8), 982–1003 (1989)
5. Fishbein, M., Ajzen, I.: Belief, Attitude, Intentions and Behavior: An Introduction to Theory and Research. Addison-Wesley, Reading (1975)
6. Gebauer, J., Shaw, M.J.: Success Factors and Impacts of Mobile Business Applications: Results from A Mobile E-Procurement Study. Int. J. Electron. Comm. 8(3), 19–42 (2004)
7. Hansen, F.: Consumer Choice Behavior: A Cognitive Theory. The Free Press, NY (1972)
8. Herzberg, A.: Payments and Banking with Mobile Personal Devices. Commun. ACM 46(5), 53–58 (2003)
9. Jaeger, S.R., Rose, J.M.: Stated Choice Experimentation, Contextual Influences and Food Choice: A Case Study. Food Qual. Prefer. 19, 539–564 (2008)
10. Lee, Y.E., Benbasat, I.: Interface Design for Mobile Commerce. Commun. ACM 46(12), 49–52 (2003)
11. Lee, Y.E., Benbasat, I.: A Framework for the Study of Customer Interface Design for Mobile Commerce. Int. J. Electron. Comm. 8(3), 79–102 (2004)
12. Liang, T.P., Wei, C.P.: Introduction to the Special Issue: A Framework for Mobile Commerce Applications. Int. J. Electron. Comm. 8(3), 7–14 (2004)
13. Lopez-Nicolas, C., Molina-Castillo, F.J., Bouwman, H.: An Assessment of Advanced Mobile Services Acceptance: Contributions from TAM and Diffusion Theory Models. I&M (in press, 2008)
14. Maamar, Z.: Virtual extension: Commerce, E-Commerce, and M-Commerce: What Comes Next? Commun. ACM 46(12), 251–257 (2003)
15. Mallat, N.: Exploring Consumer Adoption of Mobile Payments-A Qualitative Study. J. Strategic Inf. Syst. 16, 413–432 (2007)
16. Moon, J.W., Kim, Y.G.: Extending the TAM for a World-Wide-Web Context. I&M 38, 217–230 (2001)
17. Ngai, E.W.T., Cheng, T.C.E., Au, S., Lai, K.H.: Mobile Commerce Integrated with RFID Technology in a Container Depot. Decis. Support Syst. 43, 62–76 (2007)
18. Park, C.W., Iyer, E.S., Smith, D.C.: The Effects of Situational Factors on In-Store Grocery Shopping Behavior: The Role of Store Environment and Time Available for Shopping. J. Consum. Res. 15(4), 422–433 (1989)
19. Schmitt, B.H., Shultz, C.J.: Situational Effects on Brand Preferences for Image Products. Psychol. Market. 12(5), 433–446 (1995)
20. Smith, A.D.: Exploring M-Commerce In Terms Of Viability, Growth and Challenges. Int. J. Mobile Commun. 4(6), 682–703 (2006)
21. Topi, H., Valacich, J.S., Hoffer, J.A.: The Effects of Task Complexity and Time Availability Limitations on Human Performance in Database Query Tasks. Int. J. Hum.-Comput. St. 62, 349–379 (2005)
22. Van der Heijden, H.: User Acceptance of Hedonic Information Systems. MIS Quart. 28(4), 695–704 (2004)
23. Yi, M.Y., Jackson, J.D., Park, J.S., Probst, J.C.: Understanding Information Technology Acceptance by Individual Professionals-Toward An Integrative View. I&M 43, 350–363 (2006)

Modelling and Simulation of
National Electronic Product Code Network
Demonstrator Project

John P.T. Mo

RMIT University, Melbourne, Australia
john.mo@rmit.edu.au

Abstract. The National Electronic Product Code (EPC) Network Demonstrator Project (NDP) was the first large scale consumer goods track and trace investigation in the world using full EPC protocol system for applying RFID technology in supply chains. The NDP demonstrated the methods of sharing information securely using EPC Network, providing authentication to interacting parties, and enhancing the ability to track and trace movement of goods within the entire supply chain involving transactions among multiple enterprise. Due to project constraints, the actual run of the NDP was 3 months only and was unable to consolidate with quantitative results. This paper discusses the modelling and simulation of activities in the NDP in a discrete event simulation environment and provides an estimation of the potential benefits that can be derived from the NDP if it was continued for one whole year.

Keywords: EPC Network, National Demonstrator Project, FMCG industry, system simulation, inter-enterprise transactions.

1 Introduction

The National Electronic Product Code Demonstrator Project (NDP) was the first in the world to implement full Electronic Product Code (EPC) network technology across an entire supply chain for the handling inter-company transactions and movement of goods across company boundaries [1]. The NDP successfully tracked pallets and cartons and had an opportunity to demonstrate the benefits of Radio Frequency Identification (RFID) technology in the fast moving consumer goods (FMCG) supply chain. Sharing the project's learning can save Australian companies time and money [2].

The NDP involved companies from across the FMCG supply chain: Metcash, Gillette, Procter & Gamble (P&G), Nugan Estate, Capilano Honey, Visy Industries, Linfox, CHEP, VeriSign, Sun Microsystems and the Australian Food & Grocery Council (AFGC). The NDP was critical to the participants to gain understanding of the issues in EPC implementation through actual practices. It was also important to small to medium enterprises (SMEs) to learn the technology while observing the actions taken by large industry partners.

EPC is a low-cost technology, based on passive RFID devices. It is acclaimed as the successor of today's omnipresent bar codes. EPC is the basis of a distributed

C. Weinhardt, S. Luckner, and J. Stößer (Eds.): WEB 2008, LNBIP 22, pp. 60–70, 2009.

Table 1. Products used in the EPC process

Industry partners	Product
CHEP/Visy	Pallet
Gillette	Mach 3 Turbo crt 4's (R1)
	Duracell C/T AA4's (R2)
P&G	PANTENE SMOOTH & SLEEK SHMP 400ML 2000
	PANTENE SMOOTH & SLEEK COND 400ML 2750
	PANTENE COLOR REVIVAL SHMP 400ML 2250
	PANTENE COLOR REVIVAL COND 400ML 2750
	METAMUCIL SMOOTH ORANGE 283 GM 1750
	FREBREZE EXTRA STRENGTH 400 ML

architecture, called EPC Network, for the automatic identification of objects moving in the supply chain and industrial production applications. Bottani and Rizzi [3] assessed the benefits of EPC Network on fast moving consumer goods (FMCG) supply chain and concluded information flow across all parties was the most important advantage.

The NDP demonstrated the benefits of RFID technology and the use of full stack of EPC Network. It showed how EPC technology could be harnessed for tracking of pallets and cartons through the supply chain [4]. The project demonstrated benefits for all partners within the supply chain, adding to what was already understood about the savings for retailers. The sharing of learning also meant savings in time and money for Australian companies.

In the NDP, detailed use cases were established at each site specifying both the physical process and the information required at each read point. There were totally 15 use cases (11 in Gillette, 2 in P&G and 2 in Metcash) developed by the industry partners of the consortium. Use cases described how the business processes could work with the system (software) and formed the basis for implementing the middleware system in the Demonstrator. According to the use cases, components of EPC Network such as middleware, user interfaces and portal were designed to meet business requirements of the project participants.

To ensure a high probability of success, the consortium decided to simplify the material flow process by limiting the flow to certain product items. After careful consideration of the trading activities in the consortium, 6 industry partners with 9 products were decided for use in the NDP (Table 1).

The NDP achieved the objective of illustrating how the technology could be used in industrial environment. However, it did not develop a quantitative assessment of the benefits. To estimate the real benefit, this research develops a computational model that uses the industrial data to estimate the potential benefits. This paper describes the modelling and simulation analysis and discusses the findings in quantitative terms.

2 Scenario Analysis by System Simulation

Simulation is a powerful technique for solving a wide variety of problems. Harrison *et al* [5] tried to promote understanding of simulation methodology by developing an appreciation of its potential contributions to management theory. Molina and Medina [6] analysed design and operation of manufacturing enterprises using simulation tools. Analysis by simulation is to execute the behavior of a system or phenomenon under study in a virtual environment. A system is a collection of distinct objects which interact with each other. In order to study a system, only relevant information will be gathered in the system. Such a collection of pertinent information about a system is called a *model* of the system.

In our daily life, lots of problems are too complex to solve via exact mathematical analysis, such as weather, traffic jam, aircraft flight, business executive. Firstly, the system itself is too complex or the theory is not yet developed sufficiently. Secondly, there may be too many uncertainties, dynamic interactions between decisions and subsequent events, or interdependencies among variables in the system. Finally, some elaborated laboratory experiments have to be conducted, which are usually expensive and time consuming. Simulation with computer provides another way replacing the laboratory experiments. The analysis process is cheaper and faster and more importantly, efficient.

There are two different types of systems:

1. The systems in which the states change smoothly or continuously with time are called *continuous systems*. A good example is the simulation analysis by Han and Min [7] on the transmission performance of RFID.
2. The systems in which the states change abruptly at discrete points in time are called *discrete systems*. For example, Lu and Cheng [8] simulated the role of RFID in a typical manufacturing system and estimated an improvement of more than 8% was possible. Amini *et al* [9] presented a simulation study conducted in a regional hospital to investigate tactical and strategic purposes in addition to col-lateral value quality data generated by this technology.

The complexity and extent of work in the NDP presented similar issues to a pilot research. Quantitative data was difficult to capture due to other business constraints imposed to the experimental environment. This paper describes the research of using real data from the NDP as the basis of simulating the system performance if it were continued for a much longer period. The NDP is a discrete system. Each change in the NDP, such as empty pallet, flat carton inventories, loading and unloading process, customer arrivals, is called an *event*. Hence, the modelling and simulation of the NDP is a *discrete-event simulation*.

To illustrate how the NDP is modelled, we provide some background information about the NDP. The material flow process map (Fig. 1) describes the flow of physical items between the consortium partners. The material flow sequence starts from CHEP transporting pallets to P&G and Gillette. Similarly, pallets are transported from CHEP to Visy. At Gillette, products are made overseas but they are packed in different formats in Australia. Application of EPC is necessary at the carton level when the final form of delivery is made. After application of EPC, products are moved from P&G/Gillette to Metcash. This will go through the Linfox transport sys-tem but the movement of goods from Metcash distribution centre (DC) to retail out-lets, return of pallets from Metcash DC to CHEP, Visy and suppliers are not traced in NDP model after goods reach Metcash.

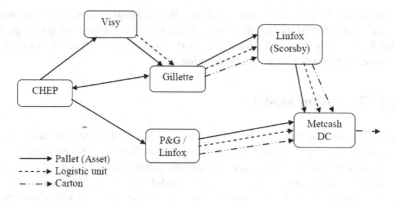

Fig. 1. NDP material flow map

In addition, tracing of information in the NDP is also important. In the information flow map (Fig. 2), P&G and Gillette place a request for pallets to CHEP.

The start of the individual transaction chain is a purchase order (PO) issued from Metcash to P&G/Gillette. Gillette places a request for flat cartons to Visy. Visy places a request for pallets to CHEP. The suppliers then issue a PO to Visy for the required number of cartons, and to CHEP for the required number of pallets. Upon delivery of the pallets and cartons, a corresponding notification will be given to the store person at the receiving company to verify the receipt of goods. Metcash's PO also initiates a series of activities at P&G/Gillette. The goods are packed and loaded on a pallet. The number of carton boxes depends on the quantity ordered. When the order is picked,

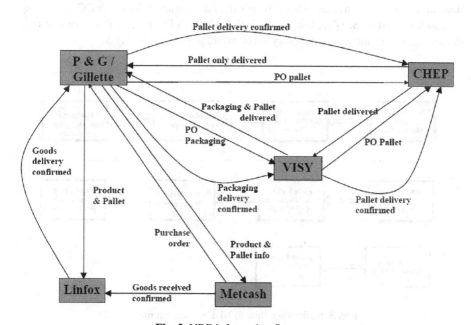

Fig. 2. NDP information flow map

the products and the pallet are confirmed and the information is sent to Metcash for confirmation and checking. The goods are passed to Linfox where the goods are handled and delivered to Metcash. Once the goods are received, Metcash confirms the receipt of goods through normal documentation.

3 NDP Simulation Model

The simulation system used in this research is ARENA [10]. This simulation system has been used extensively around the world by researchers for discrete process simulation. Creation of the NDP simulation model starts with the Create module, which is named *Metcash Inventory Control*, the first module in sub model named *Metcash Product Inventory Control*. When this entity is created, Metcash will check the inventories of all products. If the inventory is higher than a certain level, PO won't be created and the entity will go into Dispose modules. This is one kind of whole life of a flow from Create to Dispose.

If the inventory is lower than a certain level, a PO will be created and placed to the corresponding suppliers. After PO is received by supplier, plenty of flowchart modules will simulate how products are packed, wrapped, transferred, loaded and finally transported to Metcash DC. Attributes about order and products, and variables about inventory will be updated and when products are stored. This flow will be concluded by Dispose modules.

The establishment of NDP simulation model (Fig. 3) is based on the basic work flow as in Fig. 1 and the information flow in Fig. 2. At the beginning of each day, Metcash DC checks inventory (we denote as $I(t)$, where t is time) to decide whether to place an order. If the inventory level is less than a constant s, Metcash DC orders "up to" another constant S. What this means is that Metcash DC place a PO so that, if they were to arrive instantly, the inventory level would pop up to exactly S.

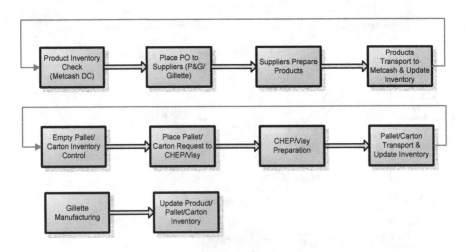

Fig. 3. Basic work flow in NDP simulation model

Therefore, if $I(t)<s$, Metcash orders $S-I(t)$ items in a PO; if $I(t)\geq s$, Metcash does nothing. This process of checking will occur again on the next day. We called this policy *(s, S) inventory models*. P&G and Gillette also use *(s, S) inventory model* to control the pallet/carton inventories. PO or requests are issued by suppliers and goods are prepared. When goods arrive at destinations, corresponding inventories will be updated immediately.

Metcash's PO initiates most of activities at P&G, Gillette CHEP and Visy. Only Gillette manufacturing is independent from Metcash's PO. However, Gillette manufacturing's activities are based on the sales forecast and the production quantity will be based on the PO quantity rather than inventory.

The NDP simulation model is further separated into five sub models. Each sub model represents a consortium member and has several functions for different work. All sub models and functions are listed in Table 2.

Table 2. NDP simulation modules

Module	Module	Product
Metcash DC	Metcash receiving process	To receive products from P&G and Gillette, transport them to designated areas
	Metcash product inventory control	To monitor and take actions controlling inventory level at Metcash
	Metcash dispatch process	NDP simulation model doesn't keep trace the pallets and cartons, so the sub-model just describes the customer arriving with some demand attributes, and update the inventories after the products are dispatched.
Gillette	Gillette manufacturing	There are two series of products in the Gillette plant. They are produced as small packs, but entities in the simulation model are pallet units.
	Gillette pack and wrap Pallets for customer order	It is a complicated function in the simulation model, as there are two important activities: packing and wrapping, and one logic control are merged.
	Gillette flat cartons receiving and empty pallets returning process	This is a simple function that flat cartons or empty pallets arrive at Gillette are transferred as stacks and pallets respectively.
	Gillette pallet and carton request	This is a logic control for Gillette requesting empty pallets and flat cartons, which is similar to Metcash product inventory control.
P&G	P&G pallets receiving process	Pallets are unloaded, transferred through reader gantry. Inventory will be updated automatically and the pallet request situation will be changed.
	P&G use cases	This function simulates the pick and pack use case at P&G.
	P&G pallet request	This is a logic control of (s, S) inventory model for P&G placing request of empty pallets, which is similar to Gillette pallet request.
CHEP	CHEP use cases	This function is to prepare empty pallets and transport them to customers
Visy	Visy use cases	This is a logic control of (s, S) inventory model for Visy placing request of empty pallets. Visy checks empty pallet inventory once a day.

4 Parameters Used in Simulation

Before the simulation is set to run, there are some important parameters to be set up. The simulation time is 360 days. Initial value of variables should be given before simulation runs, because they describe the situation at the time when the simulation runs. We assume all empty pallet and flat carton request situation and PO situation are 0, which means there is no request or PO at the start, irrespective of whether the inventories are lower than level s. All the initial values of inventories are listed in Table 3.

In order to quantify the benefits of NDP, several KPIs should be defined before simulation runs. There are two phases to evaluate the authenticity. The first phase is the time for each Process and Route. The primary data about time is based on the image transcription of NDP. Therefore, there is no doubt to the authenticity of time. The second phase is logic control of inventories. Most of activities start from inventory control. The inventory model (s, S) is used in every inventory and the focal point is to set up s and S properly. Shortage may happen because of too small s, and overstock may happen because of too large S. The $S - s$ controls the frequency of placing orders or requests. If the frequency is too high, it will cause the rising of ordering cost.

To evaluate effectiveness of EPC technology, several time values are accumulated during simulation. Processing time means the time when a PO is placed until the required products are received. It includes delays at a value added process, wait time in a queue and transfer time. The application of EPC will increase time of some process, such as placing tags on cartons, pushing cartons through gravity feedline and scanning tags on pick faces, etc. On the other hand, it will decrease time of some other process, such as administration work after products and pallet arriving, documents check, etc. It is not necessary to calculate the time for each detailed process, but the processing time including the value added delay time and wait time can indicate the change of the efficiency of the system.

The cost of labour varies slightly at different locations in the country. The actual labour cost per hour is used as shown in Table 4.

Table 3. Initial values of variables

Variable name	Initial value
P&G empty pallet inventory	30
Gillette empty pallet inventory	100
Gillette empty carton inventory	40
Visy empty pallet inventory	50
P&G product inventory	30
Gillette Mach3 inventory	15
Gillette AA4 inventory	15

Table 4. Labour cost list

Company	Labour cost/ hour
CHEP	$32
P&G	$28
Gillette	$25
Visy	$23
Metcash	$31

5 Analysis of Results

The main measure to assess the authenticity of the simulation is to examine the three plots: P&G Product Inventory, Gillette AA4 Inventory and Gillette Mach3 Inventory. The inventories rebound between proposed levels and there are rare shortages or overstocks. The plots are shown in Fig. 4, 5 and 6.

We calculate PO Processing Time in days by the function:

$$\text{PO Processing Time} = \text{VA Time} + \text{NVA Time} + \text{Wait Time} + \text{Transfer Time} \qquad (1)$$

where:

- VA Time means value added time, which is accumulated when an entity incurs a delay at a value added process.
- NVA Time means non-value added time, which is accumulated when the entity incurs a delay at a non-value added process.
- Wait time is accumulated when the entity incurs a delay at a process whose allocation has been designated as wait, or when the entity resides in a queue until the entity exits the queue.

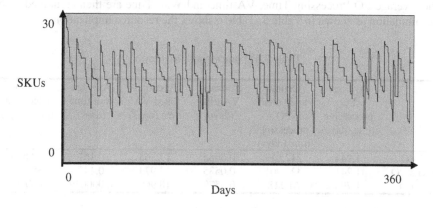

Fig. 4. The P&G product inventory plot

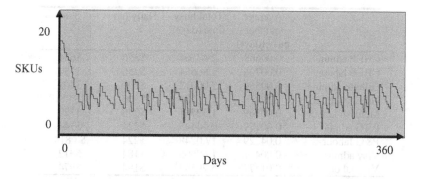

Fig. 5. The Gillette AA4 inventory plot

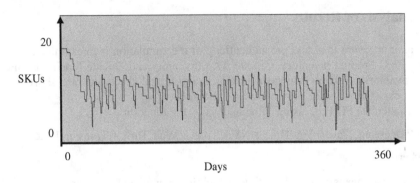

Fig. 6. The Gillette Mach3 inventory plot

- Transfer Time is accumulated when the entity incurs a delay at a process whose allocation has been designated as transfer. By default, all time spent using material handling from the Advanced Transfer panel (a conveyor or transporter) is specified as transfer.

The Average PO Processing Time, VA time and Wait Time are then computed from the simulation as shown in Table 5. Table 6 shows the resource implication:

Table 5. PO processing time (days)

	Average PO processing time (days)	Accumulated total PO processing time (days)	Average VA time (days)	Accumulated VA time (days)	Average wait time (days)	Accumulated wait time (days)
AA4 PO	1.244	242.619	0.0685	13.365	0.157	30.635
Mach3 PO	1.241	323.901	0.0535	13.973	0.147	38.236
P&G PO	1.798	61.118	0.5579	18.969	0.000049	0.00167

Table 6. Total labour cost

	Average number busy (days)	Total busy time (days)	Daily pay	Sum
CHEP admin	0.00688	2.47764	$256	$634
CHEP labour	0.00796	2.86654	$256	$734
Gillette admin	0.00556	2.00012	$200	$400
Gillette labour	2.5669	924.084	$200	$184,817
Metcash labour	0.00369	1.32761	$248	$329
P&G admin	0.00179	0.64445	$224	$144
P&G labour	0.04729	17.0248	$224	$3,814
Visy admin	0.00471	1.69695	$184	$312
Visy labour	0.01471	5.29593	$184	$974
Total cost				$192,158

The labour cost can then be evaluated by the function:

$$\text{Labour Cost} = \Sigma \text{Average Number Busy} \times 360 \times \text{Daily Pay} \tag{2}$$

The saving of \$192,158 is the overall labour cost savings if the NDP continues for a year. Other costs such as overhead and materials costs are not included. Therefore, it only represents a tiny section of the potential savings of the supply chain. Given that there are thousands of products handled by the consortium companies, the savings will be significant if the EPC technology is rolled out to the whole supply chain.

6 Conclusion

This paper gives the background of NDP and discusses some basic concepts of EPC. The NDP was executed for 3 months due to budget and resources constraints. Very limited quantitative conclusion could be drawn from the pilot study. Based on the NDP experience and the information available, the NDP is modelled in a discrete event simulation system. The computer model is simulated for analysing the potential performance of the NDP if it was run for a longer period than it was.

The NDP simulation model runs successfully and reports about entities, queues and resources were exported. According to the KPIs, relevant data during the simulation run was collected including plots and tables. PO Processing Time and Labour Cost were quantified. The simulation result shows that a direct labour cost saving of \$192,158 could be achieved if the NDP was run for one whole year. If overhead and other costs are included in the estimation, and if the EPC technology is rolled out to the whole supply chain, the savings will be substantial.

References

1. GS1 Australia, CSIRO: EPC NetworkTM Australia Demonstrator Project Report (2006), http://www.gs1au.org/
2. Attaran, M.: RFID: an enabler of supply chain operations. Supply Chain Management: An International Journal 12(4), 249–257 (2007)
3. Bottani, E., Rizzi, A.: Economical assessment of the impact of RFID technology and EPC system on the fast-moving consumer goods supply chain. International Journal of Production Economics 112(2), 548–569 (2008)
4. Mo, J.P.T.: Development of a national electronic product code network for the tracking of fast moving consumer goods. Int. J. Enterprise Network Management 2(1), 25–46 (2008)
5. Harrison, J.R., Carroll, G.R., Carley, K.M.: Simulation Modelling in Organisational and Management Research. Academy of Management Review 32(4), 1229–1245 (2007)
6. Molina, A., Medina, V.: Application of enterprise models and simulation tools for the evaluation of the impact of best manufacturing practices implementation. Annual Reviews In Control 27(2), 221–228 (2003)
7. Han, Y., Min, H.: System Modelling and Simulation of RFID. In: Auto-ID Labs Research Workshop, Zurich, Switzerland, September 23-24 (2004)

8. Lu, B., Cheng, K.: Modelling and simulation on an RFID based manufacturing system. In: Pham, D.T., Eldukhri, E.E., Soroka, A.J. (eds.) 4th Innovative Production Machines and Systems Virtual International Conference IPROMS 2008 (2008). Internet Conference on http://conference.iproms.org/
9. Amini, M., Otondo, R.F., Janz, B.D., Pitts, M.G.: Simulation Modeling and Analysis: A Collateral Application and Exposition of RFID Technology. Production and Operations Management 16(5), 586–598 (2007)
10. Kelton, W.D., Sadowski, R.P., Sturrock, D.T.: Simulation with Arena, 4th edn. McGraw-Hill, New York (2007)

Benefit Analyses of Technologies for Automatic Identification to Be Implemented in the Healthcare Sector

Mike Krey and Ueli Schlatter

Abstract. The tasks and objectives of automatic identification (Auto-ID) are to provide information on goods and products. It has already been established for years in the areas of logistics and trading and can no longer be ignored by the German healthcare sector. Some German hospitals have already discovered the capabilities of Auto-ID. Improvements in quality, safety and reductions in risk, cost and time are aspects and areas where improvements are achievable. Privacy protection, legal restraints, and the personal rights of patients and staff members are just a few aspects which make the heath care sector a sensible field for the implementation of Auto-ID. Auto-ID in this context contains the different technologies, methods and products for the registration, provision and storage of relevant data. With the help of a quantifiable and science-based evaluation, an answer is sought as to which Auto-ID has the highest capability to be implemented in healthcare business.

Keywords: Auto-ID, Supply Chain, Evaluation, Healthcare, RFID, Barcode.

1 Introduction

The German healthcare system can be devided into three main branches (Statistisches Bundesamt, 2004):

- Ambulatory Treatment, assured by 43'000 medical practitioners
- Clinical Treatment, assured by 2'200 hospitals and
- Post-operative Treatment, assured by 1'400 rehabilitation centres.

It is financed by the compulsory health insurance. With health services assured through the insurance system, current demographic changes are resulting in a steadily increasing demand for medical and nursing care.

Cost pressure, reforms and quality requirements are three keywords which are mentioned in the current debate about German healthcare. The financial framework of the German healthcare is at its limits (Jaeckel, 2004: 25-43).

The billing is calculated on a per diem basis, which means that medical insurers simply pay an agreed amount per day spent in hospital – independent of a patient's diagnosis. Any further costs are covered by the hospital, meaning the state or private hospital operators pay.

By the end of 2012 the billing by Diagnosis Related Groups (DRGs) is about to be introduced. That means that the hospital is going to be paid e.g. for an appendix operation with a fix amount and it has to cover their costs. The introduction of DRG case-based lump sums is to achieve two things:

C. Weinhardt, S. Luckner, and J. Stößer (Eds.): WEB 2008, LNBIP 22, pp. 71–82, 2009.

More transparency of all medical services offered and provided in a hospital and ideally a performance-based kind of remuneration.

In the German Federal structure, the DRGs will provide a prerequisite for more competition between the service providers because services and products delivered by hospitals can be compared, regarding cost as well as quality. National, standardised tariffs would also make it easier to achieve comparability and to promote the exchange of healthcare services between different geographical areas within Germany.

For the affected hospitals it is necessary to develop concepts and reforms to save costs and to work more efficiently. In many organizations, IT is fundamental to support, sustain and grow the business. In this context IT as a business enabler can play an important role in German hospitals.

Most of the 2'200 German hospitals are community owned and regulated by public law. These hospitals are in competition with an increasing number of privately financed hospitals. For the regulated hospitals it is difficult to make big financial investments within the normal budget. The IT budget is regulated for one year and includes e.g. labour costs, IT maintenance and small investments in hard- and software. Large IT projects can hardly be implemented by regulated hospitals without additional external financial support (Becker-Berke, 2004). In accordance with a survey by McKinsey & Company, a quarter of German hospitals won't be able to hold out against cost pressure and will have to close by the year 2020 (McKinsey & Company, 2006). For the affected hospitals it is necessary to develop concepts and reforms to save costs and to work more efficiently. As it has in the fields of logistics and trading, Auto-ID can become an important component for the solution of operational planning and optimization of processes in healthcare, with the resulting cost reductions (Middendorf, 2005). Primarily, Auto-ID can be help to optimize and support the business processes in the medical and non-medical areas of a hospital (Gillert & Hansen, 2007). Nurses and doctors will be freed from avoidable and time-consuming activities - there will be more time for patients. For example nurses are wasting 30% of their time by organising their workflow and 40% with administrative duties, so that the time for patient care is reduced to 8 minutes per patient and day (McKinsey & Company, 2006).

Currently, various technologies are coming into operation. Wireless Local Area Network (WLAN) is already firmly established in German hospitals. Other systems are still at the trial stage, such as Radio Frequency Identification (RFID) as a procedure for automatic identification (Auto-ID).

2 Goals of This Study

The evaluation of Auto-ID shows a professional approach to structured, rational selection and procurement of a system in accordance with the requirements of the healthcare sector. Various Auto-ID procedures are evaluated on the basis of healthcare requirements and their resulting use criteria. The requirements definition is based on practical experiences of the author and personal interviews with Chief Technology Officers (CTO) of six German hospitals with experience in the implementation of Auto-ID in different business contexts. Their experiences have been very different. Some implementations had the status of fundamental research in small, autonomous environments and others are funded by Auto-ID producers so that a clear consideration of costs and needs cannot be made. The focus of this work is a general list of requirements and makes no claim to be complete. The list will need adaption to a concrete business context in a hospital. The aim, after the evaluation process, is to make a valid and objective statement regarding which procedures are appropriate for application in the healthcare sector.

3 Scientific Approach and Automatic Identification Technologies Analysed

The following approach to evaluation was executed (Schreiber, 2003: 181-233):

- Defining requirements. A structured catalogue with wishes and demands on the Auto-ID was created with the help of the operating and IT department of the hospital. If necessary additional expert knowledge can help to channel the requirements process. The operating department uses relevant medical knowledge about the internal processes of the hospital or department where the Auto-ID should be implemented. The IT department is responsible for the technical input and uses knowledge for example in the fields of systems integration, project management or functional range of medical equipment.
- Establishing criteria. Based on the defined requirements for the Auto-ID, a list of criteria was created. The different criteria are grouped into levels which contain on the lowest level qualified and measureable questions with clear origin which can be answered by the responsible department members. For a rational and objective execution of the evaluation the criteria will be weighted.
- Benefit analysis. The collected detailed information for every technology is the basis on which every criterion is evaluated in terms of their degree of performance (Schreiber, 2003).
- Conclusion. Based on the result of the benefit analysis a concrete proposal was developed. The selected Auto-ID has the optimal capability of being implemented in healthcare in terms of the weighted criteria. The single Auto-ID technology with the highest value in the benefit analysis is not necessarily the exclusive optimal proposal. Under certain circumstances it can be reasonable that two or more Auto-ID technologies can be combined.

3.1 Fields of Application and Requirements to Auto-ID in the Healthcare Sector

The motivation to implement Auto-ID in heathcare business ranges from marketing purposes and advancement of clinical pathways to automatisation of clinical business processes (Becker-Berke, 2004: 16-33). The following scenarios have a deep impact on the functional range of the technology and shows that field of application for using Auto-ID in German healthcare may be different (Bultmann et al., 2002; Kern, 2006: 95-169). This list of scenarios may not be complete, but it provides an understanding of the different fields of application in healthcare business for the reader. E.g.

- Documentation support in patient treatment processes.
- Automation of staff authentication processes.
- Completely transparent supply chain process (inventory management).

- Patient identification and location assistance to ensure patient safety (patient tracking and prevention of baby theft.
- Control of cleaning intervals of medical devices.
- Optimisation in terms of finding the right clinical assets at the right time (asset tracking).
- Control of temperature throughout blood supply chain (Auto-ID in combination with sensors).

Process engineering/Process control means the logistics business processes in a hospital, such as inventory control, with mechanisms for automatic tracking of goods or medical products.

The documentation of time, date and cleaner of medical equipment which was used, for example, in a surgery, is regulated by law and statutory regulations. Authorisation and documentation processes supported by Auto-ID can help to make these standard processes easier to handle by combining them with authentication mechanism (Kern, 2006: 95-169). The result is a fully automated and paperless process.

Tracking in the healthcare business initiated a public dispute in Germany. The technology tells us what asset is in which room or part of the building at what time. The result is that valuable time previously spent searching for an asset can be reduced or even eliminated (Kern, 2006: 95-169). But data protection officers objected that tracking a patient or a staff member is an intrusion into privacy which cannot be tolerated by law.

Auto-ID can help to control the 'viability' of a patient. If the Auto-ID systems register a value below or above a defined reference value, for example, a message will be sent automatically by mobile phone to the next emergency department. Another possibility is the combination of Auto-ID with a sensor system, which controls the temperature throughout the supply chain of a blood bottle (Kern, 2006: 95-169).

Depending on the scenario in which Auto-ID will be implemented, the requirements on the functional range differs. The following list of questions gives the reader an understanding of the defined requirements on Auto-ID but may not be complete.

- How can Auto-ID hardware be affixed to medical equipment?
- Is the Auto-ID equipment resistant to water, temperature and chemical substances in medical treatment processes?
- Are there ways to integrate the technology into the existing hospital information systems (HIS) via HL-7 or CORBAmed interfaces?
- How safely can personal data be handled (Security features)?
- How does the Auto-ID fulfil the requirements for fire protection in the healthcare sector?
- What is the maximum data rate and what data volume can be handled by the technology?
- How can be guaranteed that the data is valid, persistent reliable and available?

3.2 RFID in Patient Treatment Processes and Logictics

A secure patient care and improvements in the patient treatmant processes are just two motivations for implementing Auto-ID Technologies in the heathcare sector. Most of

Table 1. Differences between Auto ID technologies in the healthcare sector and in the logistics

Patient Treatment Process	Logistics
Security & Quality in Patient Treatment Processes	Optimizations in Logistic Processes
Tracking and Information Quality	Quick Identification of Goods (Goods receiving) und Process Transparency (Multi-Tag-Handling)
Large Areas are covered by Readers	Strategic Gateways for reading the tags (goods receiving)
Many „active" Applications	Many „passive" Applications
Reuse of Transponders	One-Way Transponder
Cost Drivers: Reader	Cost Drivers: Transponder
Individual-related Data	Normally no individual-related Data

these solutions covering the increasing demand in the healthcare sector to get the relevant information, in the right quality, at the right time to the treatment process.

Optimizations in time and cost reduction are goals in the logistics and that differs fundamentally from the healthcare sector. The following table summarizes the main differences between the healthcare sector and the logistics/retail sector but may not be complete (Gillert & Hansen, 2007).

Auto-ID in healthcare sector is implemented with different intention than in logistic processes. The consequence is that the vendors for Auto-ID Technologies are doing an in creased development on hard- and software for the healthcare sector, to cover their special needs.

These needs are founded in the increased requirements of the transponder technologie which – e.g. is located in places with fluctuating temperatures, strong contamination and there integration to different wireless technologies e.g. "Bluetooth" and "WLAN" (Figure 1).

Auto-ID can improve the quality of information along the processes – the following aspects describe the increasing need of information quality (Bullinger & ten Hompel, 2007):

- Information can be send from software system like HIS (Hospital Information System) in a mobile, quick, secure and flexible way to the place where they are needed – improved information access.
- Information can be handled demand-oriented – patient-oriented information
- Information is specific, relevant and context-sensitive prepared - emergency call system

The focus in the logistics is "Multi-Tag-Handling", which makes it possible to identify a large number of tags at the same time (Figure 1).

Another specific characteristic in the healthcare sector is the technical environment. If tracking of patients and staff are requirement in a hospital it can be possible to cover large areas by readers an additional infrastructure, which means an increasing

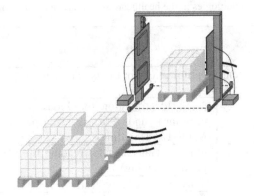

Fig. 1. Multi-Tag-Handling

number of readers (e.g. WLAN Access Points). In this context a cost-benefit analysis should be made at the beginning of the planning phase. On the other hand gateways in the logistics are positioned at strategic places (goods receiving).

Another difference is the information which is send along the process. In the healthcare sector the information is individual-related data, which have to be treated with care and whose handling is regulated by law. In the logistics we have data that is related to goods which is from the data privacy laws, unproblematic.

3.2 Auto-ID Analysed

Auto-ID contains the different technologies, methods and products for the registration, provision and storage of relevant data (Finkenzeller, 2006: 1-10). Auto-ID can play a part in the improvement of processes in healthcare business. With the help of real-time processing and automatic stock detection, for example in the supply chain, and with its ability to trace goods, the efficiency of a hospital can be sustainably impoved (Bullinger & ten Hompel, 2007).

The following Auto-ID technologies were the basis for the evaluation (Finkenzeller, 2006: 2), (Figure 2):

- Bar Code
- Optical Character Recognition (OCR)
- Chip Card
- Biometric Methods
- RFID

A distinction is drawn between four basic principles (Arnold et al., 2003):

- Mechanical and electromechanical identification systems, which use mechanical components like pins as binary storage. They are based on capacitive and inductive mechanisms for scanning.
- Magnetic identification systems, which use magnetic fields e.g. of permanent magnet (magnetic card) as storage. They require small distances for accurate scanning.

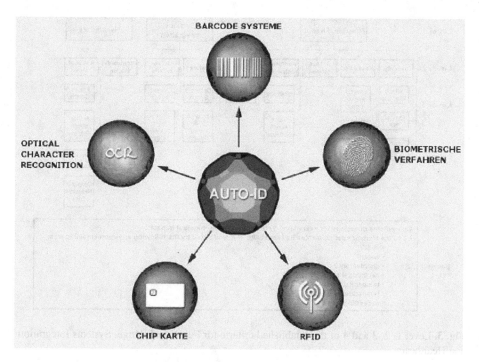

Fig. 2. Defined Auto-ID technologies (Finkenzeller, 2006: 2)

- Opto-electronical identification systems, which are able to detect the shape of an item or markings like colours, OCR or bar code.
- Electromagnetic identification systems, which use inductive waves for a touchless carrier of information. They use electrically programmable microchips to store data.

Biometric methods are additionally separated into iris identification, fingerprint and voice identification. The detailed description of every Auto-ID is left out and can be gleaned at Finkenzeller (Finkenzeller, 2006).

4 Established Criteria and Benefit Analysis

4.1 Established Criteria

To provide an efficient way of using the list of criteria from both, the IT department and the operating department of the hospital, the collected wishes and demands are assigned to four criteria levels (level 1 - 4). The highest level (level 1) is divided into the following and aggregates the lower criteria (Figure 3):

- Functional range
- Systems integration
- Healthcare
- General criteria

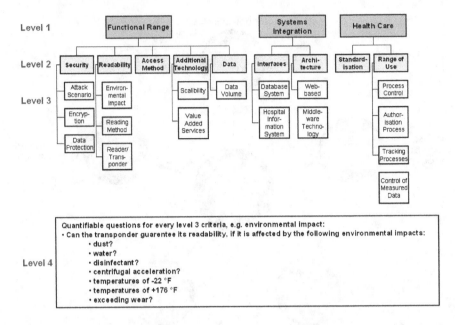

Fig. 3. Level 1, 2, 3 and 4 of the established criteria for Functional Range, Systems Integration and Healthcare

The criteria in these categories are not directly measureable or rateable and have to be separated into detailed subcriteria (level 2 & 3), (Figure 3). Level 4 deals with quantifiable questions, measureable by the department members and relating to the requirements in the systems specification (Schreiber, 2003: 146). By defining one category just for the requirements of heath care we focus on the aim of finding a valid Auto-ID which is appropriate for application to the healthcare sector specifically.

The general criteria are consciously left out of this consideration. This criteria level deals e.g. with general information about cost for the Auto-ID technology (hard- & software) and support or criteria concerning the know-how of the producer in the healthcare sector.

4.2 Benefit Analysis

The method of the paired comparison was used to give a valid weighting on every criterion (Table 2). It was used for levels one to three (level 1 - 3). Table 2 shows the paired comparison carried out for the first level. Every sum of the comparison between two criteria has the result 10. In this example the 'general criteria' are less important (expresses by '1') than criteria concerning 'heath care' (expressed by '9'). In this evaluation, the significance of the criterion 'heath care' can be seen (42%). The score in this category is influenced by the ability of the Auto-ID process to live up to context-specific expectations and its ease of integration into existing infrastructure. The weighing of the criteria was made by the author. It should be mentioned that no

Table 2. Result of the paired comparison for the first level (level 1)

Criteria (Level 1)	1 Functional Range	2 Systems Integration	3 Health Care	4 General Criteria	Points (absolute)	Relative weight %
1 Functional Range		5	2	7	14	23
2 Systems Integration	5		2	7	14	23
3 Health Care	8	8		9	25	42
4 General Criteria	3	3	1		7	12
Sum (absolute)					60	100

concrete project with predefined requirements has been the basis for the weighing decisions and the result of the paired comparison is just valid for this work and has to be reviewed and adapted if the requirements and the field where the project takes place should change. It is possible if the evaluation takes place in another context, for example when Auto-ID should be implemented in an existing environment in a hospital the criteria of 'systems integration' should get more emphasis.

The second step, after carrying out the paired comparison, is to calculate the value of benefit. In this calculation, the weight of a level obviously determines the influence of the next level down. This method guarantees that all relevant criteria are rated and aggregated to the level above. The detailed description of this method is left out and can be gleaned at Schreiber (Schreiber, 2003).

5   Conclusion

The conclusion presents an interpretation of the most important results of the evaluation and makes no claim to be complete.

The aim of the evaluation was to find a valid statement as to which procedure, in accordance with requirements, is appropriate for application to the healthcare sector.

RFID shows the highest benefit value in every aggregated level of achievement on level 1 and has good potential to place lasting emphasis on clinical processes and pathways (Figure 4).

It became clear that for a concrete project a new arrangement of the weightings has to be devised to cover all relevant project requirements as well as the context in which the project is to be implemented in the hospital. But the evaluation showed as well that it is not possible to make a single statement as to which method is the most useful for every field of application in the healthcare sector and should generally be implemented. If we take a look at level 2, RFID in authorisation (security and data) processes is not the only useful solution (Figure 5). Biometic methods have the highest benefit value in these fields. Based on this awareness a useful combination of two

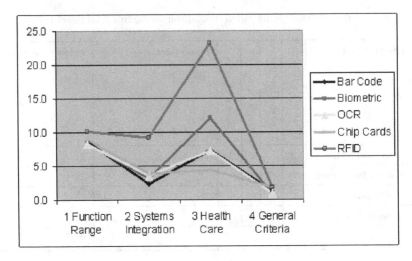

Fig. 4. Conclusion of the evaluation (Level 1)

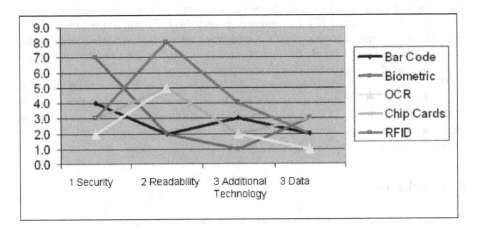

Fig. 5. Conclusion of the evaluation (Level 2)

methods - RFID and biometric methods - could guarantee a holistically successful, sustainable and well-accepted project in healthcare. The developed list of criteria is an important orientation guide for decision making but has to be reengineered if the requirements are changed.

If we take a look at level 3 - RFID has by far the highest impact in the field of applications for controlling measurable data and tracking items (Figure 6). If the field of application 'Process control' is concerned, the bar code has nearly the same impact and can have a lasting effect in areas of logistics in a hospital. That result shows that RFID keeps its relevance for the area of logistics as well for the health-care business.

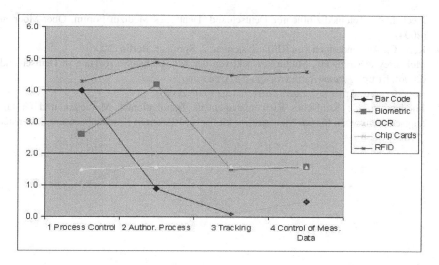

Fig. 6. Conclusion of the evaluation (Level 3)

The evaluation showed that RFID offers significant benefit potential in terms of supporting quality processes and saving money and time. It is not, however, a technical view on RFID. It should be treated as an instrument to accelerate administrative and clinical business processes and to design them in a more efficient way.

Most of the German healthcare institutions implementing RFID projects have the status of "early adopters". This denomination will soon no longer be applicable, as German hospitals are forced to make their services more attractive to patients. The increase of cost pressure in the healthcare system leads managers to lay more emphasis on return on invest (ROI) and repayment strategies. Processes have to be optimised so that costs can be saved. In this regard RFID can play an important role.

References

1. AeroScout. Case Studies online (2007),
   http://www.aeroscout.com/content.asp?page=case%20studies
   (02.03.2008)
2. Arnold, D., et al.: Handbuch Logistik. Springer, Berlin (2003)
3. Becker-Berke, S., Lautwein-Reinhard, B.: Gesundheitswesen. In: Ein Lexikon für Einsteiger und Insider, Bonn (2004)
4. Bullinger, H.J., ten Hompel, M. (eds.): Internet der Dinge. Springer, Berlin (2007)
5. Bultmann, M., et al.: Datenschutz und Telemedizin. Anforderungen an Medizinnetze (2002), http://www.datenschutz-bayern.de/verwaltung/
   datenschutzTelemedizin.pdf (26.03.2008)
6. Finkenzeller, K.: RFID-Handbuch, 4, Munich (2006)
7. Gillert, F., Hansen, W.-R.: RFID für die Optimierung von Geschäftsprozessen, Munich (2007)

8. Jaeckel, A.: Telemedizinfuehrer Deutschland. Deutsches Medizin Forum, Ober-Moerlen (2004)
9. Kern, C.: Anwendungen von RFID-Systemen, 2. Springer, Berlin (2006)
10. McKinsey & Company, Studie Perspektiven der Krankenhausversorgung in Deutschland (2006), http://www.mckinsey.de/presse/ 060502_business_breakfast.htm (30.03.2008)
11. Middendorf, C.: Klinisches Risikomanagement. Implikationen, Methoden und Gestaltungsempfehlungen für das Management klinischer Risiken in Krankenhaeusern, Muenster (2005)

An Exploratory Study of Risk Factors for Implementing Service-Oriented IS Projects

Hsin-Lu Chang[1] and Chia-Pei Lue[2]

[1] Department of Management Information Systems, National Chengchi University,
Taipei 116, Taiwan
hchang@mis.nccu.edu.tw
[2] Organization and Systems Supply Chain Division, PresiCarre Corporation,
Taipei 251, Taiwan
yanny_lue@carrefour.com

Abstract. For IS project managers, how to implement the projects successfully is always a challenge. Further, as more and more enterprises start to develop service-oriented IS projects, it is essential to assess the sources and impacts of relevant risks. This research aimed at identifying risk factors related to service-oriented IS projects and analyzing the impact of these risk factors. Applying the SIMM (service integrated maturity model) proposed by IBM, customer service systems were selected to justify the research framework. Result showed that the risk factors influencing the adoption of service-oriented systems were insufficient technology planning, lack of expertise, ineffective project governance, and organizational misalignment, listed in the order of strength of influence. The findings of this research is expected to assist managers realize the risks and the importance of these risks that have to be noticed and controlled when making decisions on service-oriented systems adoption.

Keywords: Risk management, Service-orientation, IS project management, Service integration, Customer service Systems.

1 Introduction

Failure of IS projects is common despite efforts for improvement. For example, a survey of more than 600 organizations in 22 countries showed that 49% of these organizations have experienced at least one IS project failure [1]. Also, a PIPC survey in 2005 found that 31% of IS projects failed to deliver on time and another 31% failed to deliver within budget [2]. Industrial efforts have been carried out to deal with the IS project risks. Examples include the COBIT (Control Objectives for Information and related Technology) framework proposed by the Information Systems Audit and Control Association (ISACA) and the IT Governance Institute (ITGI) [3], and the guidelines published by the Project Management Institute to define the project risk management methodology for project management [4]. Researchers have also proposed frameworks or methods for risk management and control [5][6][7][8].

Such issue becomes even more complex and important nowadays as more and more companies start to focus on the strategy of on-demand business [9], or so-called

C. Weinhardt, S. Luckner, and J. Stößer (Eds.): WEB 2008, LNBIP 22, pp. 83–95, 2009.

service-oriented enterprise (SOE) to respond to the increasing business dynamics, changing customer preferences, and disruptive technological shifts [10]. To achieve these goals, the integration between IT and the management processes needs to be assured. That is, the focus of IS projects should transform from simply replacing manpower to a higher level of integration of processes, technologies and the people managing and acting upon them. In this paper, we call these IS projects that focus on supporting SOE as "service-oriented IS projects."

Implementing these service-oriented IS projects however are not easy and involve a lot of risks [11]. Organizations need to handle challenges not only in technology but also in the business. These challenges may occur in processes, strategies, and workforces. This study therefore aims at developing a risk assessment framework for implementing service-oriented IS projects. Such framework is expected to create value for project managers in managing and running service-oriented IS projects, as well as for CEOs and top mangers in transforming their businesses into a SOEs. The research objectives are (1) to develop a risk assessment framework for service-oriented IS projects, and (2) to prioritize the risk factors that can differentiate adopters from non-adopters of service-oriented IS for better management of service-oriented IS projects.

2 Conceptual Background

2.1 IS Project Risks

Over the past few decades, a number of studies have discussed the concept of "risk" in IS projects and categorized the factors into different types or models. Ewusi-Mensah and Przasnyski proposed the three dimensions of risk (economic, organizational, and technological) and discussed the influence of each of these dimensions on the failure of IS projects [7]. Keil et al. categorized software project risks into a framework consisting of four quadrants (customer mandate, scope and requirements, execution, and environment) and two dimensions (perceived relative importance of risk and perceived level of control) [8]. Moreover, Wallace and Keil discussed the relationship between software project risks and project performance by investigating a proposed model containing six primary dimensions of risks [12]. Based on a review of 46 articles, Alter and Sherer conceptualized risk as (1) composed of different types of negative outcomes; (2) leading to loss or source of risk factors; (3) probability of negative outcomes (sometimes weighted by loss); (4) difficulty in estimating outcome; and (5) undefined or discussed using a different term such as problem or threat [13]. This study follows the description of risk as "leading to loss or source of risk factors" and more detailed description of the definitions and operationalizations will be provided below.

2.2 IS Projects and Service-Oriented Enterprises

According to Wikipedia, service-orientation (SO) is defined as a design paradigm that specifies the creation of automation logic in the form of services. Service-oriented architecture (SOA) is often viewed as an enabler of service orientation and is an architectural style based on which existing or new functionalities are grouped into atomic services. These services communicate with each other by passing data from one service to another, or by coordinating an activity between one or more services. Past researchers have discussed similar concepts of "service orientation" such as customer orientation, market orientation, and on demand (e.g., [11][14][15]). IBM consolidated these concepts and proposed the "On Demand Business Architecture" in 2004. According to IBM, on demand business refers to an enterprise whose business processes are integrated across the company and with key partners, suppliers and customers, enabling it to quickly respond to any customer demand, market opportunity or external threat [9].

To enable service orientation, companies need to develop a business strategy framework that focuses on the decisions of service strategy formulation [15][16]. To support these service strategies, an understanding of the actual business processes and underlying IT infrastructure is needed [10][17][18]. The investment of service-oriented IS projects therefore focuses on the integration of IT and business processes to enable the availability of data for decision makings. Moreover, these projects need to consider the development in connectivity, automation, and technology integration to enable extensible enterprises and dynamically reconfigure business relationships in response to market changes and business relationships [10]. It is expected that these investments have profound influence on those who work for such companies and the way their works get structured. Human capital management and optimization therefore also become a critical issue while investing these service-oriented IS projects [11][16][19].

IBM has proposed the Service Integration Maturity Model (SIMM) [20], depicting the levels of maturity of service-oriented systems. The seven levels are explained below.

- Level 1: *Data Integration.* The organization starts from proprietary and ad-hoc integration, rendering the architecture brittle in the face of change.
- Level 2: *Application Integration.* The organization moves toward some form of EAI (Enterprise Application Integration), albeit with proprietary connections and integration points.
- Level 3: *Functional Integration.* The organization componentizes and modularizes major or critical parts of its application portfolio, exposing functionality in a more modular fashion. The integration between components is done through the interfaces and contracts between them.
- Level 4: *Process Integration.* The organization embarks on the early phases of SOA by defining and exposing services for consumption internally or externally by business partners.
- Level 5: *Supply-Chain Integration.* The organization extends its influence into the value chain and service eco-system. Services form a contract among suppliers, consumers, and brokers who can build their own eco-system for on-demand interaction.
- Level 6: *Virtual Infrastructure.* The organization now creates a virtualized infrastructure to run applications after decoupling the application, its services, components, and flows. The infrastructure externalizes its monitoring, management, and events (common event infrastructure).
- Level 7: *Eco-System Integration.* The organization now has a dynamically re-configurable software architecture. It can compose services at run-time using externalized policy descriptions, management, and monitoring.

Based on our definition of service orientation, service-oriented IT projects are defined as those that aim to achieve level 4 of service integration or even higher level.

3   Research Model and Hypotheses Development

3.1   The Initial Research Model

Based on the review of relevant literature and the discussion above, the initial research model of this study was proposed as shown in Figure 1.

The independent variables were economic risks, organizational risks, and technological risks. Table 1 below provides a more detailed description of the three kinds of risks.

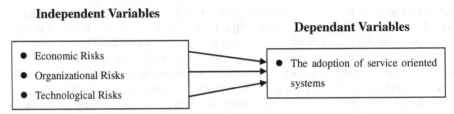

Independent Variables

- Economic Risks
- Organizational Risks
- Technological Risks

Dependant Variables

- The adoption of service oriented systems

Fig. 1. Initial Research Model

Table 1. Risk Hierarchy of Service-Oriented Projects

Risk Category	Factor	In Service-Oriented IS Projects
Economic Risk	Size Risks Resource Risks	• IT planning becomes more long-term oriented [15][17] • Lack of technology resources to support service-oriented IS projects [21]
Organizational Risk	Extent of Change Brought	• Lack of supply chain flexibility [10] • Lack of supportive processes [10][11][14][22] • Lack of supportive organization structure [11] • Lack of organizational responsiveness [23] • Lack of the modulization of user tasks [16] • Lack of user capability [15][23]
	Intensity of Conflicts	• Lack of high cohesion and morale in service development activities [16] • Lack of specific executive as the service owner for each logically connected set of services [18]
	Environmental complexity	• Lack of close communication within the new service project group [16] • Lack of close communication with customers [16] • Insufficient information sharing that coordinates new service/products development activities [16]
Technological Risk	Lack of Expertise	• Lack of knowledge in standardization [10][16][18] • Lack of knowledge in modulization [10][17][18] • Lack of IS Team knowledge in new services and products [16] • Lack of the ability to leverage managerial IS knowledge in the customer service processes [21]
	User Risks	• Lack of user involvement [8] • Lack of developing market learning and service climate knowledge for users [15][16][19][21][24]

3.2 Pretest and Revised Research Model

In preparation for the large-scale data collection, three interviews were conducted during early April 2008. The three companies selected were implementing service-oriented IS projects, with their company background shown in Table 2. Two issues were identified from the interviews following by the Delphi method: (1) Various definitions of SO systems exist among the three companies, and (2) most companies that declared to have service-oriented systems only reached the basic level of service integration. After intensive discussion, the research model was revised as shown in Figure 2 to reflect the features of service orientation.

The revised risk factors are shown in Table 3. Compared with the risk hierarchy of Table 1, size risk, resource risk, and insufficient staffing risk were consolidated and renamed "Resource insufficiency." The extent of changes and intensity of conflicts were grouped into "Organizational misalignment." Environmental complexity, environmental uncertainty, lack of commitment, and user risk were also consolidated and renamed "Ineffective project governance." Moreover, lack of expertise and inappropriate staffing were consolidated under the new name "Lack of expertise," and Technology complexity was renamed "Insufficient technology planning."

3.3 Hypotheses Development

Resource risks are associated with resource availability. If the project is not allocated sufficient resources, the project may not be accomplished in time. Therefore, Hypothesis 1 was proposed as follows.

H1: Resource insufficiency risk will negatively affect the adoption of service-oriented systems.

Since supply chain processes are derived from the integration of enterprise processes, lack of supply chain flexibility means there is neither internal enterprise flexibility nor flexibility of the connections, adding difficulties to dynamic information flows [10].

Table 2. Company Profile

Company	Role of SO	No. of Employee	Capital (NT Million$)
Company A	Solution Provider	65	65
Hospital T	Customized	4000	N/A
Corporate I	Solution Provider	1700	360

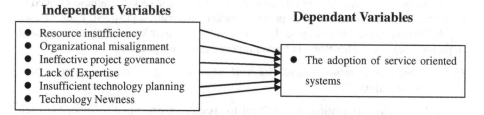

Fig. 2. Revised Research Model

Table 3. Revised Risk Factors

Risk Factor	Description
Resource insufficiency	• Can't perceive the value • Resource insufficiency in project time, staffing, budget, hardware, software
Organizational misalignment	• Lack of flexibility • Lack of supportive process • Lack of supportive organization structure • Lack of organizational responsiveness • Lack of the modulization of user tasks • Lack of user capability
Ineffective project governance	• Lack of specific executive as the service owner for each logically connected set of services • Lack of close communication within the new service project group • Lack of close communication with customers • Top management commitment • Commitment among development team members • User involvement • User attitude and user commitment
Lack of Expertise	• Lack of knowledge in standardization • Lack of knowledge in modualization • Lack of IS team knowledge in new services and products • Lack of IS team knowledge in service-oriented systems • Lack of the ability to leverage managerial IT knowledge in the customer service processes
Insufficient technology planning	• Number of links to existing systems • Number of links to future systems • Difficulty in defining the inputs and outputs of the system • Number of users outside the organization
Technology Newness	• Software newness • Hardware newness

Similarly, companies need to develop processes to support market-sensing and customer-orientation [10][11][14][22]. Moreover, service-oriented IS projects require horizontal and network-like structure based on service consumer-service provider relationship [11]. To support service-oriented IS projects, organizations need to be responsive to customer needs and competitors' actions [23]. To support modularization of service components, user tasks should be re-designed as well [16]. Besides, users within the organizations that are related to the services of the service framework need to be market responsive and able to process market information [15][23]. Lack of user capability may cause risks because there is no sufficient user knowledge to design and implement services. Therefore, H2 was proposed as shown below.

H2: Organizational misalignment risk will negatively affect the adoption of service-oriented system.

To enable service orientation, it is critical to specify an executive to supervise each logically connected set of services, and his/her responsibility is aligned with the overall enterprise governance [18]. It is also important to have close and clear communication within the new service project group when designing new services [16]. If the communication is not good enough, conflicts, misunderstandings, and unfamiliarity may cause serious risks. It is also of equal importance to have close communication with customers. Therefore, H3 was proposed.

H3: Ineffective project governance risk will negatively affect the adoption of service-oriented systems.

Lack of knowledge in modularization is also risky [10][17][18]. Modularization refers to the process of designing and packaging services into modules. Each related functions will be reorganized by usage and purpose of the services and user requirements. Without being properly modularized, these functions tend to be tightly coupled with each other, putting the competitive advantage of flexibility in peril. Lack of IS team knowledge in new services and products may also incur risks [16]. IS teams need to have the knowledge about the process, the workflow, the users, the new services, and the innovation of the tasks. Moreover, risks may occur when IS teams lack the ability to leverage managerial IT knowledge in customer service process [21]. More specifically, every industry has its unique domain knowhow, and for that reason there exist different concerns to design the new services as well as the IT infrastructures. H4 was therefore proposed.

H4: Lack of expertise risk will negatively affect the adoption of service-oriented systems.

Integration with existing systems involves implementation issues such as how to link with legacy systems, how to run the new systems without affecting the old ones, and which existing functions should remain unchanged [6] [12]. Improperly dealing with these issues may cause risks. H5 was thus proposed as follows.

H5: Insufficient technology planning risk will negatively affect the adoption of service-oriented systems.

The concept of service-oriented architecture is new, and the technology to implement it is new as well. Since the IS project involves new hardware, software, and technology, more efforts are needed to overcome the technological problems. It therefore requires more time and resources and brings about more risks than the projects using existing technologies. Based on the argument above, H6 was therefore proposed as follows.

H6: The technology newness risk will negatively affect the adoption of service-oriented systems.

4   Data Analysis

4.1   Data Collection

To test our hypotheses, we target at the companies whom have applied the concept of service integration in implementing their customer service system project. Developed upon IBM SIMM described in Section 2, four levels of service integration for customer service systems are proposed: data integration (level 1), application and functional integration (level 2), process integration (level 3), and eco-system integration (level 4). The detail definition of each level is shown in Table 4. A Web survey was conducted for data collection. The URL of a Web questionnaire was sent to 300 professionals within organizations that have implemented customer service systems. A total of 107 responses were received out of which 105 were valid.

The average number of employees in the firms was 405, capital 0.37 NT billion dollars, and annual sales 1.68 NT billion dollars. The areas covered various industries to which the complete list is available on request from the authors. For the customer service system project that has implemented in these responding companies, 44 companies have expressed that their project belongs to level 1, and 19 companies have the project belonging to level 2. Based on our definition, these companies haven't adopted service concept in there IS project, and thus we label these companies as Non-SO group. The data also shows 24 respondents have implemented the project that belongs

Table 4. Definition of Service Integration Level for Customer Service Systems

Level	Description
Data integration	The organization owns a basic enterprise website for customers to send comments and complaints. The website has an independent member system, from which customers can browse the website to join member, subscribe company e-paper, search information about the products and services, apply for services, or give comments. There is no direct connection between the website's member system and the company's inner CRM system. The employees of the customer service have to manually transform the data of the website's member system and import the data into the CRM system for further processing the requests for the customers.
Application and functional integration	The enterprise website has connections to the internal (e.g. CRM, ERP) and external (e.g. SCM) systems of the organization. There are standardized format of transformation (e.g. XML). The transformation can be scheduled as automatically executed tasks within a certain period by batch, or be designed as synchronized tasks to import data synchronously into other related systems of the organization without manual operations. The automation only refers to those data interchange with no flows (e.g. receive order form or add new member). For the processes which are involved with flows or complicated logistics should rely on manual operation or other process to be accomplished.
Process integration	For enterprise the interaction between internal/external systems becomes more automatic. It not only makes customers register the services on line and transfers data into the internal system automatically but also disposes the processes of business knowledge (e.g., identify a form which the departments belong to, understand how to dispose in different situation). For example, when a user makes an order, the system will activate the processes to fulfill the order needs automatically, if the order involves the cooperation of external factories and stores, system will sends the order information to them in order to reach the best route planning and fast to fulfill the order needs.
Eco-system integration	Any service component is modulized and independent. To fulfill customer needs, the system is able to recombine different service components to form a new one. For example, customer service system can be divided into the following service components: member service, order service, and distribution service. User can selects the service which he needs and makes the service join to his systems or processes.

to level 3, and 18 belongs to level 4. These companies are treated as adopters of service-oriented systems; we label them as SO group.

4.2 Instrument Validation

Factor analysis was conducted to assess the construct validity, using principal component analysis for factor extraction and Varimax for rotation. 13 Items with factor loadings under 0.5 was discarded, and the Cronbach's α value of the six risk factors ranged from 0.769 to 0.932. Besides factor analysis, the correlation matrix of the measurement items was inspected to assess the convergent validity. The smallest within-factor correlations were all significantly different from zero, providing positive evidence for convergent validity. Further, the between- and within-factor correlations also supported the discriminant validity of the instrument.

4.3 Mean Value Analysis

The comparison of mean values of the risk factors between Non-SO and SO groups revealed that four of the six risk factors (ineffective project governance, lack of expertise, insufficient technology planning, and organizational misalignment) were able to discriminate the adoption behavior while the other two were not (see Table 5).

Table 5. Mean Value Analysis

Risk Measure	Non-SO (N=63)	SO (N=42)	Mean Difference	Significance
Ineffective project governance	3.57	2.73	0.84	0.000
Lack of expertise	4.00	2.88	1.12	0.000
Insufficient technology planning	4.24	3.08	1.15	0.000
Resource insufficiency	4.40	4.45	-0.04	0.877
Organizational misalignment	3.62	2.90	0.72	0.002
Technology newness	4.41	4.14	0.27	0.339

As shown in Table 5, the means of the Non-SO group were higher than those of the SO group. Such finding was consistent with the hypotheses of this study. In addition, both groups showed higher-than-average resource insufficiency (4.40 for Non-SO and 4.45 for SO) and technological newness (4.41 for Non-SO and 4.14 for SO), meaning that both groups perceived high risks in these two categories.

4.4 Regression Analysis

The research hypotheses were analyzed using binary logistic regression. The result of the binary logistic regression is shown in Table 6. From the result in Table 6, ineffective project governance, lack of expertise, insufficient technology planning, and organizational misalignment were found to be significant and negatively related to the adoption of service-oriented systems, while resource insufficiency and technology

Table 6. Summary of Binary Logistic Regression Analysis

	B	S.E	Wald	Rank	df	Sig.	Exp(B)
Ineffective project governance	-0.585	0.258	5.145	3	1	0.023	0.557
Lack of expertise	-0.831	0.270	9.453	2	1	0.002	0.436
Insufficient technology planning	-0.966	0.271	12.654	1	1	0.000	0.381
Resource insufficiency	0.087	0.249	0.123	6	1	0.726	1.091
Organizational misalignment	-0.503	0.250	4.056	4	1	0.044	0.605
Technology newness	-0.126	0.248	0.259	5	1	0.611	0.881
Overall model fit	chi-square = 33.151 (p=0.000) Hosmer & Lemeshow = 12.147 (p=0.145)						

Table 7. Classification Result

		Model		
		Predicted Group		
	Number of			Percentage.
Actual Group	Cases	Non-SO	SO	Correct.
Non-SO	63	49	14	77.8%
SO	42	18	24	57.1%
Overall	105			69.5% Correct

newness were not. The reason these two factors were insignificant may be due to the fact that adoption of service-oriented systems was a challenge per se for the companies. The technology was a new concept and most companies do not have required resources. Therefore these two factors were unable to explain the difference between adoption and non-adoption. Table 7 shows how well the regression model classified SO from Non-SO groups. As shown in the table, the hit ratio of the regression model was 69.5%. As there were 63 Non-SO and 42 SO companies, the classification accuracy by random guess was $(63/105)^2 + (42/105)^2 = 52\%$ (the maximum chance criterion). Thus, it could be concluded that this model could be considered a valid predictor of the adoption of service-oriented systems. The results therefore supported four of the six hypotheses proposed (H2, H3, H4, H5), while rejecting the other two (H1 and H6).

5 Conclusion

Two major findings arose from this study and are discussed in this section.

1. *Four risk factors influencing the adoption of service-oriented systems were identified. These factors included insufficient technology planning, lack of expertise, ineffective project governance, and organizational misalignment.*

First, according to the Wald statistics in Table 6, the most influential risk factor to the adoption of service-oriented systems was "insufficient technology planning." Since service-oriented systems require integration among business, technology, process, and workforce, huge efforts are needed. Integration for service-oriented systems requires the development and deployment of integration platforms and interfaces to existing systems. The efforts to enhance the integration of service-oriented systems can be more complicated and costly than the integration of traditional information systems. This also means that well-designed adoption plan is essential to the successful of adoption. Second, developing the knowledge of technologies such as J2EE, .NET platform, WSDL, XML, and SOAP is expensive and acquiring professionals with qualified skills is also a challenging task. Even if the company chooses to outsource to software vendors, how much the vendor knows about service-oriented technology is questionable and thus needs to be evaluated. Third, due to the newness and large scale of the service-oriented concept and technology, managing a serviced oriented system project is more difficult than managing a traditional one. And since service orientation is not a purely technical problem, supports from top managers and key users are essential. Well governance and communication to realize the benefits are required. In a business environment, it is common that key users own the power to the decision of implementing a system, and the IS professionals are responsible for identifying requirements and the implementation work. A successful project is impossible without proper governance and communication structure in the business. Fourth, organizational alignment is also required because the success of the systems depends on how process, workforces, strategies, and technologies move toward the same direction. To ensure the alignment, the company structure may need to be reorganized, business processes modularized, and alternative service groups organized to make the goals consistent. If related parties are not aligned together (e.g., each department managers has their own conceptualizations on how to use IT to improve customer service), the existing processes may not be able to support customers' changing requirements. The companies may therefore encounter difficulties in collecting market and competitors' information, making it more difficult to adopt service-oriented systems successfully.

2. *Although resource insufficiency and technology newness were not essential risk factors to the adoption of service-oriented systems, they both were valued high in terms of risk.*

From the mean value analysis of Table 5, the Non-SO and SO groups rated resource insufficiency (4.40, 4.45) and technology newness (4.41, 4.14) higher than average. Although the two risk factors were not significant according to the binary logistic regression analysis shown in Table 6, the result showed that both groups perceived these two factors as high risk.

With the new technology and insufficient resource, companies who chose to implement service-oriented systems might want to build competitive advantages after successful implementation. In other word, facing the challenges of insufficient resources and technology newness, companies still decided to implement the systems in order to follow industrial trends or to sustain competitive advantages. Decision makers, however, need to proceed with implementation with great care to control the scale, budget, human resource, or functions.

Limitations exist and need to be noted though cautious steps had been taken. First, the participants of the survey were limited to IS department staff with experiences in planning/implementing customer systems, and only one participant per company was accepted. Under such strict conditions, qualified participants were hard to find and therefore small sample size was unavoidable. To mitigate this problem, we contacted as many sources of targets as possible and offered monetary rewards. Second, because no unified and agreed-upon definition of "service-oriented systems" was available, this study followed IBM's SIMM and industrial interviews and proposed four maturity levels of customer service systems. The definition of each maturity level is suggested to be further refined for future studies. Moreover, this study only considered the risks of adopting service-oriented IS projects, leaving risk control issues untouched [8]. It is also a suggested direction for future studies.

Acknowledgments. This article was based on a research project supported by the National Science Council of Taiwan under grant no. 97-2410-H-004-127. The project was also supported by Sayling Wen Cultural and Educational Foundation.

References

1. KPMG: Global IT Project Management Survey (2005), http://www.kpmg.com.au/aci/docs/irmpmqa-global-it-pm-survey2005.pdf (accessed on 2008/03/24)
2. PIPC: Global Project Management Survey (2005), http://www.pmportal.co.uk/uploads/documents/PIPCSurvey.pdf (accessed on 2008/03/24)
3. ISACA (Information Systems Audit and Control Association) (2007), http://www.isaca.org/Content/NavigationMenu/Members_and_Leaders/COBIT6/Obtain_COBIT/Obtain_COBIT.htm (accessed on 2008/03/24)
4. PMI (Project Management Institute): A Guide to the Project Management Body of Knowledge, PMBOK (2004), http://publications.ksu.edu.sa/IT%20Papers/PMP/PMBOK.pdf (accessed on 2008/03/24)
5. Boehm, B.W.: Software Risk Management: Principles and Practices. IEEE Software 8(1), 32–41 (1991)
6. Barki, H., Rivard, S., Talbot, J.: An Integrative Contingency Model of Software Project Risk Management. Journal of Management Information Systems 17(4), 37–69 (2001)
7. Ewusi-Mensah, K., Przasnyski, Z.H.: Factors Contributing to the Abandonment of. Information Systems Development Projects. Journal of Information Technology 9(3), 185–201 (1994)
8. Keil, M., Cule, P., Lyytinen, K., Schmidt, R.: A Framework for Identifying Software Project Risks. Communications of the ACM 41(11), 76–83 (1998)
9. IBM Research: Services Science: A New Academic Discipline (2004), http://www.almaden.ibm.com/asr/SSME/facsummit.pdf (accessed on 2008/03/24)
10. Gosain, S., Malhotra, A., El Sawy, O.A.: Coordinating for Flexibility in e-Business Supply Chains. Journal of Management Information Systems 21(3), 7–46 (2005)

11. Cherbakov, L., Galambos, G., Harishankar, R., Kalyana, S., Rackham, G.: Impact of Service Orientation at the Business Level. IBM Systems Journal 44(4), 653–668 (2005)
12. Wallace, L., Keil, M.: Software Project Risks and Their Effect on Outcomes. Communications of the ACM 47(4), 68–73 (2004)
13. Alter, S., Sherer, S.: A General, But Readily Adaptable Model of Information System Risk. Communications of the AIS 14(1), 1–28 (2004)
14. Narver, J., Slater, S.: The Effect of a Market Orientation on Business Profitability. Journal of Marketing 54(4), 20–35 (1990)
15. Slater, S., Narver, J.: Customer-Led and Market-Oriented: Let's Not Confuse the Two. Strategic Management Journal 19(10), 1001–1006 (1998)
16. Menor, L., Roth, A.: New Service Development Competence in Retail Banking: Construct Development and Measurement Validation. Journal of Operations Management 25(4), 825–846 (2007)
17. Weill, P., Subramani, M., Broadbent, M.: Building IT Infrastructure for Strategic Agility. MIT Sloan Management Review 44(1), 57–65 (2002)
18. Bieberstein, N., Bose, S., Walker, L., Lynch, A.: Impact of Service-Oriented Architecture on Enterprise Systems, Organizational Structures, and Individuals. IBM Systems Journal 44(4), 691–708 (2005)
19. Schneider, B., White, S., Paul, M.: Linking Service Climate and Customer Perceptions of Service Quality: Test of a Causal Model. Journal of Applied Psychology 83(2), 150–163 (1998)
20. Arsanjani, A., Holley, K.: Increase Flexibility with the Service Integration Maturity Model (SIMM) (2005), http://www.ibm.com/developerworks/webservices/library/ws-soa-simm/ (accessed on 2008/06/16)
21. Ray, G., Barney, J.B., Muhanna, W.A.: Capabilities, Business Processes, and Competitive Advantage: Choosing the Dependent Variable in Empirical Tests of the Resource-Based View. Strategic Management Journal 25(1), 23–37 (2004)
22. Day, G.S.: The Capabilities of Market-Driven Organizations. Journal of Marketing 58(4), 37–52 (1994)
23. Hult, T., Ketchen, D., Slater, S.: Market Orientation and Performance: An Integration of Disparate Approaches. Strategic Management Journal 26(12), 1173–1181 (2005)

Cloud-Based DSS and Availability Context:
The Probability of Successful Decision Outcomes

Stephen Russell[1], Victoria Yoon[2], and Guisseppi Forgionne[2]

[1] Department of Information Systems & Technology Management
The George Washington University
Washington, D.C., USA
russells@gwu.edu
[2] Information Systems Department
University of Maryland, Baltimore County
Baltimore, Maryland, USA
yoon@umbc.edu, forgionn@umbc.edu

Abstract. In an age of cloud computing, mobile users, and wireless networks, the availability of decision support related computing resources can no longer guarantee five-nines (99.999%) availability but the dependence on decision support systems is ever increasing. If not already, the likelihood of obtaining accurate deterministic advice from these systems will become critical information. This study proposes a probabilistic model that maps decision resource availability to correct decision outcomes. Grounded in system reliability theory, the probability functions are given and developed. The model is evaluated with a simulated decision opportunity and the outcome of the experimentation is quantified using a goodness of fit measure and ANOVA testing.

Keywords: Context Aware Computing, Availability Awareness, Decision Support Systems, Cloud Computing.

1   Introduction

The availability of pervasive networking, inexpensive storage, and high performance computing has created the foundation for a broad range of new approaches capable of delivering on the promise of cloud computing. The "cloud" can be defined as the environment where computing resources are hosted and used from the distributed Internet environment. Cloud computing extends the notion of desktop computing to the scalability and virtualization of distributed processing servers on the Internet. Within the cloud, an application is built using resources from multiple services and potentially from multiple locations. Cloud computing is typically implemented as a software-as-a-service model. This removes the burden of software updates and server maintenance from business and other users. One of the most significant benefits of cloud computing is that it provides a way to increase capacity or add capabilities dynamically as they are needed without investing in new infrastructure, training new personnel, or licensing new software. For many companies, the true value of cloud computing beyond the "pay as you go" model is the time to value ratio and reduced risk, compared to in-house implementations.

C. Weinhardt, S. Luckner, and J. Stößer (Eds.): WEB 2008, LNBIP 22, pp. 96–109, 2009.

A user of cloud computing services doesn't necessarily care about how they are implemented, what technologies are used, or how they are managed. The most significant concern is that there is access to it and that the service/application has a level of reliability necessary to meet the functional requirements [1]. In this context, reliability may be one of the most significant issues facing cloud computing. Very few applications have been able to achieve 100% availability. Moreover, while a cloud computing application may be 100% reliable, users' access to it may not be. This issue is complicated in the face of mobile users and access using 3G wireless networking technologies.

Consider the following example. A user gets on a train and begins conducting a session with a cloud application-based decision support system. As the train begins to move, the environmental computing conditions begin to change. If the train were to go through a tunnel, the user's connectivity may temporarily be interrupted; potentially regaining the connection when the train emerges from the tunnel. If a user were made to know that the tunnel was coming and connectivity may be lost, the user could adjust their interaction with the decision support system (DSS), or even plan their usage of the system in a manner that avoids complete or disastrous interruption, e.g. downloading data/information and interacting locally. While it may not be possible to know exactly when and for how long a session may be interrupted, it may be possible to know the likelihood of interruption occurrences and durations. The work of Russell et al. [2] has demonstrated that knowledge of computing resources' availability can affect the support provided by applications and even affect decisions associated with that use. Russell et al's research indicates that it is important to extend awareness of computing resources' such as data, network connectivity, or software applications to system users and not just implement it as an internal hardware or software algorithm.

This work extends Russell's et al's work as the basis for use with cloud computing decision support applications. Conceptually, the research in this paper seeks to develop a probabilistic model that can be used in conjunction with collected availability context data. To further the understanding of the effect of availability context information on decision making, this paper proposes a probabilistic model to describe the relationship between decision outcome accuracy and evaluates the model using a simulation. In Section 2, a discussion of existing reliability and availability-related technologies is discussed, followed by the introduction of a probabilistic reliability model for decision support systems. In section 2.3, a probabilistic model that maps decision outcome to DSS availability is presented. Section 3 explains the simulation experiment that evaluates the decision outcome model. Section 4 presents the results of this experiment followed by conclusions in Section 5.

2 System Reliability, Availability, and Decision Making

Many people confuse or interchange the concepts of system reliability and availability. Before examining availability in depth, it is helpful to have an understanding of the distinction between the two concepts. These concepts are most frequently discussed in a hardware or equipment context, but also have applicability to software. Most often associated with component or system failure, reliability is a measure of the likelihood that a system or process will perform its designed function for a specified period of time. Availability is a relative measure of the *extent* that a system can perform its designed function [3]. As a relative measure, availability includes metrics such as delays, congestion, and loading. To illustrate, the reliability of a system could be determined by the number of failures and the amount of time between them. So, if a system was broken twice as much as it was working, it would have 50% reliability. This same system would be unavailable 50% of the time. However, a system does not have to be broken to be unavailable. Consider if a system was so busy processing data that it could not handle any additional tasks. The system is not broken, it is just temporarily busy. Simply put, system availability includes system reliability, as well as delay-oriented interruptions.

Reliability and availability both affect the systems that business people have become dependent on and there has been significant research on quantifying and minimizing system outages of any sort. Much of this research has centered on computer system components or hardware. Reussner et al. [4] use rich architecture definition language (RADL) to predict component reliability through compositional analysis of usage profiles and of environment component reliability. Mikic-Rakic et al. [5] propose a fast approximating solution for relating how software systems' environmental deployment (wired, mobile, grid, etc.) will affect its availability. Henson [6] suggests a method to improve hard disk reliability by dividing the hard disk file system data into small, individually repairable fault–isolation domains while preserving normal file system semantics. Dai et al. [7] propose a model for a centralized heterogeneous distributed system and examines the distributed service reliability which is defined as the probability of successfully providing a service in a distributed environment. All of these prior works concentrate on the system itself rather than the impact of low availability. The emphasis on hardware components is typical of system availability research and seldom do these types of studies simultaneously address software service availability.

With the recent interest in web services and service composition there has been a renewed research effort concentrating on software availability. In the web service domain, hardware is seen as an underlying component, on which software functions run. These independent services are loosely coupled and assembled to perform more complex functions. As a result, the availability of software is critical to web service use and composition. Notwithstanding its general consideration as an underlying component, even in a web service context, there is an implicit emphasis on systems hardware. For example, Salas et al. [8] proposed a method for providing an infrastructure that replicates web services across hardware on a wide area network. Sung et al. [9] put forward dynamic cluster configuration using a server agent and a service description server as a solution to improve computer service availability. Other research in this area adopts the use of context information, such as physical location about the service hardware [10] or using network bandwidth reservation [11] to improve availability. Research in web service availability has primarily addressed the issue of being able to compose the set of services that are necessary to fulfill a process or function. Like research in hardware availability, little attention is given to the impact of availability on outcomes resulting from system usage.

The approach proposed in this study addresses the two limitations noted above (a focus on hardware only and the exclusion of outcome impact). This prior research provides a solid foundation for quantifying, improving, and addressing system reliability (and subsequently availability) but these works have not extended this information to decision making outcomes. By mapping system availability to decision outcomes, users of cloud computing-based DSS may be made aware of the likelihood that a successful result can be obtained from an engagement with the system, within the time constraints of the decision opportunity.

2.1 Existing Availability-Related Technologies

In a decision support context, availability should be considered not only from a systems viewpoint, but also from the perspective of decision-related resources. These resources may be models, data, services, agents, processing, output devices, other decision makers, or even the decision maker requesting support. While not all decision support systems and scenarios require external or distributed resources to provide guidance to a decision maker, most contemporary DSS utilize the benefits provided by computer networks. The introduction of networking and distributed resources adds another dimension to the issue of resource availability. As discussed above, there are many solutions to determine or quantify if hardware or a software service is reliably "on-line." However, availability goes beyond this on-off notion and encompasses more than resource online/offline - operating/failed status information.

The obvious question is: *how might details about resources' availability be obtained*? Research from other domains provides answers to this question. The first domain is high-availability computing. Research in this area has already identified methods to monitor and evaluate hardware related statuses such as power [12, 13], network characteristics [14, 15], computer components [16, 17], processing/computing load [18], and storage [19].

The second domain provides status of resources that can be considered software services. Software services provide a layer of abstraction for a full range of programmable functions and data. Research in the area of web service composition and quality of service (QoS) can provide solutions delivering awareness knowledge for these types of resources. Quality of service is often defined as the probability that a network or service will meet a defined provision contract. This probability could be used by agents to forecast the likelihood of resource interruption as well as potentially quantitatively predict outage durations. There is a significant amount of research studying applications using QoS and QoS monitoring for service level agreements, adaptation to changing system conditions, and web service composition [20-23]. Web service composition is a particularly active research area, rich with solutions for service availability, because of the critical nature of this information for process scheduling and execution planning [24, 25].

A third domain provides availability information on human users of decision support systems. From the perspective of "users as a resource," human computer interaction research has provided several availability-oriented solutions. Most of the efforts have focused on detecting *if a user is* and not necessarily *when the user will become* online and available [26-28]. However, there are probabilistic models that can provide forecasts for humans' presence and availability. Horvitz et al. [29] developed a prototype service intended to support collaboration and communication by learning predictive models that provide forecasts of users' presence and availability. To accomplish this, they collected data about user activity and proximity to multiple devices and combined this with analyzed content of users' calendars.

The research in these three domains provides reasonable methods for obtaining quantitative availability information regarding decision resources such as hardware, network, and software services (e.g. web server, database servers, and business logic applications), as well as collaborators and systems users. Because the research conducted in these other domains delivers viable solutions for this problem, the probability model proposed in this work does not focus on this issue. Instead, the model is grounded in system reliability theory, extended to decision-related resource availability, and focused on how correct decision outcomes may be a function of these resources' availability.

2.2 Decision-Related Computing Resource Availability as a System Reliability Problem

Particularly in the case of DSS, decision resource availability may be analogous to system reliability. This is because a decision resource may be the DSS itself, another system, data from some storage-system, a network communication medium, an output device (e.g. monitors, printers, etc.), collaborating system users, or even decision makers themselves. One way to view a decision resource is as a hierarchical structure of interacting functions. This hierarchical structure may have $1 - n$ levels and when the resource is a computing device, these levels would encompass hardware, firmware, and software. The underlying concept is that a decision-resource, via its hierarchy, relates to a number of sub-resources at lower levels of the hierarchy. The functions in a resource hierarchy act and interact together to provide the resource at the top of the hierarchy. Upper level functions depend on lower levels to ensure their reliability and availability.

Figure 1 illustrates a generalized hierarchy. While every level may not be necessary for every resource, the level dependencies are evident. Consider an example where a DSS provides guidance by presenting information on a graphical map, e.g. a spatial DSS. This DSS may require data from a remote website that converts street addresses to latitude and longitude. This remote website/data would be considered a resource. This resource depends on a hierarchy of dependent functions to be able to serve its purpose. Examining Figure 1, without power/electricity, there is no connectivity or anything else above power. Without connectivity the data in storage cannot be delivered. Without storage, processing cannot occur; there is nothing to process. Without processing, the software cannot operate, and if the software (web server, address-to-lat/long converter, or host operating system) fails, the resource cannot respond to the DSS's request. There is an implicit dependency from top to bottom but

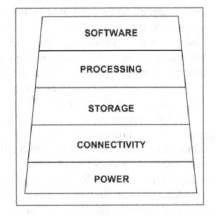

Fig. 1. Decision resource hierarchy

not the other way. It is possible to not have connectivity, yet have power available and so on.

Typically the availability of components, software, and systems is given in terms of its likelihood of being available; not the inverse (the likelihood it is *not* available). In the reliability practice there is a concept called 5 nines that refers to uptime (availability). If a system is said to have 5 nines reliability it is available 99.999% of the time. This translates to being *unavailable* 31.5 seconds per year. This measure is complicated in systems where there are dependencies, as is the case with a decision resource. The hierarchical dependence seen in a decision resource would suggest that the probability of a resource being available can be viewed as the product of the levels in its hierarchy. Each item in the hierarchy is independent unto itself but dependent on the level below it. Therefore, if each hierarchy level's availability is given in terms of it its potential availability (the likelihood it is available), probability theory can be applied. Because the function at each level in the hierarchy is independent in terms of its availability and dependent on lower levels in terms of its unavailability, the multiplicative rule of probability applies. Equation (1) shows the generalized form.

$$P(A \cap B) = P(A)P(B) \tag{1}$$

Building on this theory and applying it to Figure 1, let W=Power, C=Connectivity, G=Storage, O=Processing, and T=Software. The probability of availability for each level in the hierarchy can be given according to Table 1. Because availability is most commonly expressed in positive terms (i.e. uptime instead of downtime) the focus of Table 1 is on the probability that each level *is* available. Due to the dependency on lower levels, the probability that each level *is not* available would be additive. Table 1 shows the probability that each level in the hierarchy is determined by multiplying the previous levels' probability by the current level's probability and the overall availability of the decision resource is given by the probability of the topmost level. This leads to the generalized equation shown in (2) where $P(R)$ represents the probability of the decision resource (R), and F represents the function at each level, for all levels $i=1$ through n.

$$P(R) = \prod_{i=1}^{n} P(F_i) \tag{2}$$

Table 1. Hierarchy level availability probability

LEVEL	FUNCTION	FUNCTION PROBABILITY	LEVEL PROBABILITY
1	POWER	P(W)	P(W)
2	CONNECTIVITY	P(C)	P(W) * P(C)
3	STORAGE	P(G)	P(W) * P(C) * P(G)
4	PROCESSING	P(O)	P(W) * P(C) * P(G) * P(O)
5	SOFTWARE	P(T)	P(W) * P(C) * P(G) * P(O) * P(T)

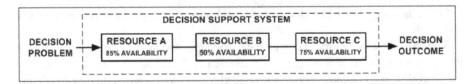

Fig. 2. A DSS with dependent resources

Extending the generalized resource availability equation in (2), all of the resources necessary for decision support can be accounted for similarly as a set of dependent resources. In this case, all the resources are necessary for the system to provide direct advice and therefore dependent in the context of the DSS provided solution. It follows that the availability of the system is given by Equation (3), where $P(S)$ denotes the availability of all the decision resources and $P(F)$ is the resource level availability, for all levels $i=1$ to n, for all resources $r=1$ to t.

$$P(S)=\prod_{r=1}^{t}\left(\prod_{i=1}^{n}P(F_i)\right)_r \tag{3}$$

Figure 2 shows a DSS that has 3 dependent resources. To illustrate with the earlier example, Resource A would represent data stored in a data warehouse. Resource B is the address to latitude and longitude web service, and Resource C would be the local processor that provides the graphical mapping. The availability of the DSS's guidance for this decision problem would be: $.85 * .50 * .75 = .319$, or 31.9% availability.

Figure 2 however, does not account for redundant resources. A redundant resource duplicates the functionality of another resource. Introducing redundant resources generally increases the overall system availability because dependencies are distributed across multiple resources. In this context, parallel resources are introduced. The availability of redundant resources (or redundant levels within a resource) is given by Equation (4), where $P(RR)$ represents the availability of the redundant resource, for all resources comprising the redundant resources $r=1$ to t. Redundant levels of a resource hierarchy follows this same formula replacing $P(R)$ with the probability of the redundant level's function availability.

$$P(RR)=1-\prod_{r=1}^{t}(1-P(R_r)) \tag{4}$$

A generalized equation can be given to describe DSS that have redundant or alternate resources as shown in Equation (5). In equation (5), probabilities for redundant resources $P(X)$, are calculated separately from non-redundant resources $P(R)$. As previously discussed, the multiplicative rule of probability applies for all resources. If there are no redundant resources, this portion of the problem is removed from the equation. Similarly, if all the resources are redundant, the part of the equation that determines the availability of non-redundant resources is removed. Each redundant resource's *unavailability* is calculated over resource $j=1$ to v. Then that value is subtracted from 1; giving the availability of the composite redundant resource. That result is then multiplied by other redundant resources $q=1$ to u to determine the availability of all redundant resources.

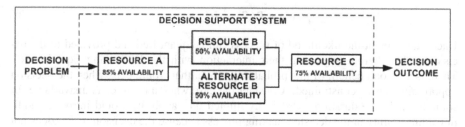

Fig. 3. A DSS with dependent and redundant resources

$$P(S)=\left(\prod_{r=1}^{t}P(R_r)\right)\left(\prod_{q=1}^{u}\left(1-\left(\prod_{j=1}^{v}\left(1-P(X_i)\right)\right)\right)_q\right)$$ (5)

Figure 3 extends the DSS in Figure 2 with redundancy in resource B. Illustrating again with the earlier example, Resource A would represent data stored in a data warehouse and Resource C is the local processor providing graphical mapping. Resource B remains the address to latitude and longitude service; only this time there is more than one provider from where the address to lat/long conversion can be obtained. To determine the probability of DSS guidance availability $P(S)$, the probability of the redundant resource must first be determined and then applied as a single value to the remainder of the system. Because all of the redundant resources must fail before the availability of that resource is reduced, the calculation's use of the likelihood of the resource being *unavailable* takes this into account. The availability probability of the redundant resource (B) in Figure 3 is: *1 - ((1-.50) * (1-.50)) = .75*. Once this is calculated, the problem is the same as the previous example, except .75 is used for resource B: *.85 * .75 * .75 = .478*, or 47.8% availability.

The overall resource availability $P(S)$ provides a deterministic value for the likelihood that the DSS can supply advice based on the necessary resources. In a data-oriented decision support context, where the DSS provides guidance that is assumed to be correct based on this data, the overall resource availability can be directly mapped to the probability of accurate decision guidance outcomes.

2.3 Decision Outcome as a Function of Resource Availability: A Probabilistic Model

The equation shown in the previous section is part of the necessary probabilities to predict outcome success. Equation 5 will provide the likelihood of decision resource availability. This assumes that if available, the DSS will provide a correct and exact answer to the decision problem. However, it is possible for the decision maker to make the correct choice without assistance from the DSS. Therefore, the complete probability of successful outcome must include the probability the decision maker makes a choice without assistance from the DSS. Equation (6) defines the probability of a correct decision outcome $P(C)$ as: the probability decision-resources are available $P(S)$, plus the probability that the decision maker selects the correct answer from the possible alternatives $P(A)$ without the decision support system.

$$P(C) = P(S) + P(A) \tag{6}$$

Uncertainty about the likelihood of success can be quantified and provided to the decision maker, before beginning their interaction with the DSS using Equation (6). There is a second benefit of this probability model that would exist when the decision opportunity is time constrained. Consider the case when a resource is unavailable for some limited time duration. Ordinarily limited unavailability would introduce additional uncertainty in the decision making process because the decision maker does not know when or if the unavailable resource will become available. The decision maker has to decide whether or not to wait for the resource to become available or to proceed without the assistance of the DSS. Given the probabilistic model shown in Equation (6), the decision maker could make that wait-don't wait decision with insight into the resource's availability. The uncertainty could be further reduced, if the specific resource probability (as opposed to the probability of all the resources) was provided to the decision maker.

3 Experimental Evaluation

More than ever, decision makers depend on data to make and justify their decisions and the general assumption is that the data is accurate and the DSS will provide a correct answer [30, 31]. As mobile and cloud computing environments increasingly become the norm and system resources become more likely to be distributed (e.g. service oriented architectures, computing grids, and distributed databases) the relevance of the research in resource availability will be progressively more significant. As a result, this study raises the research question: does the availability of decision-related resources map to decision outcomes in a probabilistic manner? Based on the above discussion and the probabilistic model presented in Section 2.3, the following alternate hypothesis is formulated:

> Decision-related resource availability maps to accurate decision outcomes according to the following probability: $P(C) = P(R) + P(A)$, where $P(C)$ is the probability of correct decision outcome, $P(R)$ is the probability decision-resources are available, and $P(A)$ is the probability that the decision maker chooses the correct answer without the decision support system.

To evaluate the probabilistic model, it is desirable to have a scenario where the DSS provides deterministic (go/no-go, yes/no, or singular answer) guidance in support of a decision opportunity. Further, the decision needs to be based on selection from possible data alternatives, where the data resource may be unavailable. For purposes of evaluating the above hypothesis, a simulation of a stock trading decision was modeled. Stock purchasing was chosen because it is representative of the decision opportunities identified above and easy to understand for a broad range of audiences.

A decision problem was constructed where a stock is purchased from the list of Standard & Poor's 500 stocks (S&P 500). The decision maker has a simple strategy for deciding which stock to purchase. In equity trading, there is a concept that volume precedes price [32] and this is the purchasing strategy that the decision maker employs. The DSS has the capability to identify from the list of 500 which stock has the highest volume for the time of purchase and this is the correct advice provided. To provide this advice, the DSS requires a resource that specifically identifies the stock with the highest volume for the purchase period. To choose a stock the decision maker requests the highest volume stock for the DSS and always takes the provided advice, if available. If the DSS is unable to provide advice, the decision maker selects a stock from the list of 500 stocks.

A precise and explicit model of the decision problem and simulation was programmed in Matlab. This software provided a robust programming environment where the simulation could be created and evaluated. The resource that provided the high-volume stock selection was coded with 5 hierarchy levels according to Figure 1. Each of these levels was coded with a probability between 0 and 100% that would be determined randomly at run time. The equation shown in (5) was coded to determine the overall resource availability probability. This probability was compared to an "outage" variable whose value was also set randomly. If the outage variable value was lower than the resource availability probability, the resource was considered unavailable. The decision maker was also coded as part of the simulation and always took the advice offered by the DSS. When the advice was not available, the simulated decision maker chose a stock randomly from the list of 500.

A run of the simulation consisted of the generating the availability probabilities, the outage value, and a single decision outcome. For each run, the availability status of the resource and subsequently the DSS advice, was recorded, with the correct stock and the stock selected by the decision maker. Several executions of the simulation were made of varying run sizes from one hundred to one million.

4 Results

The results were collected and analyzed using SPSS. Correct decision outcomes were coded as one and incorrect as zero. The resource availability status was coded similarly: one for available and zero for unavailable. The probability that the resource was available was determined for each run-size and then applied to the probability model to forecast the expected decision outcome accuracy. For example, in the case of the run of 100 decisions, the resource was available only 3% of the time. Applying this value to the probability model shown in Equation (6) leads to an expectation of 3 correct outcomes, given by: $(3/100) + (1/500)*100 = 3.2/100$. Since the measurement of correct outcomes must be an integer value, the model results were rounded to the whole number: 3 correct and 97 incorrect outcomes in the run-size with 100 runs. This same calculation was performed for each of the run-size sets and used as input to Pearson's Chi-Square Goodness of Fit Test for each. Pearson's Chi-Square Goodness of Fit Test evaluates how close observed values are to those that would be expected from a model [33]. Table 2 shows the results of this test, with the expected (EXP.) column being the calculated values from the availability model.

If the computed Chi-Square value is large (generally greater than 1), then the observed and expected values are not close and the model is a poor fit to the data. As is evident in Table 2, the test statistic values are small for every run-size indicating the

Table 2. Pearson's Chi-Square goodness of fit results

RUN-SIZE	PCNT. AVAIL.	OUTCOME	EXP.	OBS.	RES.	CHI-SQ.	ASYMP SIG.
100	3.00%	Correct	3	4	1	.344	.558
		Incorrect	97	96	-1		
1,000	2.80%	Correct	30	32	2	.137	.711
		Incorrect	970	968	-2		
10,000	3.29%	Correct	349	345	4	.048	.827
		Incorrect	9,651	9,655	-4		
50,000	3.08%	Correct	1,639	1,630	9	.051	.821
		Incorrect	48,361	48,370	-9		
100,000	3.09%	Correct	3,285	3,254	31	.302	.582
		Incorrect	96,715	96,746	-31		
500,000	3.11%	Correct	16,565	16,532	33	.068	.794
		Incorrect	483,435	483,468	-33		
1,000,000	3.12%	Correct	33,158	33,103	55	.094	.759
		Incorrect	966,842	966,897	-55		

model is a good fit. The Chi-Square test was also used to evaluate the hypothesis. In a Chi Square Goodness of Fit Test, a small significance indicates that the observed distribution does *not* conform to the hypothesized distribution [34]. In all of the runs the asymptotic significance was above an alpha = .05 level of significance indicating that the distributions are the same; supporting the alternate hypothesis. A second analysis of the expected and observed results' distribution was conducted using a one way ANOVA test. The results of the ANOVA test yielded a between groups sum of squares of .038 with an alpha level = 1. This result is consistent with and supports the goodness of fit test.

5   Conclusion

This study proposes that cloud computing applications would benefit if availability-related context information could be known. The first step in this research was to determine if it is possible to map system availability to system usage/benefit. As this study illustrates, there is a probabilistic relationship between decision support-related computing resource availability and correct decision outcomes when the decision is structured, the data is correct, and the DSS provided guidance is deterministic. When availability is less than guaranteed, the ambiguity in resource availability inserts additional uncertainty in the system usage process. By providing a measure of the likelihood of a correct outcome and details about the availability of individual computing resources, users can make informed choices regarding the potential for support from cloud based computing applications.

While the model demonstrated in this paper provides a tool for quantifying the likelihood of correct outcomes, the real benefit of the model may be realized when availability information is extended to the decision maker. In this sense, the model should be incorporated in client hardware and software that utilize cloud computing services. The model is also dependent on collected availability context data. As such, it should be tied to other context-related technologies such as location. This approach would allow the model to be used for predictive purposes. The research in this paper represents a reasonable first step in addressing availability issues related to cloud computing, but as it is implemented as a simulation it has the limitations of the simulation scenario. A future study is planned to operationalize the model within a mobile client. This future study will incorporate network sensing with GPS for location data and extend the model with a real world cloud computing application.

References

1. Buyya, R., Sulistio, A.: Service and Utility Oriented Distributed Computing Systems: Challenges and Opportunities for Modeling and Simulation Communities. In: 41st Annual Simulation Symposium (ANSS-41), Ottawa, Canada, pp. 68–81 (2008)
2. Russell, S., Forgionne, G., Yoon, V.: Presence and Availability Awareness for Decision Support Systems in Pervasive Computing Environments. International Journal of Decision Support System Technology 1 (2008)
3. Bhagwan, R., Savage, S., Voelker, G.: Understanding Availability. In: Peer-to-Peer Systems II (IPTPS 2003), Berkeley, CA, USA, pp. 256–267 (2003)
4. Reussner, R.H., Schmidt, H.W., Poernomo, I.H.: Reliability Prediction for Component-Based Software Architectures. Journal of Systems and Software 66, 241–252 (2003)
5. Mikic-Rakic, M., Malek, S., Medvidovic, N.: Improving Availability in Large, Distributed Component-Based Systems Via Redeployment. In: Dearle, A., Eisenbach, S. (eds.) CD 2005. LNCS, vol. 3798, pp. 83–98. Springer, Heidelberg (2005)
6. Henson, V., Ven, A.v.d., Gud, A., Brown, Z.: Chunkfs: Using Divide–and–Conquer to Improve File System Reliability and Repair. In: 2nd Workshop on Hot Topics in System Dependability (HotDep 2006), Seattle, WA, USA (2006)
7. Dai, Y.S., Xie, M., Poh, K.L., Liu, G.Q.: A Study of Service Reliability and Availability for Distributed Systems. Reliability Engineering & System Safety 79, 103–112 (2003)
8. Salas, J., Perez-Sorrosal, F., Martinez, M.P., Jimenez-Peris, R.: Ws-Replication: A Framework for Highly Available Web Services. In: 15th International World Wide Web Conference, Edinburgh, Scotland. ACM, New York (2006)
9. Sung, H., Choi, B., Kim, H., Song, J., Han, S., Ang, C.-W., Cheng, W.-C., Wong, K.-S.: Dynamic Clustering Model for High Service Availability. In: Eighth International Symposium on Autonomous Decentralized Systems (ISADS 2007), Sedona, AZ, USA. IEEE Computer Society, Los Alamitos (2007)
10. Ibach, P., Horbank, M.: Highly Available Location-Based Services in Mobile Environments. In: Malek, M., Reitenspiess, M., Kaiser, J. (eds.) ISAS 2004. LNCS, vol. 3335, pp. 134–147. Springer, Heidelberg (2005)
11. Xu, J., Lee, W.: Sustaining Availability of Web Services under Distributed Denial of Service Attacks. IEEE Transactions on Computers 52, 195–208 (2003)
12. Chakraborty, S., Yau, D.K.Y., Lui, J.C.S., Dong, Y.: On the Effectiveness of Movement Prediction to Reduce Energy Consumption in Wireless Communication. IEEE Transactions on Mobile Computing 5, 157–169 (2006)

13. Rahmati, A., Zhong, L.: Context-for-Wireless: Context-Sensitive Energy-Efficient Wireless Data Transfer. In: 5th International Conference on Mobile systems, Applications and Services, San Juan, Puerto Rico, pp. 165–178 (2007)

14. Shahram, G., Shyam, K., Bhaskar, K.: An Evaluation of Availability Latency in Carrier-Based Wehicular Ad-Hoc Networks. In: Proceedings of the 5th ACM international workshop on Data engineering for wireless and mobile access, Chicago, Illinois, USA. ACM Press, New York (2006)

15. Roughan, M., Griffin, T., Mao, M., Greenberg, A., Freeman, B.: Combining Routing and Traffic Data for Detection of Ip Forwarding Anomalies. ACM SIGMETRICS Performance Evaluation Review 32, 416–417 (2004)

16. Brown, A., Oppenheimer, D., Keeton, K., Thomas, R., Kubiatowicz, J., Patterson, D.A.: Istore: Introspective Storage for Data-Intensive Network Services. In: The IEEE Seventh Workshop on Hot Topics in Operating Systems, Rio Rico, AZ, USA, pp. 32–37 (1999)

17. Weatherspoon, H., Chun, B.-G., So, C.W., Kubiatowicz, J.: Long-Term Data Maintenance in Wide-Area Storage Systems: A Quantitative Approach. In: University of California, Berkely, Electrical Engineering & Computer Sciences Department, Berkely, CA, USA (2005)

18. Zhoujun, H., Zhigang, H., Zhenhua, L.: Resource Availability Evaluation in Service Grid Environment. In: 2nd IEEE Asia-Pacific Service Computing Conference (APSCC 2007), Tsukuba Science City, Japan. IEEE Computer Society, Los Alamitos (2007)

19. Blake, C., Rodrigues, R.: High Availability, Scalable Storage, Dynamic Peer Networks: Pick Two. In: The 9th conference on Hot Topics in Operating Systems (HOTOS 2003), Lihue, HI, USA, p. 1 (2003)

20. Thio, N., Karunasekera, S.: Automatic Measurement of a Qos Metric for Web Service Recommendation. In: 2005 Australian Software Engineering Conference, Brisbane, Australia, pp. 202–211 (2005)

21. Loyall, J.P., Schantz, R.E., Zinky, J.A., Bakken, D.E.: Specifying and Measuring Quality of Service in Distributed Object Systems. In: First International Symposium on Object-Oriented Real-Time Distributed Computing (ISORC 1998), Kyoto, Japan (1998)

22. Ali, A.S., Rana, O., Walker, D.W.: Ws-Qoc: Measuring Quality of Service Compliance. In: International Conference on Service Oriented Computing (ICSOC 2004), New York, NY, USA (2004)

23. Menasce, D.A.: Composing Web Services: A Qos View. IEEE Internet Computing 8, 88–90 (2004)

24. Peer, J.: Web Service Composition as Ai Planning - a Survey, University of St. Gallen (2005)

25. Pistore, M., Barbon, F., Bertoli, P., Shaparau, D., Traverso, P.: Planning and Monitoring Web Service Composition (2004)

26. Muhlenbrock, M., Brdiczka, O., Snowdon, D., Meunier, J.L.: Learning to Detect User Activity and Availability from a Variety of Sensor Data. In: Second IEEE Annual Conference on Pervasive Computing and Communications (PerCom 2004), Orlando, FL, USA, pp. 13–22 (2004)

27. Danninger, M., Kluge, T., Stiefelhagen, R.: Myconnector: Analysis of Context Cues to Predict Human Availability for Communication. In: 8th international conference on Multimodal interfaces, Banff, Alberta, Canada (2006)

28. Begole, J.B., Matsakis, N.E., Tang, J.C.: Lilsys: Sensing Unavailability. In: 2004 ACM conference on Computer supported cooperative work, Chicago, Illinois, USA (2004)

29. Horvitz, E., Koch, P., Kadie, C.M., Jacobs, A.: Coordinate: Probabilistic Forecasting of Presence and Availability. In: The Eighteenth Conference on Uncertainty and Artificial Intelligence, Edmonton, Alberta, Canada, pp. 224–233 (2002)

30. Covin, J.G., Slevin, D.P., Heeley, M.B.: Strategic Decision Making in an Intuitive Vs. Technocratic Mode: Structural and Environmental Considerations. Journal of Business Research 52, 51–67 (2001)
31. Amaro, H., Blake, S.M., Morrill, A.C., Cranston, K., Logan, J., Conron, K.J., Dai, J.: HIV Prevention Community Planning: Challenges and Opportunities for Data-Informed Decision-Making. AIDS and Behavior 9, 9–27 (2005)
32. Fontanills, G.A., Gentile, T.: The Stock Market Course. John Wiley & Sons, New York (2001)
33. Chernoff, H., Lehmann, E.L.: The Use of Maximum Likelihood Estimates in X2 Tests for Goodness-of-Fit. The Annals of Mathematical Statistics 25, 579–586 (1954)
34. Plackett, R.L.: Karl Pearson and the Chi-Squared Test. International Statistical Review 51, 59–72 (1983)

Do Clouds Compute?
A Framework for Estimating the Value of Cloud Computing

Markus Klems, Jens Nimis, and Stefan Tai

Forschungszentrum Informatik (FZI)
Haid-und-Neu-Str. 10-14, 76131 Karlsruhe, Germany
{klems,nimis,tai}@fzi.de
http://www.fzi.de

Abstract. On-demand provisioning of scalable and reliable compute services, along with a cost model that charges consumers based on actual service usage, has been an objective in distributed computing research and industry for a while. Cloud Computing promises to deliver on this objective: consumers are able to rent infrastructure in the Cloud as needed, deploy applications and store data, and access them via Web protocols on a pay-per-use basis. The acceptance of Cloud Computing, however, depends on the ability for Cloud Computing providers and consumers to implement a model for business value co-creation. Therefore, a systematic approach to measure costs and benefits of Cloud Computing is needed. In this paper, we discuss the need for valuation of Cloud Computing, identify key components, and structure these components in a framework. The framework assists decision makers in estimating Cloud Computing costs and to compare these costs to conventional IT solutions. We demonstrate by means of representative use cases how our framework can be applied to real world scenarios.

Keywords: Cloud Computing, Utility Computing, Grid Computing, Valuation, TCO.

1   Introduction

On-demand provisioning of compute services, along with a cost model that charges consumers based on actual service usage, has been an objective in distributed computing research and industry for a while. Cloud Computing promises to deliver on this objective: consumers are able to rent (virtualized) infrastructure as needed, deploy applications and store data on the infrastructure, and access the applications and data via Web protocols on a pay-per-use basis. For our purposes, we define Cloud Computing as follows: Building on compute and storage virtualization technologies, and leveraging the modern Web, Cloud Computing provides scalable and affordable compute utilities as on-demand services with variable pricing schemes, enabling a new consumer mass market.

C. Weinhardt, S. Luckner, and J. Stößer (Eds.): WEB 2008, LNBIP 22, pp. 110–123, 2009.

In addition to the technological challenges of Cloud Computing, there is a need for Cloud Computing providers and consumers to implement an appropriate model for business value co-creation. Cloud Computing providers must support variable, competitive pricing schemes. Similarly, Cloud Computing consumers must carefully evaluate costs and compare these to alternative, conventional IT infrastructure solutions. In this paper, we introduce a framework for estimating the value of Cloud Computing. We discuss the need for valuation specific to Cloud Computing, identify key components, and structure these components in a framework. The framework primarily assists decision makers in understanding Cloud Computing solutions.

2   Definitions and Classification

Grid Computing, defined as follows, may provide a highly available, reliable infrastructure for serving compute utilities, and thus relates to our understanding of Cloud Computing.

"A computational grid is a hardware and software infrastructure that provides dependable, consistent, pervasive and inexpensive access to high-end computational capabilities." [6].

Both Grid Computing and Cloud Computing implement the more general model of Utility Computing. However, the motivation and approaches to realize an infrastructure that serves compute utilities are considerably different. Grid Computing evolved in a scientific community as a means to solve computationally challenging tasks in science and industry. Although Clouds can also be used for large-scale batch jobs, they focus on very different applications. Emerging in a commercial environment, the main purpose of Cloud Computing is to provide a platform to develop, test and deploy Web-scale applications and services.

Foster proposed a simple checklist to characterize a Grid as a system that "coordinates resources that are not subject to centralized control ... using standard, open, general-purpose protocols and interfaces ... to deliver nontrivial qualities of service" [7]. By contrast, we can observe that today's Cloud Computing services are backed by massive data centers under the centralized control of single providers within the same administrative domain, such as Amazon, Google, Microsoft, and others. While Grid Computing is concerned with negotiating and managing shared resources, Cloud Computing relies on much simpler consumer-provider interactions.

Different names have been proposed in order to differentiate between different levels of Cloud Computing service complexity. For lower-level services the term Infrastructure-as-a-Service (IaaS) has been established, whereas higher-level services are labeled Platform-as-a-Service (PaaS). Typical IaaS offerings include Amazon's Elastic Compute Cloud (EC2) and Simple Storage Service (S3), Joyent's Accelerator and Rackspace's Mosso, whereas typical PaaS offerings are Google's App Engine or Salesforce's Force.com. IaaS is about basic, "raw" compute services (compute power, storage and networking) in form of dynamically provisioned virtualized computers. Third parties can build on and utilize these basic services to create complementary, composable service offerings. Examples include Scalr, a redundant, self-curing, self-scaling hosting environment built on top of Amazon's EC2, or the Aptana Cloud providing an IDE for Joyent's IaaS offerings. Google's App Engine, on the other hand, comes with its own SDK that lets developers deploy Python applications into the Google Cloud. App Engine is a PaaS offering with limited options for third-party application development, system management, and information management solutions.

3   Objective

The main purpose of our paper is to present a basic framework for estimating value and determine benefits from Cloud Computing as an alternative to conventional IT infrastructure, such as privately owned and managed IT hardware. Our effort is motivated by the rise of Cloud Computing providers and the question when it is profitable for a business to use hardware resources in the Cloud. More and more companies already embrace Cloud Computing services as part of their IT infrastructure or as a testbed for technology innovations. However, there is no guide to tell when outsourcing into the Cloud is the way to go and in which cases it does not make sense to do so. Our work introduces a more systematic, methodical valuation approach to Cloud Computing that considers both economic and technical aspects.

Valuation is an economic discipline of estimating the value of projects and enterprises. Corporate management relies on valuation methods in order to make reasonable investment decisions. Although the basic methods are rather simple, like Discounted Cash Flow (DCF) analysis, the difficulties lie in appropriate application to real world cases. Our approach to estimating the value of Cloud Computing services uses ideas from relative valuation with market comparables as described by Titman and Martin [23]. The main difference of our approach is to propose calculating a "cost metric" instead of a "valuation metric" and then estimate the value in terms of opportunity costs. Thereby one can valuate the benefit that Cloud Computing services provides over the best alternative technology.

4   Approach

A novel valuation framework dedicated to Cloud Computing is proposed. Previous work from related fields like Grid Computing can not be applied, as different applications are being addressed. While Grid Computing primarily assists scientists with computationally expensive problems, Cloud Computing addresses the needs of businesses building and deploying applications that are of varying scale and complexity and which utilize the Web. Although back-end technologies may be similar, the target groups and typical use cases for Grids and Clouds are very different.

Figure 1 illustrates our framework for estimating the value of IaaS offerings. In the following, we describe in more detail the steps suggested with the framework.

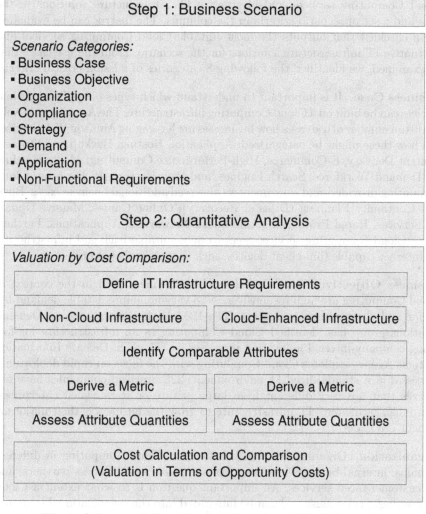

Fig. 1. A framework for estimating the value of Cloud Computing

In our current research, a set of tools is being developed in support of the steps in the framework.

4.1 Business Scenario

In a first step, we suggest to model a business scenario in order to evaluate the use of Cloud Computing services within the scope of a specific project. For this purpose, it is necessary to capture essential properties of the scenario. Such a descriptive approach is rather qualitative by nature but can be extended to map into quantitative metrics and thus be used in the second step of our framework. We propose that the decision maker creates a matrix with available Cloud Computing services and alternative IT infrastructure solutions in the rows and a set of scenario criteria in the columns. The matrix can be evaluated like a checklist that outputs the most suitable Cloud Computing services and alternative IT infrastructure solutions for the scenario. From the use cases that we examined, we identified the following 8 categories of mission-critical criteria.

Business Case. It is important to understand which types of applications and services can be built on a Cloud Computing infrastructure. The Amazon.com website lists a number of use cases how businesses are leveraging Amazon Web Services and how these might be categorized: Application Hosting, Backup and Storage, Content Delivery, E-Commerce, High-Performance Computing, Media Hosting, On-Demand Workforce, Search Engines, and Web Hosting [1]. For other Cloud Computing providers and consumers we observed additional business cases: Business Continuity Planning (Disaster Recovery), Online Games, Massive Updating Services, Rapid Prototyping, and Social Networking Applications. Furthermore, Cloud Computing services seem to be a suitable back-end infrastructure for Internet-capable thin-client devices, such as mobile phones or netbooks.

Business Objective. Typical business benefits mentioned in the context of Cloud Computing are high responsiveness to varying, unpredictable demand behavior and shorter time to market. The IBM High Performance on Demand Solutions group has identified Cloud Computing as an infrastructure for fostering company-internal innovation processes [5]. The U.S. Defense Information Systems Agency explores Cloud Computing with the focus on rapid deployment processes in a standardized IT environment [22]. Start-up companies have objectives that are very different from large private or state-owned enterprises: affordable, "scale-out" IT infrastructure to grow the business is their major argument pro Cloud ([1], [12]).

Organization. Organizations can benefit from Cloud Computing in different domains: internal business processes, collaboration with business partners, and for customer-faced services. An important question is to what extent a Cloud Computing service must and can be integrated into the organizational structure of an enterprise, and how a Cloud might be used to leverage communication and collaboration with business partners and customers.

Compliance. The shift from personal and business data into the Cloud where it is processed and stored must comply with privacy laws and regulations, such as the Federal Data Protection Act in Germany. If it is prohibited by law to store application and user data outside national borders then a Cloud Computing service with data centers in other countries cannot be used. Legal aspects could also make a Cloud application more expensive due to different security policies that must be followed.

Strategy. Developing an application for the Cloud or migrating an existing application into the Cloud comes with the risk of vendor lock-in and dependency on the vendor's pricing policy. Low-level Cloud Computing services, such as Amazon's EC2, seem less prone to this kind of risk than high-level PaaS offerings, such as Google's App Engine. Migrating an application that has been deployed on a Xen-virtualized Amazon Machine Image to another IaaS provider who uses similar hardware virtualization or to a conventional IT infrastructure might require some work. However, an application that is designed to run on Google's App Engine and that relies on Google's special-purpose interfaces and services will be much more difficult or even impossible to migrate to alternative environments.

Demand. Services and applications in the Web and corporate networks can roughly be divided into two categories: services that deal with somewhat predictable demand behavior and those that must handle unexpected demand volumes, respectively. Services from the first category must be built on top of scalable infrastructure in order to adapt to changing demand volumes. The second category is even more challenging, since increase and decrease in demand cannot be forecasted at all and sometimes occurs within minutes or even seconds.

Traditionally, the IT operations department of an organization must master the difficulties involved in scaling corporate infrastructure up or down. In practice it is impossible to constantly fully utilize available server capacities, which is why there is always a tradeoff between resource over-utilization, resulting in bad user experience, and under-utilization, leading to negative financial performance [20]. The IT department dimensions the infrastructure according to expected demand volumes and in a way such that enough space for business growth is left. Moreover, emergency situations, like server outages and demand spikes must be addressed and dealt with. Associated with under- and over-utilization is the notion of opportunity costs. The opportunity costs of under-utilization are measured in units of wasted compute resources, such as idle running servers. The opportunity costs of over-utilization are the costs of losing customers or being sued as a consequence of a temporary server outage.

Expected Demand: Seasonal Demand. An online retail store is a typical service that suffers from seasonal demand spikes. During Christmas the retail store usually faces much higher demand volumes than over the rest of the year. The IT infrastructure must be dimensioned such that it can handle even the highest demand peaks in December.

Expected Demand: Temporary Effect. Some services and applications are short-lived and targeted to single or seldom events, such as Websites for the Olympic Games 2008 in Beijing. As seen with seasonal demand spikes, the increase and decrease of demand volume is somewhat predictable. However, the service only exists for a comparably short period of time, during which it experiences heavy traffic loads. After the event is finished, the demand will decrease to a constant low level and the service might be shut down eventually.

Expected Demand: Batch Processing. The third category of expected demand scenarios are batch processing jobs. In this case the demand volume is usually known beforehand and does not need to be estimated.

Unexpected demand: Temporary Effect. This scenario is similar to the "expected temporary effect", except for one major difference: the demand behavior cannot be predicted at all or only short time in advance. A typical example for this scenario is a Web start-up company that becomes popular over night because it was featured on a news network. Many people simultaneously rush to the Website of the start-up company, causing significant traffic load and eventually bring down the servers. Named after two famous news sharing Websites this phenomenon is known as "Slashdot effect" or "Digg effect".

Application. Application-specific requirements comprise for example the runtime environment, database technology, Web server software and additional software libraries as well as load-balancing and redundancy mechanisms. A Cloud Computing infrastructure that comes with a pre-configured runtime and software libraries that facilitate integration into social network sites would for example be a good choice for a situational social networking application.

Non-Functional Requirements. In addition to application-specific requirements, non-functional requirements must be addressed as well: security, high availability, reliability, scalability, Quality of Service and so on. These requirements are obviously related to the above mentioned aspects, such as business objectives, application, demand, and so on.

4.2   Quantitative Analysis

In the second step of our framework, we suggest to conduct a quantitative analysis of the business scenario by means of valuation methods. The valuation of Cloud Computing services must take into account costs as well as cash flows resulting from the underlying business model. Within the context of our valuation approach we suggest a cost comparison between "Cloud-Enhanced" IT infrastructure and the best alternative "Non-Cloud" IT infrastructure investment. Based on this cost comparison, the benefits of Cloud Computing technology can be measured as opportunity costs.

Define IT Infrastructure Requirements. First of all, the decision maker must identify mission-critical requirements of the IT infrastructure according to the criteria of the business scenario (section 4.1). On the basis of these requirements she must decide which Cloud Computing services and alternative IT infrastructure solutions are most suitable for the scenario.

Non-Cloud vs. Cloud-Enhanced IT Infrastructure. This is probably the most challenging task in our approach to value Cloud Computing technology. The decision maker must model two infrastructure environments that are suitable to fulfill the criteria of the business scenario. The first IT infrastructure does not use Cloud Computing services (Non-Cloud infrastructure) whereas the second infrastructure does (Cloud-Enhanced infrastructure). The Non-Cloud infrastrucure could be pure on-premise IT infrastructure or a Grid Computing service. The Cloud-Enhanced infrastructure might be a Cloud Computing service, such as Amazon's EC2 or a combination of conventional on-premise IT infrastructure plus additional Cloud Computing services to capture demand spikes. If there is no possibility to realize the business scenario without Cloud Computing services, then the value of Cloud Computing must be estimated with alternative methods, such as a DCF analysis. For example, applications for Salesforce's platform Force.com can not be deployed in an alternative environment. The value of such an application should therefore be measured in terms of expected cash flows instead of opportunity costs.

Identify Comparable Attributes. It is necessary to identify key attributes that indicate fulfillment of the business scenario requirements and that can be measured or estimated for the Non-Cloud and the Cloud-Enhanced infrastructure, respectively. These comparable attributes can be derived from a subset of the business scenario criteria. Examples of comparable attributes are storage capacity, processing power or results from application load testing and stress testing. These attributes are needed in order to make Non-Cloud and Cloud-Enhanced infrastructures comparable.

Derive a Metric Based on Comparable Attributes. A "cost metric" can then be calculated by dividing the cumulative infrastructure costs by the amount of "attribute units" used over time. The metric will usually be different for Non-Cloud and Cloud-Enhanced infrastructure, respectively, and reflect the infrastructure's capability to meet business scenario criteria, such as demand behavior or Quality of Service. A Scorecard method could be used in order to map the qualitative criteria of the business scenario into quantitative "costs". Thereby, risk factors can be captured by the calculation.

For a full-fledged data center, Koomey, et al. showed that Gartner's Total Cost of Ownership (TCO) provides a good tool for cost calculations [13]. The cost model comprises direct costs, such as Capital Expenditures for the facility, energy and cooling infrastructure, cables, servers, and so on. Moreover, there are Operational Expenditures which must be taken into account, such as energy, network fees and IT employees. Indirect costs comprise costs from failing to meet business objectives, e.g. timely rollout or quality of service. There is no easy way to measure these factors and approaches will vary from case to case. One could for example compare cash flows that result from failing to deliver certain business objectives with cash flows that are expected to be earned when business objectives are met. If the introduction of a service offer is delayed due to slow deployment processes, the resulting monetary deficit can be calculated with a DCF valuation method.

Assess Attribute Quantities. In order to calculate the costs for Non-Cloud and Cloud-Enhanced infrastructure, respectively, one need to measure or estimate each attribute for both environments. Then multiply the measured "units" of an attribute with the corresponding cost metric of the Non-Cloud and Cloud-Enhanced infrastructure, respectively, and compute a cost estimate for the Non-Cloud and a cost estimate for the Cloud-Enhanced infrastructure. Since there can be more than one relevant attribute, it is necessary to repeat the calculation for each attribute and then aggregate the value of all cost estimates.

Costs Calculation and Comparison. By means of a comparison between the cost aggregates of the Non-Cloud and the Cloud-Enhanced IT infrastructures it is finally possible to calculate the value of using Cloud Computing services in terms of opportunity costs. If the aggregate costs of the Non-Cloud infrastructure exceed the aggregate costs of the Cloud-Enhanced infrastructure then obviously the value is positive; otherwise it is negative and the Non-Cloud infrastructure is preferable.

5   Evaluation and Discussion

We demonstrate by four representative use cases how our framework can be applied to real world scenarios. Today, the adoption of Cloud Computing technology is mainly driven by small and medium-sized Web start-up companies. Due to their small size, low capitalization and short company history, start-ups usually do not have access to a reliable and scalable IT infrastructure. With Cloud Computing services, they circumvent market barriers in form of up-front costs and scarce hardware technology skills. Companies can enter new markets and compete with established companies in business segments, such as content delivery, multimedia services, media hosting, storage and backup services, search technology, and Web 2.0 applications, all of which require outstanding back-end capabilities.

Enterprises currently experiment with Cloud Computing technology with the primary objectives to foster innovation and reduce time-to-market of new products through rapid prototyping and short deployment cycles.

The first two use cases, "New York Times TimesMachine" and "Major League Baseball", are good examples of how and why Cloud Computing technology is applied in established corporations. The other two examples, "Powerset Search Engine" and "Jungle Disk", demonstrate how Cloud Computing technology opens up new business opportunities for start-up companies. We only apply the qualitative part (section 4.1) of our framework because we have no exact quantifiable information about technical requirements of each use case.

5.1   New York Times TimesMachine

In autumn 2007 New York Times senior software engineer Derek Gottfrid worked on a project named TimesMachine. The service should provide access to any New York Times issue since 1851, adding up to a bulk of 11 million articles which had to be served in the form of PDF files. Previously Gottfrid and his colleagues had implemented a solution that generated the PDF files dynamically from already scanned TIFF images of the New York Times articles. This approach worked well, but when traffic volumes were about to increase significantly it would be better to serve pre-generated static PDF files. Faced with the challenge to convert

4 Terabyte of source data into PDF, Derek Gottfrid decided to make use of Amazon's EC2 and S3. He uploaded the source data to S3 and started a Hadoop cluster of customized EC2 Amazon Machine Images (AMIs). With 100 EC2 AMIs running in parallel he could complete the task of reading the source data from S3, converting it to PDF and storing it back to S3 within less than two days.

Within our framework the business scenario can be described as follows. The business case is "high performance computing", organizational aspects comprise "enterprise scenario" and "high lead times to purchase new infrastructure hardware", no known compliance issues are involved, the primary business objective is "cost efficiency", enterprise strategy does not play a role, demand is "expected: planned batch job", application-specific requirements are "special-purpose software libraries (iText PDF Library, Java Advanced Image Extension)" and there are no important non-functional technical requirements.

5.2 Major League Baseball

MLB Advanced Media is the company that develops and maintains the Major League Baseball Web sites. During the 2007 season, director of operations Ryan Nelson received the request to implement a chat product as an additional service to the website. He was told that the chat had to go online as soon as possible. However, the company's data center in Manhattan did not leave much free room for new servers. Since there was no time to order and install new machines, Nelson decided to call the Cloud Computing provider Joyent. He arranged for 10 virtual machines in a development cluster and another 20 machines for production mode. Nelson's team developed and tested the chat for about 2 months and then launched the new product. When the playoffs and World Series started, more resources were needed. Another 15 virtual machines and additional RAM solved the problem.

The business scenario: the business case is "application hosting (chat product)", organizational aspects are "enterprise scenario" and "outsourced infrastructure in a data center", compliance issues are not reported, the primary business objectives are "try out new products quickly and turn them off if they are not successful", strategy considerations comprise "need for a more flexible infrastructure provider", demand is "expected: seasonal with temporary spikes", application-specific requirements are "suitable environment for the chat product" and non-functional requirements include "high reliability, availability and scalability". Ryan Nelson found that Joyent provided a suitable IaaS offering; without Cloud Computing services, the next best alternative would have been to buy additional rack space and data center connectivity (bearing the risk that the product cannot be rolled out in time).

5.3 Powerset Search Engine

The semantic search engine Powerset is a good use case to show how Cloud Computing services can be employed by a start-up company as cost-efficient, scalable infrastructure. Paul Hamman, VP Datacenter Operations for Powerset, explains that alternative IT infrastructure solutions to Cloud Computing, such as renting servers or Grid Computing technology were to expensive and only scaled well for batch jobs. Therefore Powerset decided to roll out on Amazon's EC2 because it met the requirements in terms of functionality, flexibility and scalability.

The business scenario can be described as follows. The business case is "search engine", the organization is a "start-up company", compliance does not play an important role, the primary business objective is "cost efficiency", strategic considerations are not mentioned, demand is "unexpected with temporary spikes", application-specific requirements include a "highly flexible development and deployment environment", and non-functional requirements are "high availability and scalability". Without Cloud Computing services, the best alternative IT infrastructure to Amazon's EC2 would probably have been to rent servers, although Paul Hamman points out that it would not have scaled well.

5.4   Jungle Disk

Jungle Disk is a start-up company that managed to develop a client application for data storage and backup in Amazon's S3 in less than 30 days. The company's business model is to charge its users a small extra amount for each Gigabyte of data stored in Amazon's Cloud Computing infrastructure. The company adds value to the existing Cloud Computing service by providing for a better user interface.

The business scenario: The business case is "network-centric storage and backup", the organization is a "start-up company", compliance must address "data protection concerns", the primary business objective is to "provide value-add services on top of existing Cloud Computing services", strategic considerations might be the "Cloud provider attitude towards third-party developers", demand is "unexpected und unpredictable", application-specific requirements include "external access to Cloud interfaces", and the most important non-functional requirements are "high availability and scalability". This scenario could not have been accomplished without the existence of Cloud Computing offerings and can therefore not be valuated by means of an infrastructure cost comparison.

6   Related Work

Various economic aspects of outsourcing storage capacities and processing power have been covered by previous work in distributed computing and Grid Computing ([4], [10], [21], [11]). However, the methods and business models introduced for Grid Computing do not apply for Cloud Computing, which, as we argued before, addresses different use cases.

With a rule of thumb calculation Gray points to the opportunity costs of distributed computing in the Internet as opposed to local computations, i.e. in

LAN clusters [10]. In his scenario 1 USD equals 1 GB sent over WAN or alternatively eight hours CPU processing time. Gray reasons that except for highly processing-intensive applications outsourcing computing tasks into a distributed environment does not pay off because network traffic fees outnumber savings in processing power. Calculating the tradeoff between basic computing services can be useful to get a general idea of the economies involved. This method can easily be applied to the pricing schemes of IaaS providers. For 1 USD in 2008 the Web Service Amazon EC2 offers around 6 GB data transfer or 10 hours CPU processing[1]. However, this sort of calculation only makes sense if placed in a broader context. Whether or not computing services can be performed locally depends on the business scenario and criteria, such as application type. It might for example be necessary to process data in a distributed environment in order to enable online collaboration.

Thanos, et al. evaluate the adoption of Grid Computing technology for business purposes in a more comprehensive way [21]. The authors shed light on general business objectives and economic issues associated with Grid Computing, such as economies of scale and scope, network externalities, market barriers, etc. In particular, the explanations regarding the economic rationale behind complementing privately owned IT infrastructure with Utility Computing services point out aspects that are also important in the context of our valuation framework. Cloud Computing just like Grid Computing implements the more general model of Utility Computing. However, the business scenarios described by Thanos, et al. only partially apply to those we can observe in Cloud Computing. Important benefits associated with Cloud Computing, such as a developer-oriented environment for application development, testing and deployment, different usage patterns as pointed out by Bégin in [3], time to market requirements and other business scenario criteria are not covered.

7 Conclusion and Future Work

Cloud Computing is an emerging trend of provisioning scalable and reliable services over the Web as computing utilities. Early adopters of Cloud Computing services, such as start-up companies engaged in Web-scale projects, intuitively embrace the opportunity to rely on massively scalable IT infrastructure from providers like Amazon. However, there is no systematic, dedicated approach to measure costs and benefits of Cloud Computing that could serve as a guide for decision makers to tell when outsourcing IT resources into the Cloud makes sense.

We have addressed this problem and developed a valuation framework that serves as a starting point for future work. Our framework provides a step-by-step guide to determine the benefits from Cloud Computing, and in particular

---

[1] According to the US Amazon Web Service pricing in July 2008 one GB of outgoing traffic costs $0.17 for the first 10 TB per month. Running a small AMI instance with the compute capacity of a 1.0-1.2 GHz 2007 Xeon or Opteron processor for one hour costs $0.10 USD.

Infrastructure-as-a-Service, from understanding relevant business scenario criteria to quantitative valuation. We identify key components, such as business objectives, organization and compliance, strategy, demand, and technical requirements. Based on a qualitative business scenario analysis and a quantitative cost comparison, the value of Cloud Computing services can be estimated in terms of opportunity costs. Four well-known use cases of Cloud Computing adopters serve as a means to discuss and evaluate the validity of our framework. All scenarios illustrate how Cloud Computing can be leveraged as an alternative to or in combination with conventional IT infrastructure.

In future work, we will develop additional valuation methods that can be applied within the context of our framework in order to provide a more detailed quantitative analysis in addition to qualitative decision support. Furthermore, it is necessary to evaluate cost models that might serve as a template for estimating direct and indirect infrastructure costs that are connected to the business scenario criteria. We expect further changes and differentiation in pricing models of various Cloud Computing providers. Their analysis and the combination of different Cloud Computing offerings, also by means of emerging Cloud Computing marketplaces, will be integrated in our framework.

References

1. Amazon Web Services, Customer Case Studies,
   http://aws.amazon.com/solutions/case-studies
   (retrieved October 30, 2008)
2. Aptana Cloud IDE, http://www.aptana.com/cloud (retrieved October 30, 2008)
3. Bégin, M.: An EGEE Comparative Study: Grids and Clouds - Evolution or Revolution? Grids for E-Science, CERN (2008)
4. Buyya, R., Stockinger, H., Giddy, J., Abramson, D.: Economic Models for Management of Resources in Peer-to-Peer and Grid Computing. In: SPIE International Symposium on The Convergence of Information Technologies and Communications, Denver, CO (2001)
5. Chiu, W.: From Cloud Computing to the New Enterprise Data Center. IBM High Performance On Demand Solutions (2008)
6. Foster, I., Kesselman, C.: The Grid: Blueprint for a New Computing Infrastructure. Morgan Kaufman Publishers, San Francisco (1998)
7. Foster, I.: What is the Grid? A Three Point Checklist. GridToday (2002)
8. Gartner TCO, http://amt.gartner.com/TCO/index.htm (retrieved August 27, 2008)
9. Google App Engine, http://code.google.com/appengine/ (retrieved October 30, 2008)
10. Gray, J.: Distributed Computing Economics. In: Computer Systems Theory, Technology, and Applications, A Tribute to Roger Needham, pp. 93–101. Springer, Heidelberg (2004)
11. Hwang, J., Park, J.: Decision Factors of Enterprises for Adopting Grid Computing. In: Veit, D.J., Altmann, J. (eds.) GECON 2007. LNCS, vol. 4685, pp. 16–28. Springer, Heidelberg (2007)
12. Joyent Inc., http://joyent.com (retrieved October 30, 2008)

13. Koomey, J., Brill, K., Turner, P., Stanley, J., Taylor, B.: A Simple Model for Determining True Total Cost of Ownership for Data Centers. The Uptime Institute, Santa Fe (2007)
14. Klems, M.: The Cloud Computing Ecosphere: Main Companies and Applications Classified, http://virtualization.sys-con.com/node/611926 (retrieved July 31, 2008)
15. Major League Baseball, Use Case, http://www.networkworld.com/news/2007/121007-your-take-mlb.html (retrieved October 30, 2008)
16. Microsoft Azure Service Platform, http://www.microsoft.com/azure (retrieved October 30, 2008)
17. New York Times TimesMachine, Use Case, http://open.nytimes.com/2007/11/01/self-service-prorated-super-computing-fun/ (retrieved October 30, 2008)
18. Salesforce Force.com, http://www.force.com (retrieved October 30, 2008)
19. Scalr framework, http://code.google.com/p/scalr (retrieved October 30, 2008)
20. Schlossnagle, T.: Scalable Internet Architectures. Sams Publishing (2006)
21. Thanos, G., Courcoubetis, C., Stamoulis, G.: Adopting the Grid for Business Purposes: The Main Objectives and the Associated Economic Issues. In: Veit, D.J., Altmann, J. (eds.) GECON 2007. LNCS, vol. 4685, pp. 1–15. Springer, Heidelberg (2007)
22. Pentagon's IT Unit Seeks to Adopt Cloud Computing. New York Times.com, http://www.nytimes.com/idg/IDG_852573C400693880002574890080F9EF.html?ref=technology (retrieved October 30, 2008)
23. Titman, S., Martin, J.: Valuation. The Art & Science of Corporate Investment Decisions. Addison-Wesley, Reading (2007)

Analyzing Members' Motivations to Participate in Role-Playing and Self-Expression Based Virtual Communities

Young Eun Lee and Aditya Saharia

Graduate School of Business
Fordham University
113 W. 60th street, New York, NY 10023
eyolee@fordham.edu, saharia@fordham.edu

Abstract. With the rapid growth of computer mediated communication technologies in the last two decades, various types of virtual communities have emerged. Some communities provide a role playing arena, enabled by avatars, while others provide an arena for expressing and promoting detailed personal profiles to enhance their offline social networks. Due to different focus of these virtual communities, different factors motivate members to participate in these communities. In this study, we examine differences in members' motivations to participate in role-playing versus self-expression based virtual communities. To achieve this goal, we apply the Wang and Fesenmaier (2004) framework, which explains members' participation in terms of their functional, social, psychological, and hedonic needs. The primary contributions of this study are two folds: First, it demonstrates differences between role-playing and self-expression based communities. Second, it provides a comprehensive framework describing members' motivation to participate in virtual communities.

Keywords: Virtual communities, motivation to participate, conceptual framework, online survey.

1 Introduction

Computer mediated communication has introduced a new form of human social life called *Virtual Communities,* where a group of people interact primarily via computer-mediated communications for educational, professional, social, and other purposes [1]. 84% of United States Internet users (close to 100 million individuals) are members of virtual communities, such as work-related associations, affiliation communities, political organizations, and entertainment groups [2]. Along with the rapid growth and expansions of the Web 2.0 tools, many different types of virtual communities have emerged, such as email lists, website bulletin boards, Usenet newsgroups, real-time online-chat systems, web-based chat rooms, multiplayer virtual games, and multi-user domains [3].

Among these virtual communities available, multiplayer virtual games and multi-user domains are distinguished from the rest: They are special forms of real-time

C. Weinhardt, S. Luckner, and J. Stößer (Eds.): WEB 2008, LNBIP 22, pp. 124–134, 2009.

computerized conferencing, where participants, using pseudonymous personas called avatars, role-play for socialization, entertainment, education and commerce purposes [2-4]. While members of other types of virtual communities (e.g., Usenet newsgroups) may use pseudonyms to remain anonymous, members of the multiplayer virtual games and multi-user domains use disguised identities, not only to hide their real identities, but also to enjoy the experience of playing the role of a different persona in a "game-like" simulated environments [4, 5].

The rapid growth of role-playing communities is sharply contrasted with another type of fast-growing virtual community, whose main use is to express oneself, such as Facebook and MySpace.com. Members of those virtual communities share a detailed personal, self-composed history with other members. For instance, through "My Profile" in Facebook, they describe details about their day and post pictures of themselves [6]. The in-depth profiles of members that have become open to the public have raised serious privacy concerns among critics (http://www.foxnews.com/story/0,2933,293115,00.html). Such concerns, however, have not refrained members from posting their personal details, presumably because members want to supplement their face-to-face interactions by sharing their personal details online [7].

The mode by which the identity and information about a member is conveyed to others, is an important factor in the community formation [6]. We claim that members of these two types of virtual communities have different sets of motivations driving them to virtual communities. Dholakia et al. (2004) have argued that different factors influence members' participation in distinct types of virtual communities, as the goals members want to achieve differ across virtual communities. However, very little empirical evidence exists that distinguishes the different types of communities. This is particularly true in terms of using pseudonyms represented by avatars and investigated factors influencing members' participations in those communities [6].

In this light, the first goal of our study is to categorize two types of virtual communities and contrast factors that drive members' participation in these two virtual communities. We herein call virtual communities in which members maintain their identities and post personal details to enhance their offline relationships with other members as "Self-Expression-based Virtual Communities (SEVC)." Facebook and MySpace are examples of the SEVC. On the other hand, virtual communities where members create pseudonyms, called avatars, to enjoy the life of a different persona are called "Role-Playing-based Virtual Communities (RPVC)" in this study. Examples of RPVC include SecondLife, Habbo Club, and World of Warcraft.

A number of studies have been conducted to identify factors influencing members' participation in a virtual community, as participation is vital for the communities' existence and success [8]. Previous research has investigated participation from diverse perspectives, such as gift economy [9], social identity theory [6, 10], self-efficacy theory [11], social capital theory [12], playfulness [13], perceived usefulness and facilitating conditions [7]. Despite a large number of relevant studies, few provide a comprehensive theoretical framework to explain members' participation in virtual communities [8]. Furthermore, some of the studies, which employed quantitative methods, have reported inconsistent and ambiguous results. Therefore, the second goal of our study is to propose a comprehensive theoretical framework that explains member participation in virtual communities.

The rest of this paper is organized as follows. Section 2 introduces our research model and hypotheses. Section 3 describes the research method that will be used to test our hypotheses, including the methodology, measures, and statistical analyses. Lastly, Section 4 concludes with anticipated results and their contributions to theory advancement and implications to practice.

2   Hypotheses Development and Theoretical Background

In this section, we first define SEVCs, RPVCs, and participation in more detail. Then, we provide a theoretical framework proposed by Wang and Fesenmaier (2004), upon which we contrast motivations for participation across SEVCs and RPVCs.

2.1   Distinction between SEVC and RPVC

The distinction between SEVC and RPVC is pivotal in this study. We argued earlier that SEVC and RPVC are differentiated in that the former assumes that members maintain their real identities and the latter assumes that members use disguised identity. However, we should also note that not all members use these virtual communities in the way they were originally designed. For instance, an individual may create a disguised identity, to become a member of a SEVC for certain networks (e.g., school or region) to steal important information and intellectual properties from the networks. Likewise, many enterprises are using SecondLife as themselves for business purposes [5]. For instance, Apple built a store that exactly mimics the real Apple store in New York City. Obama, the 2008 US democratic presidential nominee, maintains campaign details in Second Life, apparently revealing his own identity. However, in this paper, we focus on members of SEVCs who maintain their own identities to express themselves and members of RPVCs who play different roles than themselves (Table 1).

2.2   Definition of Participation in Virtual Communities

Our goal is to investigate factors influencing "participation." Previous research has defined participation as members' acts of contributing to the community by posting messages and participating in community real-time meetings. Therefore, participation is distinguished from the act of joining communities. Participation is also distinguished from lurking, the behavior that does not contribute to the community, but simply involves reading posted messages [8].

Granted that Li and Lai's definition s valid in most bulletin-board based virtual communities, it needs to be more refined in the context of RPVCs for two reasons. First, "posting messages" is not one of the main activities members perform. Many RPVC members would rather "talk" virtually through instant messaging than post messages in bulletin boards to communicate with other members. Second, "participating in real-time meetings with other members" is also not sufficient to describe RPVC participation, because members of RPVCs may be engaged in many solitary activities not intended for interactions with others at certain point of time. For instance, they may spend time building and decorating their simulated home by themselves. These types of solitary activities were not considered "participation," as

Table 1. Examples of Virtual Communities

SEVCs	RPVCs
Facebook (www.facebook.com) • An online community that aims to connect students through schools, clubs, interests, and regions. **LinkedIn (www.linkedin.com)** • One of the most popular "business-oriented social networking site" with over 24 million registered users spanning 150 industries. **MySpace (http://www.myspace.com)** • A popular social networking site in the US. • For self-expression & reconnection with friends. **Xanga (www.xanga.com)** • A web community targeted at teenagers. It permits weblogs, photos and video sharing, as well as meeting new friends and connecting with old ones.	**Gaia Online (www.gaiaonline.com)** • "Part forum, part gaming site, part virtual world" (Mashable), with over 3.5 million users. • Inspired by anime and manga, targeted at youth. **Lineage (http://www.lineage.com/)** • A by-subscription fantasy multi-player role-playing game with over 1 million active users (Wikipedia). **Second Life (www.secondlife.com)** • "An online society within a 3D world, where users can explore, build, socialize and participate in their own economy." **World of WarCraft (http://www.worldofwarcraft.com/index.xml)** • Multi-player role-playing game, with 62% of the market share in the multi-player role game domain.

the previous definition assumed all activities are intended for interactions with other members, as shown in "attending real-time meetings with other members." We therefore expand the definition of "participation" from the narrow set of actions, such as posting messages in bulletin boards or attending real-time meetings, to the frequency and length of logging in to virtual communities to maintain their *visible online presence*. More specifically, "visible online presence" includes posting messages, attending real-time meetings with other members in SEVCs, *plus*, and maneuvering avatars for both solitary and interactional purposes in RPVC.

2.3 Factors Influencing Members' Participation in Virtual Communities

Wang and Fesenmaier (2004) have asserted that four main needs drive members' participation in virtual communities: functional needs, social needs, psychological needs, and hedonic needs. We apply their framework to this study, because it contains a broad set of motivations that can explain our expanded notion of participation, as opposed to narrowly-defined participation as "posting messages." In addition to the four needs claimed by Wang and Fesenmaier, we included facilitating conditions as a factor that influences members' actual participation behavior (Figure 1).

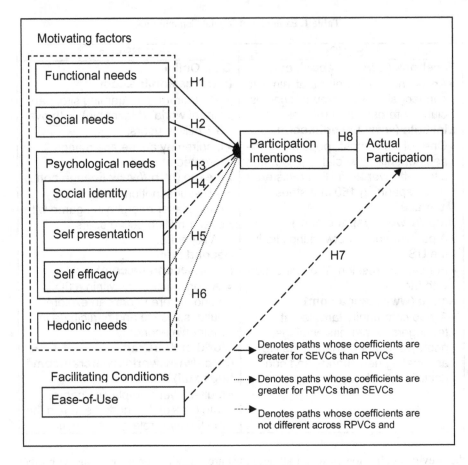

Fig. 1. Research Model

Functional needs refer the specific activities and goals members aim to fulfill in virtual communities [14]. These needs entail transactions to buy and sell products or services, provide support for gathering information to seek knowledge or to facilitate decision-making. Functional needs are often called "perceived consequences [15]," and "purposive values [6]," and have been found to influence members' intentions to participate in virtual communities.

We argue that functional needs play a greater role in member participation in SEVCs than RPVCs, because, trust in, and credibility of, the source is vital for electronic transactions and information gathering, which lacks physical interactions [16]. Therefore, members would want to collect information or purchase products or services from those whose identities are known transparently inside the community.

SEVC members' identities are revealed to other members. More importantly, many SEVCs provide features for connecting friends or message boards, which can function as a reputation mechanism. A reputation mechanism establishes trust among members and fosters social interactions [6]. In contrast, RPVCs do not require members to publish their identities, nor provide a reputation mechanism. As a result, members are likely to participate in SEVCs to fulfill their functional needs, but less likely in RPVCs. Therefore, we posit the following:

H1. The degree to which functional needs positively affect members' participation intentions will be greater for SEVCs than for RPVCs.

Social needs include the purposes of online communities, such as socializing, forming relationships, and attaining the trust of others [14]. Social needs are supported by Social Capital Theory, which explains members' willingness to contribute to virtual communities, from the perspective of social capital creation and appropriation. Social capital includes trust, culture, social support, social exchange, social resources, and social networks [17]. Support, help, and assistance obtained from these social resources are important assets for members in the long term [14]. Needs for such social resources drive members to participate in virtual communities [9].

We assert that such social needs are more apparent drivers for members of SEVCs, than RPVCs. SEVC's primary function is to enable members to express and promote themselves in their social network and to connect with other members. On the other hand, RPVCs guarantee members' anonymity and, therefore, RPVC members may not expect their social networks inside RPVCs to benefit their real lives. As a result, we contend:

H2. The degree to which social needs positively affect members' participation intentions will be greater for SEVCs than RPVCs.

Psychological, in addition to functional and social needs can be met in virtual communities. By joining a community, where it be physical or online, people fulfill a number of psychological needs [18]. Bressler and Grantham (2000) argued that psychological needs are the reasons that enable communities to become such a powerful organizing force in the world of commerce. One defines his/her self-concept in a community in three ways: (1) by identifying oneself as a member of a community (explained by Social Identity Theory), (2) by presenting self-image to other members (Self-Presentation Theory), and (3) by believing that s/he is capable of exerting control over their own functioning and/or external resources (Self-Efficacy Theory) [19].

Social identity theory argues that a person views himself/herself as a member of a reference group in his/her attempt to define himself/herself [10]. For instance, a person identifies himself/herself as an "American;" by doing so, the person tries to embody the characteristics of "Americans." Individuals categorize themselves as members of a reference group, conform their behaviors to the group, and share beliefs, norms, and cultures of the group [2]. A number of studies have found that needs for building social identity are a strong motivator for people to participate in virtual communties [2, 6, 10].

It is hard to imagine that the person who is motivated to identify himself/herself as a member of a reference group will want to remain anonymous in the group. In other words, a person who wants to identify himself/herself as a member of certain group is likely to express himself/herself as a member, rather than disguise himself/herself as someone else. Therefore, we assume that the influence of one's needs of social identification, for participation intentions, is greater for SEVCs than RPVCs:

H3. The degree to which the needs for social identity positively affect members' participation intentions will be greater for SEVCs than RPVCs.

While the literature has paid substantial attention to social identity theory in virtual communities, very few studies have been conducted from the perspectives of self-presentation. Self-presentation consists of behaviors intended to manage the impressions that observers have of actors [20]. Self-presentation is often used interchangeably with impression management, in that both are defined as an attempt to control the images presented to others, usually to increase the power of the individual [20]. Neglect of self-presentation may be attributed to the fact that text-only web-based forums do not provide a variety of options to present members to others. However, with the proliferation of broadband Internet, RPVCs have become equipped with avatars, which enable members to express themselves with abundant choices, and SEVCs to furnish their websites with a number of multi-media options, fulfilling members' needs for self-presentation.

Nevertheless, given the lack of prior research, we do not attempt to provide our expectations on which type of virtual communities – either SEVCs or RPVCs – fulfills members' needs for presenting themselves, to a greater degree. SEVCs allow members to demonstrate their unknown talents and portray their images favorably [12]. Likewise, RPVC members may enjoy expressing visual images and characters of their disguised persona in the virtual space [21]. Therefore, without previous research or theory, we are not able to compare the impact of the needs for self-presentation on the participation intentions between SEVC and RPVC. Instead, we provide the null hypothesis as follows:

H4. There will be no difference in the degree to which the needs for self-presentation positively affect members' participation intentions between SEVCs and RPVCs.

Self-efficacy refers to "people's beliefs about their capabilities to produce effects to exercise control over their own functioning and over events that affect their lives [22]." As beliefs in personal efficacy affect life choices, level of motivation, and quality of functioning, people strive to have a robust sense of efficacy to sustain the perseverant effort needed to succeed [23]. As such, community members use virtual communities as a channel in which they can demonstrate their self-efficacy to others and to themselves [12].

However, not all members have the expertise that exceeds others in a given subject matter [24]. Also, many members of SEVCs may already know each other directly, or through mutual connections, and hence, they may not want to boast themselves excessively, because it may hurt their reputations [24]. In contrast, in RPVCs, members are not known to one another, and hence, they are allowed to experience the fictional life of someone else who is more competent than themselves. Therefore, we hypothesize:

H5. The degree to which the needs for self-efficacy positively affect members' participation intentions will be greater for RPVCs than SEVCs.

Members participate in virtual communities for their own enjoyment and entertainment purposes [14]. The hedonic perspective views members as those people who seek pleasure through enjoyment, entertainment, amusement, and fun [25]. Hedonic needs, such as enjoyment and pleasure, have been found to influence members' participation in virtual communities [13, 26].

We argue that RPVCs provide members with the opportunity to explore a new world of fantasy and entertainment, where they can try out new personas and engage in role-playing games where everything seems possible [14]. In contrast, participants in SEVCs may feel peer pressure, as many people do in their face-to-face social networks, and hence, without participation in that network, an individual may not be able to connect with their peers. SEVC members may also feel apprehensive about the peer judgment of their postings [24]. Therefore, although participation in SEVCs is voluntary, the peer pressure and evaluation apprehension may hamper the fun aspect of participation. Therefore, we argue that hedonic needs play a greater role in RPVCs, rather than SEVCs:

H6. The degree to which hedonic needs positively affect members' participation intentions will be greater for RPVCs than SEVCs.

Lastly, members' intentions to participate in virtual communities will be led to their actual participation behavior, if conditions to facilitate their participation are met. We adopt the ease-of-use of features employed by virtual communities. Ease-of-use refers to the degree to which users expect the system to be free of effort [27]. We expect that ease-of-use will influence members' participation behavior.

H7. Perceived ease-of-use will positively affect members' actual participation behavior.

3   Research Method

3.1   Questionnaire Development

We borrowed measures previously tested by the research, to represent our functional needs [6], social needs [12], social identity [6], hedonic needs [15], ease-of-use [27], participation intentions and actual participation behaviors [15]. However, these measures are revised and reworded to reflect the purpose of this study. We were not able to find measures appropriate for self-presentation and self-efficacy. Hence, we will develop a measure for each construct, based upon the Lee et al. (1999) self-presentation tactic scale and the Harrison et al. (1996) self-efficacy scale. The Lee et al. self-presentation tactic scale is appropriate for our study, as it contains items for ingratiation, entitlement, enhancement, and exemplification, which are applicable to the context of virtual communities. The Harrison et al. self-efficacy measure not only deals with general self-efficacy, but also social efficacy, i.e., self-efficacy perceived in a social context, which is applicable to the context of virtual communities.

3.2   Data Collection

The data will be collected using an online survey, the URL of which will be distributed via e-mail to current active members of virtual communities. Only members of SEVCs and RPVCs listed in Table 1 will be recruited. Also, respondents will be either those who maintain their real identities in SEVCs or those who use pseudonyms in RPVCs. In the case where a respondent is a member of both types of virtual communities, s/he will be asked which type of virtual communities s/he most frequently visits and s/he will be asked to only answer questions about the one they visit more frequently.

3.3 Data Analyses and Sample Size

We will use the Partial Least Squares (PLS) method to analyze the data, because it is a powerful method of analysis that has minimal demands on measurement scales, sample size, and residual distributions [28]. The requirement of the sample size is at least ten times the largest number of structural paths directed at any one construct [29]. The largest number of paths to any construct (intentions to participate in virtual communities) in our model is six. In addition, we will divide the sample into SEVCs and RPVCs to compare the influence of each hypothesized path. Therefore, a sample of at least 120 cases for the entire sample (thus 60 cases for the split sample) will be required.

4 Conclusion

In this paper, we have provided a framework that explains antecedents of participation in virtual communities. Particularly, we identified RPVCs and SEVCs: RPVCs provide members with role-playing experience with a different persona while SEVCs enable users to express themselves to enhance their offline social networks. We argue that functional and social needs along with the needs for social identity are more strongly associated with members' intentions to participate in SEVCs than RPVCs. The needs for enhancing self-efficacy and hedonic needs have greater impact on participation intentions for RPVCs than SEVCs. We did not compare the magnitude of impact that the needs for self-presentation have on participation intentions between SEVCs and RPVCs, due to lack of prior studies. We anticipate that facilitating conditions, represented by ease-of-use, will influence members' actual participation behavior.

By identifying primary needs of members of distinct types of virtual communities, we are able to provide developers with specific design guidelines which inform them of the features that are more effective than others in increasing members' participation. First, if satisfying functional needs turns out to be a more significant criterion for SEVCs than RPVCs, a developer for SEVCs can add features that fulfill functional needs, such as safe checkout processes for e-transactions and bulletin-boards designed for knowledge-sharing among members. On the flip side, RPVC developers may not need these features as much, because these are not the main drivers of RPVC participation. Members of RPVCs do not act as themselves. Therefore, their experience as someone else may not be evolved into their real lives. In other words, they may sample and purchase products in a store inside a simulate environment, but they do so to enjoy the experience of buying products they normally would not buy in their real lives. This is particularly important implication to community builders as many enterprises nowadays explore business opportunities in RPVCs by promoting their products and luring consumers to their stores. However, whether such experience inside a virtual environment will lead to consumers' real-life purchases is still questionable.

Instead, RPVC developers may want to improve features that will make users' role-playing experience more enjoyable, if our expectation on the stronger association between hedonic needs and participation intentions in RPVCs is supported. Also, if our expectation on the stronger association between the needs for self-efficacy and participation intentions in RPVCs is supported, then, RPVC developers may want to expand options of creating avatars. For now, most options of creating avatars are limited to their appearances: e.g., hair and eye color, height, clothes, and accessories. To these, RPVC developers may add options that represent characters, occupations, skills, and expertise. For instance, if a member chooses an avatar of professor in IS, the avatar can integrate enterprise applications and improve business processes. The knowledge necessary for being an IS professor can be provided as built-in functions inside the avatar (e.g., your chosen professor has the ability to integrate enterprise applications. Use this option when you're asked to solve business problems caused by fragmented systems). Therefore, the user does not need the necessary knowledge; all s/he needs to do is to choose one of these options based upon detailed instructions that come with the avatar.

Contributions of this study to theory advancement are two-folds. First, this is the first study that distinguished virtual communities in terms of users' identities – whether or not online identities match members' real identities. This distinction is particularly important as we have seen two contrasting types of virtual communities – role-playing and self-expression based – grow rapidly. Also, although different motivators are expected to drive members to participate in different types of virtual communities, very little empirical studies have classified virtual communities and empirically tested difference across them [6]. The second contribution of this study is that it provides a comprehensive framework that explains motivations to participate in virtual communities. Although many studies have been investigated this issue, they have focused on certain factors, such as social identity, while neglecting other factors, such as self-presentation, self-efficacy, which have been identified as important drivers of building self in Social Psychology. This study provides a comprehensive framework that includes all these relevant factors and hence can be building blocks for future studies.

References

1. Rheingold, H.: The Virtual Community: Homesteading on the Electronic Frontier. MIT Press, Cambridge (2000)
2. Pentina, I., Prybutok, V.R., Zhang, X.: The Role of Virtual Communities As Shopping Reference Groups. Journal of Electronic Commerce Research 9, 114–123, 125, 127–136 (2008)
3. Catterall, M., Maclaran, P.: Researching Consumers in Virtual Worlds: A Cyberspace Odyssey. Journal of Consumer Behaviour 1, 228 (2002)
4. Mennecke, B., Roche, E.M., Bray, D.A., Konsynski, B., Lester, J., Rowe, M.: Second Life and Other Virtual Worlds: A Roadmap for Research. In: International Conference on Information Systems, Montreal (2007)
5. Hemp, P.: Avatar-Based Marketing. Harvard Business Review 84, 48–57 (2006)
6. Dholakia, U.M., Bagozzi, R.P., Pearo, L.K.: A Social Influence Model of Consumer Participation in Network- and Small-group-based Virtual Communities. International Journal of Research in Marketing 21, 241–263 (2004)
7. Koh, J., Kim, Y.-G., Butler, B., Bock, G.-W.: Encouraging Participation in Virtual Communities. Communications of the ACM 50 (2007)
8. Li, H., Lai, V.S.: The Interpersonal Relationship Perspective on Virtual Community Participation. In: International Conference on Information Systems, Montreal, Canada (2007)
9. Kollock, P.: The Economics of Online Cooperation: Gifts and Public Goods in Cyberspace in Communities in Cyberspace. Routledge, London (1999)
10. Bagozzi, R.P., Dholakia, U.M.: Intentional Social Action in Virtual Communities. Journal of Interacitve Marketing 16, 2–21 (2002)

11. Wang, Y., Fresenmaier, D.R.: Assessing Motivation of COntribution in Online COmmunities: An Empirical Investigation of an Online Travel Commnity. Electronic Markets 13 (2003)
12. Wasko, M.M., Faraj, S.: Why Should I Share? Examining Social Capital and Knowledge Contribution in Electronic Networks of Practice. MIS Quarterly 29, 35–58 (2005)
13. Sledgianowski, D., Kulviwat, S.: Social Network Sites: Antecedents of User Adoption and Usage. In: America's Conference on Information Systems, Toronto (2008)
14. Wang, Y., Fesenmaier, D.R.: Towards Understanding Members' General Participation In and Active Contribution to An Online Travel Community. Tourism Management 25, 709–722 (2004)
15. Limayem, M., Hirt, S.G.: Force of Habit and Information Systems Usage: Theory and Initial Validation. Journal of the Association for Information Systems 4, 65–97 (2003)
16. Kim, D., Benbasat, I.: The Effects of Trust-Assuring Arguments on Consumer Trust in Internet Stores: Application of Toulmin's Model of Argumentation. Information Systems Research 17, 286–300 (2006)
17. Wang, Y., Fesenmaier, D.R.: Assessing Motivation of Contribution in Online Communities: An Empirical Investigation of an Online Travel Community. Electronic Markets 13, 33 (2003)
18. Bressler, S.E., Grantham, C.E.: Communities of Commerce: Building Internet Business Communities to Accelerate Growth, Minimize Risk, and Increase Customer Loyalty. McGraw Hill, New York (2000)
19. Baumeister, R.F., Cairns, K.J.: Repression and Self-Presentation: When Audiences Interfere With Self-Deceptive Strategies. Journal of Personality and Social Psychology 62, 851–862 (1992)
20. Lee, S.-J., Quigley, B.M., Nesler, M.S., Corbett, A.B., Tedeschi, J.T.: Development of a Self-Presentation Tactics Scale. Personality and Individual Differences 26, 701–722 (1999)
21. Kim, Y.J., Baker, J., Song, J.: An Exploratory Study of Social Factors Influencing Virtual Community Members' Satisfaction with Avatars. Communications of the AIS 20, 567–593 (2007)
22. Bandura, A.: Self-Efficacy. In: Ramachaudran, V.S. (ed.) Encyclopedia of Human Behavior, vol. 4, pp. 71–81. Academic Press, New York (1994)
23. Bandura, A.: Social Foundations of Thought and Action: A Social Cognitive Theory. Prentice-Hall, Englowood Cliffs (1986)
24. Ardichvili, A., Page, V., Wentling, T.: Motivation and Barriers to Participation in Virtual Knowledge-sharing Communities of Practice. Journal of Knowledge Management 7, 64–77 (2003)
25. Hoffman, D.L., Novak, T.P.: Marketing in Hypermedia Computer-Mediated Environments: Conceptual Foundations. Journal of Marketing 60, 50 (1996)
26. Gupta, S., Kim, H.-W.: Developing the Commitment to Virtual Community: The Balanced Effects of Cognition and Affect. Information Resources Management Journal 20, 28–43 (2007)
27. Venkatesh, V., Davis, F.D.: A Theoretical Extension of the Technology Acceptance Model: Four Longitudinal Field Studies. Management Science 46, 186–204 (2000)
28. Chin, W.W., Newsted, P.R., Hoyle, R.H.: Structural Equation Modeling Analysis with Small Samples Using Partial Least Squares. In: Anonymous (ed.) Statistical Strategies for Small Sample Research, pp. 307–341. Sage publications, Inc., Thousand Oaks (1999)
29. Keil, M., Tan, B.C.Y., Wei, K.-K., Saarinen, T., Tuunainen, V., Wassenaar, A.: A Cross-Cultural Study on Escalation of Commitment Behavior in Software Projects. MIS Quarterly 24, 299–325 (2000)

Evolution of Virtual Communities*

Eunyoung Cheon and JoongHo Ahn

College of Business Administration,
Seoul National University, Seoul, 151-916, Korea
{echeon, jahn}@snu.ac.kr

Abstract. As the capabilities of technologies are enhanced and users become diversified, virtual communities have evolved from BBS to a new phenomena—virtual world. This study describes the evolution of VCs in three generations by three dimensions. Facing new challenges in new VC generation, VC platform providers need to adopt new approaches. The authors discuss important factors of future VCs. The field for VCs in the future will become more sophisticated and competitive.

Keywords: Virtual Community, Computer-Mediated Communications, Social Networks, Internet, Virtual World.

1 Introduction

The exponential technical advances and digital revolution made people possible to do business or anything else with other parties anywhere and anytime on the globe. The new technologies related to being digital, mobile, personal and virtual amplify and turbocharge the flattening process of the world [Friedman, 2006]. The development of microprocessor reduced the size and the price of computers and made powerful computers more available to common people. The birth of the Internet and ease of computer-mediated communication were accelerated to eliminate the gaps among different parts of the world. The globe becomes a more connected place. Face-to-face meeting is no longer the only option to socialize with other people who live in another side of the globe. Computer-supported social networks have released human interactions from the bond of spatial constraint [Wellman, 2005]. Online relationship associates people with another form of community—virtual community.

The term, virtual community (VC), refers to various social networks interacting via digitized communication. It is commonly used to describe various forms of computer-mediated communication among large groups that exchange information, enjoy hobbies, chat, etc., as people do in the real world [Igbaria, 1999]. We define VC as networks of individuals or business partners that share common interests and satisfy their own needs in the form of digitized communication on a technical platform.

---

* This research was supported by the **Ministry of Knowledge Economy**, Korea, under the Information Technology Research Center support program supervised by the Institute of Information Technology Advancement. (grant number **IITA-2008-C1090-0801-0031**)

C. Weinhardt, S. Luckner, and J. Stößer (Eds.): WEB 2008, LNBIP 22, pp. 135–143, 2009.

When the capabilities of technologies are enhanced and users are diversified, new forms of communication and interaction become possible.

Whereas people interacted with other people through text-based environment like Bulletin Board System (BBS) in 1980s, recent VCs are available in animated 3D environment with streaming media technology. Within the streaming 3D VCs like Second Life, Entropia Universe, There, etc. (often called as virtual world), members live in the skin of an avatar that is designed by themselves and interact with other people simultaneously. Improved environment—simulating real word with 3D animation— of VC enables people to behave very similarly as they do in the real world and also creates new business opportunities to various industries. We call this newly formed VC as "Virtual World Community (VWC)."

As VC evolves from BBS to a new phenomenon—VWC, very little research has been conducted on describing related issues and phenomena in its evolution over time. For the purpose of defining and describing the evolution of VCs, we reviewed various articles both in academic and practical journals, case studies, and empirical evidence. The studies we have made indicate the existence of three generations of growth in evolution of VCs. Our purpose here is to describe the three generations with key characteristics of each one of them and provide future trend.

2 Theoretical Background

In describing the evolution of VCs, we inspect their distinct patterns. Based on a review of literature and on observations of activity in VCs, three dimensions are considered in describing each generation: environment richness, population diversity, economic activity. Environment richness implies social presence theory and media richness theory. Social presence considers the degree in which a medium allows a user to build interpersonal relationships with other users. Media with a high degree of social presence are regarded as being warm, personal, sensitive, and sociable [Short et al., 1976]. Media richness theory states that there is a fit between the uncertainty and equivocality of tasks and the richness of media [Daft and Lengel, 1986]. It suggests that richer formats of communication media lead to better communication than less rich communication media.

Synchronicity is also an important factor related to interaction in VCs. Synchronicity regards the degree to which a medium enables real-time interaction (Hoffman and Novak, 1996). Synchronous technology design, compared to asynchronous technology design, can enhance users' perception of social presence (Blanchard, 2004). Applying theses theories, environment richness here refers to a user's perceptual dimension of being physically present in interacting with others. Technological factors like the qualities of interface, technical abilities related to connection speed, bandwidth, processing power, and storage capacity, and synchronicity are examined in the dimension of environment richness.

As young groups of computer and information literate join the workforce, they will engage in employing information, communication, and transportation technologies [Igbaria, 1999]. Having enlightened and diversified participants is important to the evolution of virtual society [Igbaria, 1999]. Various kinds of users in a community will support the sociability and interactions among users better. Users are a primary source of resources for most VCs. Researchers have shown that the size of a community matters in encouraging existing community members to interact. Having many sources of resources available is important to provide benefits for individuals and these benefits are the basis for a community to attract and retain members [Butler, 2001]. Considering the impact from diversified users in VCs, we here examined population diversity which refers to various kinds of users, characterized based on age, sex, education levels, computer literacy, and citizenship, and size of a VC.

Online users have created various forms, such as C2C or B2C, of commercial markets. Online markets deal with tangible (e.g. books, cars, electronics) and intangible (e.g. services, virtual items) products. The Internet and WWW (World Wide Web) enabled people to get information easily and revolutionized the ways how people do shopping. Abundant product choices are available to online consumers. Many future B2C commercial transactions will be generated in VCs [Bressler and Grantham, 2000]. Considering the importance of commercial transactions online, we here examined economic activity which refers to economic actions like buying and selling goods.

3 Evolution of VC

Advances in computing hardware and capabilities of telecommunication networks have powered software platforms. With state of the art computer technology, software platforms can support more features and functions to provide powerful and diversified services to the users. These software platforms revolutionized various industries and also altered how people interact with other people. The recent VCs under Web-based platforms are also likely to change the way people interact when compared to text-based platforms in the past. As related technologies like hardware, software, telecommunication, and networking become advanced, VCs can have more complex functions in communicating online. The platform nature of VCs has been transformed from text-based interface to 3D-animated interface. The three generations in the evolution of VCs are portrayed in Table 1, considering three dimensions mentioned above.

Table 1. VCs' evolution

	VC 1.0	VC 2.0 & 2.5	VC 3.0
Environment Richness	Thin	Medium	Thick
	◄───►		
Population Diversity	Low	Medium	High
	◄───►		
Economic Activity	Limited	Supported	Sophisticated
	◄───►		
Examples	BBS(Bulletin Board System), ISCABBS (Iowa Student Computer Association BBS), Newsgroups, Private discussion forums	Blogs, Compuserve, AOL, Yahoo; CyWorld, MySpace	Virtual worlds (e.g. Second Life, Entropia Universe, The Sims Online, Habbo Hotel, There, etc.)

3.1 VC1.0

The first public bulletin board system, Computerized Bulletin Board System (CBBS), was developed by Ward Christensen in the end of 1970s [Christensen and Suess, 1989]. By the mid-1980s, a number of public BBSes ran on simple software. Users are connected to a text-based platform through low speed MODEM dial-up connection. Through text-based platforms like BBS, people exchange information (usually called "posting") by typing the words with a keyboard and fetching the documents via FTP. Because the interface of VC is not user-friendly, participating in VC requires a certain level of computer skills. To avoid hefty long distance phone bills, users often connect to local BBS. And usually, BBS organizes meetings from time to time to let its users meet face to face. Unfriendly user interface and local connection limit the diversity of population. People represented by different user IDs are able to discuss through message boards, text chat rooms, and download files. Because users are identified only by a user ID and communicate based on textual media format, users are very limited to express themselves. Some members buy goods from or sell goods to other members. Because VCs do not support commercial transactions online, members often meet face-to-face to complete the transaction. These factors limit commercial activities on VC.

3.2 VC2.0

With the debut of the Internet, HTTP (Hypertext Transfer Protocol) and software OS, Windows, Internet Portal Websites such as Yahoo!, AOL or MSN, replaced the role of BBS. In the beginning of 1990s, AOL 1.0 for MS Widows 3.x was launched. Instead of command lines based on the standard terminal program, VCs supported by Websites with proprietary software are able to offer richer a media format, a graphical user interface (GUI). Compared to VC1.0, the environment richness was enhanced in this era. Globalization is also important factor here just like in the business world. VCs begin to link people from various countries at low connection cost via the Internet and allow greater involvement to be affordable. Furthermore, information is updated real-time and provides richer graphic and text contents, compared to the VC 1.0 era. However, users still use IDs to represent themselves that are characterized as impersonal. In addition, commercial activities are limited because online payment system is not mature.

3.3 VC2.5

With the increase of connection speed to the Internet, users are able to upload and download large media files such as photo, music, even video. VCs supported by Web-based platforms, can have a richer environment in exchanging information. With the desire to express personal style, users are opted to new Web-based VC platforms such as CyWorld, Myspace, Facebook, and Bebo. At the end of 1990s, CyWorld pioneered personalized virtual space. These platforms allow users to create their personal homepages and use any color of their choice on the background, insert digitized media like pictures and music, and download or upload the information by a simple mouse-click.

For instance, CyWorld (www.cyworld.com) by SK Communication in Korea let users design their personal homepage (called as "minihompy") with digitized graphics, audio, and messages without learning HTML, Web Publishing Programs, or Photoshop. Furthermore, CyWorld introduced "avatar," a character which appears on the user's minihompy to represent the user. While users in VC2.0 still use personalized IDs, users in this generation of VC can reflect their own personal characteristics to design avatars and minihompy better than before.

Furthermore, users can purchase ready-made articles (item for avatars, background music, etc.) to dress up their avatars or add into the minihompy without any hassle. The easiness of building a personal space with fabulous digital contents and expressing personal style in this environment has allured a vastly diversified population (for example, youngsters and women) to this platform. And now even, politicians and celebrities use VCs to reach the people there. VCs in this era open commercial markets and enable advertisers and businesses to reach their members. For instance, CyWorld supports CyWorld market where members can sell or buy goods and make the transactions among members and between members and companies. Facebook welcomes advertisers and businesses to target the members in its VC. With better IT capability, enhanced environment richness, increased diversity of population, and supported economic activity, VC2.5 has begun to merge the digital and physical space.

3.4 VC3.0

Software platforms empowered by recent information technologies and telecommunications accelerate the process of creating the new shape of VCs. Recent VCs appear as VWCs which simulate the real word with fantastic atmosphere. With easy access via the Internet and powerful streaming media technology, lots of people under the skin of avatars are able to meet and interact with many other people at one time in VWCs. VWCs that mix reality with fantasy were not only infeasible but also unimaginable ten years ago.

Recent virtual worlds simulated by avatars have appeared in two major forms. First one is the massively multiplayer online games (MMOGs), like Lineage and World of Warcraft. This world has rules for players, and multiple players fight each other to achieve their goals. Distinct from MMOG, second one is VWC primarily focused on social networking which is interested in this article. It provides platforms where users participate in an open-ended play. There are no rules and steps needed to go forward. Furthermore, all digital contents in this virtual world are even created and owned by users.

VWCs in this generation try to simulate the real world beyond the physical limitations. While VC2.5 is based on 2D Web, many VWCs like Second Life, Entropia Universe, The Sims Online, There, and Habbo Hotel provide a new form of VC, streamed-3D VC. Among them, Second Life (www.secondlife.com), launched in 2003, has received biggest attention by various people and organizations. It is an Internet-based virtual world that provides advanced level of VC services. As mentioned by Philip Rosedale, founder and CEO of Linden Lab, Second Life offers a truly collaborative, immersive, and open-ended entertainment experience. Users here can design themselves, create surrounding 3D virtual environments, run businesses and events, interact with others, and live in the community as its residents. No matter how well people communicate via e-mail, instant messaging and chat rooms, a gap still exists among communicators. Nevertheless, online communication through virtual worlds resembles offline face-to-face communication more and bridges the gap among the communicators. Users in VWC possess multiple ways to interact with others when compared to VC2.0.

Moreover, users are given intellectual rights to their creations and are able to sell them for profit, thus opening up a strong economic connection from between VC and the real world. The ownership of digital property fosters a very open-ended, creative atmosphere. Property rights build large-digital item markets, as already seen in MMOGs. Additionally, it allows the evolution of user-created contents. When Second Life was launched in 2003, the virtual world had nothing inside; there was nothing to see. However, as of July, 2008, Second Life has about ninety-two hundreds islands (of more than 1,714km2, close to the size of Maui Island, Hawaii) designed by users.

The possibility that users can grow their wealth and status in VC and translate their wealth directly to the real world will likely allure more users and hook them into the platform. Many of VWC platforms make it possible to exchange virtual currency produced in its world for real things. In the Entropia Universe and Second Life, users can exchange virtual currency to real world cash at fluctuating rates. The realistic economic settings become a big part of virtual worlds. Any resident in this VWC can become an entrepreneur: they can build, sell, buy, and own digital creations within the world. They are free to profit off of digital business activities. The mixture of virtual commerce and real world creates huge opportunities to sell products and services, catching the attention of huge corporations like IBM, Intel, NIKE, BMW, etc. Economic activities of VC in this generation are becoming increasingly sophisticated as they are expanding in terms of monetary value and number of participants involved.

4 Beyond VC3.0

VCs become just like the multisided markets. The software platform run by the operator of VC serves two or more distinctive customer groups. The platform connects people at low cost and provides participants rich environments for social networking. For instance, VWC provides the platform for distinctive groups: members, advertisers, sellers, and buyers. Similar to the case of software platforms [Evans et al., 2006], most the successful virtual communities have exploited network effects among the participants in their community. As the number of participants in the community increases, the value of the platform increases and the platform will attract other groups like advertisers and marketers. Various corporations attempt to build their images and brands, test their products and designs, and conduct business operations toward the population of the community.

VCs have recently evolved as a new paradigm, shared 3D environment and are creating various opportunities for economic activity. For VC platform providers, emerging challenges demand new approaches. New business models based on rapid and flexible responses to users' needs and more creative thinking about platform's ecosystem will emerge as a competitive VC platform. BBS was all about VC in the past but was replaced by AOL or Yahoo!, which supports graphic and text-based open platform via the Internet. Then, AOL or Yahoo! was replaced by CyWorld or MySpace, which offer enhanced 2D environment with video and audio. And now

VCs, with streamed-3D virtual worlds and truly collaborative environment have appeared as the next phase of social networking.

Similar to the case of the multisided markets, the operators of VC need to have strategies to attract more members and make VC successful. For instance, right pricing structures to attract more participants and well-balanced relationships between various groups generating benefits to all sides (participants) on VC are required. Since members are critical sources of resources, bigger size of community membership can access to more resources. Larger communities are more capable of providing valuable benefits to their members because the availability of resources is dependent on benefit provisions [Rafaeli and LaRose, 1993]. Therefore, users are willing to pay more for access to a bigger network. Though people need to pay a subscription fee to get full experience, some VWC providers allow people to join and enjoy the virtual world for free. This approach has boosted the number of membership in its community.

Besides the pricing structure to increase participants, VWCs can also welcome developers who like to cope with the platform by opening the codes for all pieces. Anyone would examine and modify the software that let the users view and navigate Second Life. Linden Lab intends to offer all participants freedom and openness to work with Second Life. These radical approaches performed by Second Life have brought them more participants to its platform and speeded up improvements. The rapidly increasing population of Second Life residents and expanded virtual world environments has even started to attract various corporations to pursue huge business opportunities in there.

VC 3.0 is becoming a mixture of community and economic activities and huge companies are involving VCs more than before. However, we need to remember primary function of VC, being a social network. The sovereign core of VC is communication at will. Under the skin of an avatar, created as a representation of a person, he or she walk around the virtual world and meet people in broadly varying contexts. The VC offers abundant social networking experience among people around the globe. VWC which simulates the complexity of real world enough offers endless wonders and possibilities of VC and resources lead the members to explore the VWC. Members will be glued to the screen to project their creation, the avatars.

Furthermore, a VC that digitally simulates the real world in a fantastic way will offer its users more pleasure to explore the virtual world. Some people would like try to do something that can not be done in the real world. Everyone can even fly and teleport from one place to another in virtual worlds. An old woman may transform herself into young and sexy woman through her avatar and interact with others. These possibilities enabled by virtual worlds will be fabulous for people who want to have unordinary experiences. Persistent virtual environments with VC will create values for users to explore the world, achieve what they want, and reward themselves for what they did.

As shown in the previous section, technology enables VCs' evolutionary advancements toward new trends. Availability of distributed computing, the Internet, and streaming media technologies creates "distributed simulation," the virtual world in which people collaboratively interact simultaneously as they do in the real world. However, a long-run perspective on VC needs to be considered as there can be many technical challenges to be handled. For instance, as the population of a VC grows, computing capacity to handle heavy traffic needs to be increased. The growth of recent VWC will depend heavily on the platform provider's technical strength in server infrastructure and software to run streaming-3D contents.

5 Conclusion

We have proposed the three generations of evolution of VC. Over time, technical capability is enhanced, and it becomes feasible to instill into VC platform's nature and make VC evolve. Virtual communication's transition from a text-based platform to streamed-3D virtual world has profoundly changed how people interact within VC.

As we have seen in the evolution of VC, users are flocking to a VC that can provide better platform. The popularity of joining VC is escalating because of low cost in getting connected, due to technology advancement and valuable benefits of being a community member. User interface is getting easier to use to create UCC (User Created Contents), alluring diversified population to VC. The variety and number of interesting content is increasing exponentially. Furthermore, users can share their digital content with others or sell them for profit. VC is even getting attention from the corporate world.

Therefore, these phenomena will accelerate the expansion of VC's ecosystem both in social and economical aspects. More people will hinge on the platform, new opportunities will be created, and the community will continuously evolve. However, we do not assume that early generation of VC will extinct upon the arrival of new generation. As long as VC platform provider has a concern for providing better environment, satisfying the users' needs, the VC will not phase out. All generations of VC can coexist. The field for VC in the future will become more sophisticated and competitive. Whether VC can survive from growing pains or not is in question. We hope what was presented here will help both practitioners and researchers in reviewing the growth of VC and issues relevant to the field of VC.

References

1. Blanchard, A.: Virtual behavior settings: an application of behavior setting theories to virtual communities. Journal of Computer-Mediated Communication 9(2) (2004)
2. Bressler, S.E., Grantham, C.E.: Communities of Commerce. McGraw-Hill, New York (2000)
3. Butler, B.S.: Membership size, communication activity, and sustainability: a resource-based model of online social structures. Information Systems Research 12(4), 346–362 (2001)
4. Christensen, W., Suess, R.: The Birth of the BBS. Chinet, http://chinet.com/html/cbbs.php
5. Daft, R.L., Lengel, R.H.: Organizational information requirements, media richness and structural design. Management Science 32(5), 554–571 (1986)
6. Evans, D.S., Hagiu, A., Schmalensee, R.: Invisible engines: how software platforms drive innovation and transform industries. MIT Press, Cambridge (2006)
7. Friedman, T.L.: The world is flat: a brief history of the twenty-first century. Farrar, Straus and Giroux, New York (2006)
8. Hoffman, D., Novak, T.: Marketing in hypermedia computer-mediated environments: conceptual foundations. Journal of Marketing 60(3), 50–68 (1996)

 9. Igbaria, M.: The driving forces in the virtual society. Communications of the ACM 42(12), 64–70 (1999)
10. Rafaeli, S., LaRose, R.J.: Electronic bulletin boards and "public goods" explanation of collaborative mass media. Communication Research 20(2), 277–297 (1993)
11. Short, J., Williams, E., Christie, B.: The Social Psychology of Telecommunications. John Wiley and Sons Ltd., London (1976)
12. Wellman, B.: Community: from neighborhood to network. Communications of the ACM 48(10), 53–55 (2005)

The Future of Professional Communities of Practice

Murray Turoff and Starr Roxanne Hiltz

Distinguished Professors Emeritus and Emerita
Information Systems Department
New Jersey Institue of Technology
turoff@njit.edu, hiltz@njit.edu
http://is.njit.edu/turoff, http://is.njit.edu/hiltz

Abstract. Thirty four professionals who are part of a community of practice in the field of health related emergency response management provided information about the sources of information that they currently use the most, as well as their unmet information needs, and the kinds of information systems tools they would like to have. This professional community relies heavily on the Web, but they report severe information overload, in terms of not easily being able to find the kinds of information they want, amid the deluge of information that is there. In particular, they would find a system that uses social tagging and social recommender system features to be very useful for accessing relevant documents in the "gray literature." We suggest that services such as these will be increasingly important for professional communities in general.

Keywords: Information Overload, Emergency Management, communities of practice, professional communications, recommender systems.

1 Introduction

In many professional communities of practice, traditional books and journals are inadequate means for obtaining current, relevant information about practical problems. Instead, the members are moving online, towards more collaborative knowledge building, and forming virtual communities of practice. In this paper, we will describe some results of a study of members of the community of practice concerned with health-related issues of emergency preparedness and response. We use the results of this study to suggest the kinds of information system support that is needed and hopefully will emerge to serve the needs of not only this specific community, but also other professional communities of practice with a need for current, vetted, and practical (action-oriented) information.

As defined by Wenger, et al (2002), "Communities of practice are groups of people who share a concern, a set of problems, or a passion about a topic, and who deepen their knowledge and expertise in this area by interacting on an ongoing basis." "Their involvement in their community is based on interest in the topic, not on formal affiliation. Their relationships are collegial rather than hierarchical" (Wenger, 2003, pg. 1). Fontaine (2001) describes them as housing "the valuable knowledge and practice of

C. Weinhardt, S. Luckner, and J. Stößer (Eds.): WEB 2008, LNBIP 22, pp. 144–158, 2009.

how things really get done in an organization." The professional association that meets face to face is a traditional community of practice; increasingly, communities of practice are moving online, instead of or in addition to using traditional means of communication such as meetings and newsletters, and thus can be referred to as "virtual communities of practice" (White, Hiltz, and Turoff, 2008.)

The authors recently completed a study for the National Library of Medicine (NLM) on the information seeking behavior of professionals in health-related Emergency Preparedness and Management. About half of the 34 respondents to a qualitative "networking inquiry" were associated with medical and public health concerns (Turoff and Hiltz, 2008). This was a highly interdisciplinary group comprised of emergency practitioners (7), health-related professionals (10), academics (7), librarians (3), and international professionals (7). All but three respondents provided their name, affiliation, and brief background information and are named as contributors in the report. The major research questions are:

- What sources of information are most valuable to this community of practice?"
- What kinds of information do they need that they are unable to find now?
- What kinds of information systems features do they want to support their needs?

The full report published on the Web provides all the details on the inquiry methodology and an appendix of all the responses to the ten open- ended questions, categorized by the above backgrounds. The effort was very much like the first round of a Delphi process (Linstone and Turoff, 1975) dedicated to exposing the current situation, the issues, and the resulting requirements for using information technology to improve current problems.

The intent of this paper is to give some insight relevant to understanding the potential future of "virtual communities of practice" with respect to the use of the Web. In part this is also based upon prior work in understanding scientific "invisible colleges" and their usage of computer mediated communications on the EIES (Electronic Information Exchange System) beginning in the mid 1970s and extending into the early nineties (Hiltz and Turoff, 1978, 1993). Based upon this assortment of sources, we will offer some hypotheses about the likely future of professional communications that the current evolution of the Web is rapidly making possible, along with underlying economic trends.

In the remainder of this paper, we briefly describe the methodology followed in the study. We then present some of the key quotations that illuminate the current status of information overload experienced by these emergency response professionals, and items on their "wish list." Finally we try to put this study into the context of other studies of online communication structures to support professional communities and/ or emergency response, and to present our projections about future information systems to support such communities.

2 Overview of the NLM Report

This paper focuses on the results of our study (Turoff and Hiltz, 2008) of professionals in the health and medical emergency management field.   However, we feel strongly that the results generalize to a great many communities of professional practice, as information overload is probably one of the implicit causes of the creation of such Web based groups.

2.1 Method

Data collection took place during the period form September to December 2007. Beginning with an initial list of expert informants identified by NLM and the study investigators, a "snowball" sampling technique was used, in which each expert was asked to suggest other appropriate participants in the study. Approximately 100 professionals involved in emergency preparedness and management were invited to participate, from which we obtained 34 completed responses. The initial persons invited were chosen to be in diverse specialty areas of the general topic.

We used an innovative data collection strategy which we call a "networking inquiry," a name chosen not only because we used the initially identified experts' professional networks to locate additional experts for inclusion, but also because we used computer networks (email) for the majority of the recruitment, data collection, and other interaction with participants. The first few participants were personally interviewed, following an interview guide with open ended questions, a process that took an hour or more. However, this proved unsatisfactory for a number of reasons. First of all, the respondents are very scattered, so travel was time consuming and not practical. Secondly, the respondents could not remember, off the top of their heads, the details of all the web sites and publications they use; they needed time to think and gather these. Therefore, we sent the list of questions to the remaining invitees, asking them to take as long as they needed to provide the information requested. We also used email to answer any questions about the study, and to send the draft report to all participants for their comments and possible additions or corrections before publication.

The methodology is thus most like the first round of a Delphi study, which uses written responses from groups of experts representing different stakeholders or roles. This is a qualitative methodology that is designed to identify concerns, rather than to quantify how many members of the community of practice share each concern or support each suggestion. Three to five experts in a specific area are usually sufficient to cover the range of qualitative insights about a given issue or topic within their specialty (Linstone and Turoff, 1975). Like a Delphi, the objective of this study is "collective (or collaborative) intelligence," a body of knowledge and ideas that is richer than any that could be obtained from a single expert within a given professional group, dealing with the topic as a whole. We will use quotes from the contributors to illustrate some of the results of this study pertinent to the subject of this paper. After reviewing the results, only three participants desired not to have their names listed as contributors to the final report. This seemed to be due to employer policies on public statements rather than disagreement with the report.

2.2 Information Overload in Emergency Preparedness and Management

The first qualitative questions dealt with asking about specific "Current Sources of Information" and "Desired Sources." A clear result is the current very general condition of information overload (Hiltz and Turoff 1985). A search of the web for Emergency Preparedness, Emergency Management, and Business Continuity produces over nine million hits. One has to join only a few of the various related message lists to get recommendations to read dozens of new documents announced every week from numerous "authoritative" sources. It is not only too much information but also the lack of the tools to help the professionals find the sorts of things they want, as illustrated in the following quotes.

> *Unfortunately I have found that it takes somebody knowledgeable (me) to go through all the various resources and pull out what is useful. I also am a generalist in terms of interest in all things medical/public health, with a strong interest in everything else available in the homeland security field*

> *I think the problem is not resources; it is finding the right ones and then knowing which resources are authoritative. A web search on any given topic will likely turn up multiple resources.*

> *Just as it is important to be able to obtain information; [it] must be relevant. This emphasizes the need for "peer-reviewed" materials that do not necessarily have to be present in a journal form (peer-reviewed web sites may do fine).*

> *"I am currently unable to avoid information overload. I simply do not have the time to actively search the internet, read, let alone quickly scan specific websites, journals, and books. Unfortunate, but true! Usually the only electronic sources of information I look at, other than email are material that is "pushed to me" -- for example, information feeds (RSS) from Alertnet, ReliefWeb, etc. and Google."*

A medical professional wants *"best practices with summaries if I wanted to know what the best way to handle an event is."* Another noted that an unmet need is *"Information about what other organizations are doing. What supplies, equipment, medications and personnel are "in the pipeline" on route to a disaster scene? Unfortunately, we are still depending on traditional (read: antiquated) means of communication."* Another wants more *"Disaster 'After Action Reports', especially where lessons were NOT learned and the same deficiencies were present over time."*

This need for the "nitty gritty" details are also expressed as:
"What the FEMA planning course calls "implementing information" Standard Operating Guidelines (SOGs), equipment lists, job action sheets, MOUs (Memorandum of Understanding). There is a lot of clinical information, much of which is redundant, and not enough logistics and management info (by comparison)."

> Desired is: *"A database with Disaster related instruments:*
> *Pre Disaster HVA (Hazard Vulnerability Assessments) instruments.*
> *Psychosocial Assessment tools*
> *Post Disaster Response Assessment instruments.*
> *A database with National/State/City protocols and intervention plans*
> *A data repository with National/State/City disaster drill data*
> *A centralized data repository with raw data published or research in progress."*

"I find the on-line publication "Big Medicine" (grass roots effort) is an excellent source of straightforward unvarnished information. There in fact is a significant overload of information with insufficient concrete actions. This is especially true of DHS (Department of Homeland Security) *and HHS* (Health and Human Services). *There is a profound lack of leadership at the Federal Level."*

In other words, the kinds of resources needed, but not available, deal not with published literature, but with information, particularly about procedures and tools to support these procedures, that must be contributed, gathered, and vetted by peers who are actually on the "front lines" of emergencies. This material, not in professional journals, is often referred to as the "gray literature." The combination of a great deal of material and a low signal to noise ratio of material, with the "gray literature" largely ignored by traditional information science efforts, leads to a feeling of information overload shared by most of the members of this professional group. For example, there is no national database that tries to gather and make available local emergency plans whereby emergency managers can compare different planning alternatives for improving their own.

2.3 Information Diversity and Sharing

Since this is a highly interdisciplinary profession concerned with every societal function that can be impacted by natural and man made disasters, a wide range of topics are sought by the many different concerns. The literally hundreds of topics and websites listed by the respondents are very diverse. Furthermore there is a clear desire to share useful information with others, as shown in the quotes below.

2.3.1 What Is Available?

"I review GAO reports, Federal Guidance on Disaster Preparedness and subscribe to (and write for) the on line publication, "Big Medicine... I am not an academic, but rather an operational person who is delighted to share my experience with others."

"I used to go to national libraries in both Canada and the US to find... specific authors, books, or articles that I had found through other sources. However, I no longer do so. My success rate through libraries was on the order of ¼ to 1/3... I now go to Google first. More often than not, Google points to a Wikipedia article with 100% of what I'm looking for. On other occasions, I can find most of what I'm looking for through other links, resulting in an overall success rate approaching 90%, in about one-third of the time."

"My sources of information and knowledge are highly diverse, rather than tied to specific journals. I am connected to a handful of national and global knowledge management networks. These often point to useful or interesting articles in various professional and scientific journals. I may pose a specific question to these networks to get me started on a search. This often results in a pointer to a web site with what I'm looking for."

"There is a general lack of publicly available manuals and online training programs for disaster management. Also needed are publicly available algorithms

for specific disasters. These can be easily accomplished by introducing national organizations for disaster management, organizing courses in disaster manage-ment and providing databases of material... They could be supplemented with a moderated forum for exchanging experiences."

2.3.2   What Is Not Available?

"Detailed after action reports put out by state and local public health agencies describing the management actions taken to respond to an incident, including the resources used and what actions were especially effective and which ones were not."

"If I were to have access to the type of resources, services, or types of informa-tion that you describe above, I would want to be assured that there was some degree of "Quality Control" and "Attribution." Documents or reports, from rec-ognized organizations, stating clearly the date and source of every document and facilities to validate the information, allowing users to assign their credibil-ity. Hopefully, there will be peer pressures resulting from the use of this infor-mation by respected individuals and organizations in the emergency health relief community... A critical mass of participation and data is needed before such dynamics can take hold."

"Different pieces of information exist at different levels of the emergency relief "information pipeline," but not in a form which is easily accessible or immedi-ately made available to emergency personnel. We need some means to consoli-date, filter, organize, and redistribute such information and other existing sources of data to the right people, at the right time, in the right format, etc."

"This will be difficult to achieve on a large-scale. It would require a very knowledgeable individual to do the organizing, indexing, clustering, processing, and/or filtering. Basically, a "documentalist" who will retrieve only the relevant information on behalf of the users. Will also need an expert such as an epidemi-ologist to consolidate data from a variety of sources, formats etc., and most importantly to synthesize information."

"Finally, we need to have some form of "Feedback monitoring" - A constant reassessment of the methods and effectiveness of those methods to determine if they are achieving its objectives - questionnaire, listservs, etc."

"Applicable federal documents as we go through the new National Response Framework, the National Response Plan, the TCLs (Target Capabilities Lists), all those kind of things. They are huge huge documents that nobody in their right mind has the ability to read. An index that says here are all the federal documents but divided in a certain way and again walking you through so that it starts with the strategy and goes down to the universal task lists. Something that makes that easy, an index that makes that easy. So that's the federal plans. Best practices with summaries so if I wanted to know what the best way to handle an event is I could easily find the best practices but not have to read the whole document to do that."

"I would like to see more community-based approaches to material, particularly using social tagging to create a more grounded taxonomy – the one we currently

have is heavily predefined by the Cluster system. An aggregator of academic publications that might be useful in disaster response, from a range of journals in different topic areas, would be very useful in helping the humanitarian community to access this expertise – at the moment, it's just too difficult and costly for us to stay up on current research."

"You may wish to consider Google's approach and/or folksonomies or tagging. There's a couple of really fascinating videos on YouTube that talk about Web 2.0 and organizing information. One on the Information Revolution and the other on Web 2.0... Unfortunately, our IT security people have deemed both YouTube and Facebook to have no valid business purposes, so I can't simply send you the URL."

"Also a mechanism to get questions answered in one place that then shares the info back to all for future.... Our agency's action plan contained sections that would have been useful to others developing plans, but they could not be shared."

"Resources for coping with information overload, broadly defined, due to the plethora of types and sources of information. As one of our international experts put it, "Just as it is important to be able to obtain information; [it] must be relevant. This emphasizes the need for... peer-reviewed materials that do not necessarily have to be present in a journal form (e.g., peer-reviewed web sites may do fine)."

"Collections of practitioner documents in specific areas such as plans, best practices, training materials, and requirements and design studies for support systems of all sorts. Many localities do not have adequate resources to pay for these and national level documents do not deal adequately with local situations. Having a compilation to compare and evolve current plans, training, and other preparedness activities would be quite valuable."

2.4 Grassroots Community Efforts

One of the other interesting results was the exposure of a number of efforts undertaken by volunteer individuals or groups. In some cases these were professionals working at a regular job for a local, state, or federal agency or they were consultants who contributed to information gathering efforts that were free to the practitioner community. These were in some cases group efforts to create newsletters, blogs, forums, and websites useful to various specialties in the field. They had characteristics of what we think of as open source community groups. We list here only a few popular examples:

2.4.1 Website List for Community Services
One of the practitioners who responded, Gregory Banner of DHHS, has been collecting useful websites for many years. His list of sites is on the Web:

http://www.ynhhs.org/emergency/us_dhhs_web_sites.pdf

Currently this has over 1500 websites (and over 70 pages if printed), is continuously updated, and each one has an abstract and is assigned to one or more categories. Due to various messages lists this site is known to most emergency managers.

2.4.2 An international Mental Health Website from Sweden

This website, in seven languages, is a very comprehensive collection of mental health information for the public. It is developed and maintained by both psychologists and psychiatrists as largely an open source effort on an international scale. It includes online consultation with professionals, discussion forums organized around a particular problem area, and extensive regular updates from all around the world, all vetted by Swedish professionals.

http://web4health.info

The above site is for public access to expert vetted information on all forms of mental health problems. In recent years it has started to include trauma problems and advice focusing on disaster victims.

2.4.3 Communities of Practice

Communities of practice are characterized by not only creating websites for dissemination but also by employing some form of collaborative software that allows meaningful complex discussions to take place. We have chosen a few examples from what appear to be very popular and respected examples in the emergency practitioner community.

Big Medicine. This network gathers and disseminates information for emergency practitioners in the health and medical field. It is operated by a team of volunteers comprised of both practitioners and consultants. The effort has two websites: one for publishing and indexing the newsletter and the second for group collaboration and the exchange of information:

http://www.bigmedicine.ca/index.htm
http://bigmedicine.collectivex.com/main/summary

ISCRAM (http://iscram.org) was formed in 2004 for professionals interested in the problems of developing better information systems in the emergency field (Van de Walle and Turoff 2006). ISCRAM started as a workshop in 2004 in Brussels and it now has over 2000 online members worldwide and its international meeting in 2008 in Washington DC had around 300 attendees. ISCRAM provides a forum for those concerned with general emergency information system R and D challenges.

All Hands Information Portal. This news collection and distribution site allows practitioners to contribute, utilizes volunteers, and is supported by a consultant firm made up of practitioners. It has an editor that reviews contributions before they are entered and insures they get properly categorized into the topic areas. The website is designed to help reduce the problem of overload by providing tools for practitioners to deal with information proliferation. The all hands community net has both blogs and forums, as do many of the others.

http://www.all-hands.net/ *Editor: Steve Davis steve@all-hands.net*

2.5 Grassroots Community Efforts (Continued)

There is a sizable effort taking place to create and to involve local citizen communities in all the phases of Emergency Planning and Preparedness and to set up what amounts to local community based social networks (Sutton, et al 2008; Shneiderman and Preece 2007; Palen, Hiltz, and Liu, 2007; Liu et al 2008). There has been a lack of integration of public agencies and citizen help groups into the functions of planning, mitigation, preparedness, training, and command and control (Turoff et al 2008) and this leads to incomplete and unrealistic efforts at many emergency functions such as evacuation, alerting, and early preparation after detection of an approaching threat. On line social networks are beginning to fill in some of the gaps that occur after the disaster with respect to tracking refugees, utilizing shelter and emergency treatment facilities.

3 Interpretations of the Results

The observations we would make based upon the above and all the comments contributed are:

- Currently literature in this area is very scattered, especially the gray literature.
- Many types of gray literature are considered critical to practitioners and some of them are not collected and organized in any systematic library science approach.
- Static indexes are not going to satisfy the users at the practitioner level and even the academic level because the current the field is evolving and changing.
- Users have turned to social networks to help alleviate information overload and are attracted to services that support the underlying social networks.
- Users want to have control over their abilities to filter and organize their material.
- Users also want more professional help to aid their information seeking processes.
- There are too many sources competing for being" the source" and this lack of organizational cooperation is a major challenge to overcome.
- A professional library could be the logical mediator between organizations.
- Grassroots based services worldwide are undergoing rapid development.
- Collaboration capabilities (e.g., social recommender systems) are expected by practitioners and they have begun to gravitate to systems that provide them.
- A form of recommender system on gray literature documents recommended by users could be explored as an appropriate method to allow user involvement.
- An approach to users contributing and evaluating "best practices" is another obvious recommender type of approach if the system can integrate local factors for the individual user.
- Structuring and visualization approaches to provide quick access to complex information should receive considerable attention to service the practitioner community.
- AI approaches can also be very useful if the users have control over setting what are sometimes very unique needs and requirements or training the AI in a feedback process.

- Collaborative tagging was mentioned a number of times by the respondents and seems to be one example of the desire to have involvement in the process of tailoring the systems serving them.

Our role for NLM was to gather the problems, issues, and requirements but not to recommend solutions in this particular effort. Just about all the participants might be considered very computer literate but not Information System professionals. For the purpose of this paper we would like to express here the solutions we see for this community of practice. We hypothesize that what this community of practitioners really want and what can be designed is a collaborative recommender system with a knowledge structure that they can evolve and which will be under control of a large vetted community of contributors and service a much wider community of user practitioners. We would expect such a system to service many thousands of users concerned with any phase of Emergency Preparedness and Management. Some of the properties of this system would be:

1. Documents to be included are nominated by any vetted contributor
2. Comments on the utility can be made and attached to the document as a discussion thread
3. Anyone can vote on the utility of the document and change their vote based upon the discussion changing their viewpoint.
4. Votes are reported and organized by the specialty areas of the voters established through the vetting process (an idea borrowed from the Delphi process)
5. Users can look up documents by specialty area of the voters and the resulting ratings
6. Collaborative tagging should be implemented to continually update and expand an index.
7. Users would be able to form groups of common interest based upon similar ratings of documents.
8. Users would be able to establish group discussions which a volunteer moderator could summarize in a type of Wiki to make available useful insights and wisdom.
9. The history of documents and their usage as well as those of contributors, raters and users would also be tracked to be able to evaluate the status of the system and publish insights on its utility.

While the system would start with an index put together by some representative group of the contributors, there would also be a social tagging procedure allowing ongoing modifications and additions to the index by the contributor community. The general area of users supplying index terms is often referred to as "folksonomies" and a recent review (Stock, 2007) refers to the benefits and problems with this approach. We feel for groups of experts this has to be a collaborative type approach where there is some sort of Delphi-like consensus among participants (Turoff et al, 2002; Linstone and Turoff, 1975). In the original collaborative tagging game on the web to develop index terms for pictures (http://espgame.org), two people who did not know each other (anonymously) were required to independently propose terms (other than those already in use for the picture). Only if they both proposed the same term did that term become a new key word or phrase for the given picture. In the system being proposed here users would be able to include personal keys for documents for their own use. If "n" users added the same key for a document that key would become a public index term for the given document. A human editor would have to veto terms such as "to read" or "to review."

The use of personal keys has a long history of use in communications oriented systems to aid people in locating things they have seen for later use (Hiltz and Turoff, 1985, 1978, 1993; Johnson-Lenz, 1980; Turoff et al, 1993). Also important is the observation that a system allowing users to establish indirect communications can become an important laboratory tool for understanding user cognitive processes (Hiltz, et al, 1982) such as the choices of terms for retrieval. A system like this, supporting a community of experts, can become a laboratory tool for information scientists to use the products of the user actions for improving the formal index efforts for that body of technical knowledge – evolutionary knowledge bases.

The number of contributors for this community is probably in the range of a few thousand. However, there would be a much large community of observers who would make use of the results. There would be an editor and/or editorial committee that would allow non-contributors to make suggestions for documents to be included with an accompanying justification and also to submit comments on documents which would be reviewed before adding by the editor. In fact, there would probably be a process for a user to become a contributor by a demonstration of effort or by being the author of a number of well rated documents. The contributions of the professionals to documents, discussions, and tags would allow a social matching function to aid small groups of practitioners to form small communities in very specific topic areas. The ability to detect small social communities emerging in asynchronous online class discussions was documented in a recent thesis for a significant number of online courses (Saltz et al 2004, 2007).

In 1982, Turoff and Hiltz pointed out that one of the results of the EIES (Electronic Information Exchange System (Turoff, 1978; Hiltz and Turoff, 1978) field trials from 1976 on was that systems to exchange scientific findings among invisible colleges would look different than journal articles. While there seem to be more journals then ever, costs are becoming prohibitive, even for libraries, and other alternatives such as "open access" communities (Poynder, 2008) are spreading. Many of the journal replacements demonstrated on EIES, such as TOPICS (Johnson-Lenz and Johnson-Lenz, 1980), were an early form of professional based recommender system (Hiltz and Turoff 1985; Turoff et al 1993).

One of the key features of TOPICS was a public membership list for the 100-150 members that showed how many questions each member had asked the group to respond to and how many answers they had provided to the questions of others. The clear peer pressure message that worked very well was: "If you want help on your problems, you have to help others on their problems." The system proposed in this paper should provide a similar status membership list to encourage appropriate credit for contributions to the community.

Besides the collaborative systems established by professionals we have seen a number of social networking systems taking a role in disasters and sometimes producing information that is more up to date and timely than the authorities. One recent example was the Virginia Tech shooting and the rapid determination of the identification of the actual causalities (before the authorities) by Facebook groups (Vieweg et al 2008). It demonstrated the concept of collaborative intelligence (Hiltz and Turoff, 1978, 1993). Other grassroots efforts for major disasters such as Katrina included the tracking of missing people and updated information on shelters or other resources (Palen and Hiltz 2007). Local emergency management professionals are very concerned with the need to insure active local community participation in planning and preparing for possible disaster situations. What practitioners in Emergency Management desire to see is the establishment of a "culture of preparedness" in local communities. The true first responders are usually the local citizens who quickly undertake to help their neighbors.

4 Conclusions and Observations

The Emergency Preparedness and Management practitioner community in the U.S. and worldwide is a very dedicated, loosely coupled network of professionals that is deeply concerned with their performance and ability to deal with disasters of any type. The phenomenon of "threat rigidity" is well known in this community and one of the major factors in bringing this about is losing a sense of being able to make good decisions under the pressures and stress of reacting quickly and correctly to the events occurring in a disaster (Plotnick and Turoff, 2008; Turoff et al 2008). The worst impact of the current situation is a feeling among many that the information really needed to improve their plans and local ability to react is out there somewhere, but they cannot find it or it exists but is not collected and being made available.

According to HRT (High Reliability Theory), that is supposed to be the operational principle for organizations that must deal with disasters, everyone must expose and share errors no matter how small and collectively the organization needs to work to correct even the smallest error least it grow in the future to something major. Unfortunately in the current atmosphere among agencies in government and private companies such as utilities, the practice seems to be more like "let's not expose mistakes least we be criticized." HRT is really a restatement of a much older theory (The Science of Muddling Through by Lindblom, see Turoff et al. 2009). A recommender system that allows anonymous contributions (Linstone and Turoff, 1975) would go a long way to begin to allow professionals to accomplish what the organizations responsible for Emergency Management do not seem to want to do. Collecting the errors that occurred is exactly what some of the comments of the participants called for in the original study.

The motivation in other professional fields may not be quite so intense. However, unless a new researcher is part of an existing invisible college that regularly exchanges draft papers or has the funds to attend appropriate conferences, she or he is unlikely to succeed in the long term by only reading published journal papers. The fact that an increasing number of universities are putting PhD theses on the Web is a signal of the movement to open access and one of the sources benefiting professionals. A field such as IS in a relatively short time has grown to be a very diverse community with significant overlaps between AIS, ASIS, TIMS, ACM, and the IEEE Computer Society. The actual narrow topic areas that most researchers work in cut across these professional organizations and their journals. There are already examples of features like collaborative tagging being added as open source features to existing social networks. It is very likely that some of these social networks will attract both communities of practice and academic oriented "invisible colleges" unless the professional societies start to offer online support for the sort of collaborative recommender system we have outlined in this paper. A number of professional communities have already set up memberships on various social networks as a trial effort. Whether they stay there will depend a great deal on what sort of collaborative recommender features become available.

There is also quite a bit of related work in adding decision support capabilities to the evaluation of items such as documents for communities of practice and even social networks (White, et al 2008, 2007, Turoff et al 2002). One recent example is the emergence of the Wikimapia which has already been put to use by some emergency managers to create a database of concerns and resources for their locality. Such a tool can be used by any citizen in a given area to collaborate on gathering any possible problem, concern, or resource based upon the knowledge of those in the community who may have appropriate skills or prior experiences that provide them insight. Support for such collaborative gathering and rating of resources is at the heart of what we see as the future of online services for communities of practice.

Acknowledgments. The research reported here was partially supported by the National Library of Medicine. The opinions expressed are solely those of the authors and do not necessarily reflect those of the National Library of Medicine. We wish to thank Stacey Arnesen, Barbara Rapp, and Elliot Siegel for their contributions and suggestions on the original effort and the final report. We also wish to thank Connie White for her review of this paper.

References

1. Fontaine, M.: Keeping Communities of Practice Afloat: Understanding and fostering roles in communities. Knowledge Management Review 4, 4 (2001)
2. Hiltz, S.R., Turoff, M.: The Network Nation: Human Communication via Computer. Addison Wesley Advanced Book Program, Reading; revised edition. MIT Press (1978/1993)
3. Hiltz, S.R., Turoff, M.: Structuring Computer-Mediated Communication Systems to Avoid Information Overload. Communications of the ACM 28(7), 680–689 (1985)
4. Hiltz, S.R., Turoff, M., Johnson, K.: Using a Computerized Conferencing Systems as a Laboratory Tool. SIGSOC Bulletin 13(4) (1982)
5. Hughes, A., Palen, L., Sutton, J., Liu, S.B., Vieweg, S.: Site-seeing in disaster: An examination of on-line social convergence. In: Proceedings of the 5th International ISCRAM Conference, Washington, DC (2008)
6. Johnson-Lenz, P., Johnson-Lenz, T.: LegiTech/EIES: Information Exchange Among State Legislative Researchers. In: Henderson, M., MacNaughton, J. (eds.) Electronic Communication: Technology and Impacts, AAAS Selected Symposium 52, pp. 103–111. Westview Press, Boulder (1980)
7. Linstone, H., Turoff, M.: The Delphi Method: Techniques and Applications. Addison Wesley Advanced Book Program, Reading (1975), http://is.njit.edu/turoff (accessed on August 18, 2007)

8. Liu, S.B., Palen, L., Sutton, J., Hughes, A.L., Vieweg, S.: In search of the bigger picture: The emergent role of on-line photo sharing in times of disaster. In: Proceedings of the 5th International ISCRAM Conference, Washington, DC (2008)
9. Palen, L., Hiltz, S.R., Liu, S.: Citizen Participation in Emergency Preparedness and Response. Communications of the ACM special issue 50(3), 54–58 (2007)
10. Plotnick, L., Turoff, M.: Mitigating Threat Rigidity in Crisis. In: van de Walle, B., Turoff, M., Hiltz, S.R. (eds.) Information Systems for Emergency Management. A volume in the Advances in Management Information Systems monograph series (Editor in Chief: Zwass, V.). M.E. Sharpe Inc., Armonk (expected, 2009)
11. Poynder, R.: Open Access: Doing the Numbers. Open and Shut Blog (2008), http://poynder.blogspot.com/2008/06/open-access-doing-numbers.html (accessed on Wednesday, 11 June 2008)
12. Saltz, J., Hiltz, S.R., Passerini, K., Turoff, M.: Visualizing online Interaction to increase Participation in Distance Learning Courses. IEEE Internet Computing 11(3), 36–44 (2007)
13. Saltz, J.S., Hiltz, S.R., Turoff, M.: Student Social Graphics: Visualizing a student's Online Social Network. In: Proceedings of the CSCW 2004 (Computer Supported Cooperative Work), Chicago, Illinois, November 6-10, pp. 596–599 (2004)
14. Shneiderman, B., Preece, J.: Public Health: 911.gov. Science 315, 949 (2007)
15. Stock, W.B.: Folksonomies and science communications. Information Services and Use (27), 97–103 (2002)
16. Sutton, J., Palen, L., Shklovski, I.: Backchannels on the front lines: Emergent uses of social media in the 2007 Southern California wildfires. In: Proceedings of the 5th International ISCRAM Conference, Washington, DC (2008)
17. Turoff, M.: The EIES Experience: Electronic Information Exchange System. Bulletin of the American Society for Information Science 4(5), June 9-10(1978)
18. Turoff, M., Hiltz, S.R., White, C., Plotnick, L., Hendela, A., Xiang, Y.: The Past as the Future of Emergency Preparedness and Management. Journal of Information Systems for Crisis Response and Management 1(1), 12–28 (2009)
19. Turoff, M., White, C., Plotnick, L., Hiltz, S.R.: Dynamic Emergency Response Management for Large Scale Decision Making in Extreme Events. In: Proceedings of the ISCRAM Conference, Washington, DC (2008)
20. Turoff, M., Hiltz, S.R.: Information Seeking Behavior and Viewpoints of Emergency Preparedness and Management Professionals Concerned with Health and Medicine, Report to the National Library of Medicine (February 2008), http://is.njit.edu/turoff (accessed on 6/14/08)
21. Turoff, M., Chumer, M., Van de Walle, B., Yao, X.: The Design of a Dynamic Emergency Response Management Information System (DERMIS). Journal of Information Technology Theory and Application (JITTA) 5(4), 1–35 (2004)
22. Turoff, M., Hiltz, S.R., Cho, H.-K., Li, Z., Wang, Y.: Social Decision Support Systems. In: Proceedings of the 35th Hawaii International Conference of System Sciences, HICSS 2002. IEEE press, Washington (2002)
23. Turoff, M., Hiltz, S.R.: The Electronic Journal: A Progress Report, invited paper presented to the Association of American Publishers, New York, September 1979; published in the Journal of the American Society for Information Science 33(4), 195–202 (1982)
24. Turoff, M., Hiltz, S.R.: User Behavior Patterns in the Electronic Information Exchange System. In: Proceedings of the ACM Annual Meeting, Washington DC, December 4-6 (1978)
25. Turoff, M., Hiltz, S.R., Bahgat, A.N.F., Rana, A.: Distributed Group Support Systems. MIS Quarterly 17(4), 399–417 (1993)

26. Van de Walle, B., Turoff, M., Hiltz, S.R. (eds.): Information Systems for Emergency Management, In the Advances in Management Information Systems monograph series (Editor-in-Chief: Vladimir Zwass). M.E. Sharpe Inc., Armonk (expected spring 2009)
27. Van de Walle, B., Turoff, M.: Decision Support for Emergency Situations. In: Burstein, F., Holsapple, C. (eds.) Handbook on Decision Support Systems. International Handbook on Information Systems Series. Springer, Heidelberg (2008) (this chapter is open on the Web)
28. Van de Walle, B., Turoff, M.: ISCRAM: Growing a global R&D Community on Information Systems for Crisis Response and Management. International Journal of Emergency Management 3(4), 364–369 (2006)
29. Vieweg, S., Palen, L., Liu, S., Hughes, A., Sutton, J.: Collective Intelligence in Disaster: An Examination of the Phenomenon in the Aftermath of the 2007 Virginia Tech Shooting. In: Proceedings of the 5th International ISCRAM Conference, Washington, DC, USA (2008)
30. Wenger, E., McDermott, R., Snyder, W.: Cultivating communities of practice: a guide to managing knowledge. Harvard Business School Press, Boston (2002)
31. Wenger, E.: The Public Involvement Community of Practice at Health Canada: A Case Study. The Consultation Secretariat, Communications, Marketing & Consultation Branch, Health Canada (2003)
32. White, C., Hiltz, S.R., Turoff, M.: United We Respond: One Community, One Voice. In: Proceeding of the ISCRAM 2008 Conference, Washington, DC (2008), http://iscram.org
33. White, C., Turoff, M., Van de Walle, B.: A Dynamic Delphi Process Utilizing a Modified Thurstone Scaling Method: Collaborative Judgment in Emergency Response. In: Proceedings of 4th Information Systems on Crisis Response Management, Delft, Netherlands, May 13-16 (2007)
34. Wikimapia, http://www.wikimapia.com

A Feature-Reinforcement–Based Approach for Supporting Poly-Lingual Category Integration

Chih-Ping Wei[1], Chao-Chi Chen[2],
Tsang-Hsiang Cheng[3], and Christopher C. Yang[4]

[1] Institute of Service Science, National Tsing Hua University, Hsinchu, Taiwan, ROC
[2] Institute of Technology Management, National Tsing Hua University, Hsinchu, Taiwan, ROC
[3] Department of Business Administration, Southern Taiwan University, Tainan, Taiwan, ROC
[4] College of Information Science and Technology, Drexel University, Philadelphia,
Pennsylvania, USA
cpwei@mx.nthu.edu.tw, bluechaochi@gmail.com,
cts@mail.stut.edu.tw, Chris.Yang@ischool.drexel.edu

Abstract. Document-category integration (or category integration for short) is fundamental to many e-commerce applications, including information integration along supply chains and information aggregation by intermediaries. Because of the trend of globalization, the requirement for category integration has been extended from monolingual to poly-lingual settings. Poly-lingual category integration (PLCI) aims to integrate two document catalogs, each of which consists of documents written in a mix of languages. Several category integration techniques have been proposed in the literature, but these techniques focus only on monolingual category integration rather than PLCI. In this study, we propose a feature-reinforcement-based PLCI (namely, FR-PLCI) technique that takes into account the master documents of all languages when integrating source documents (in the source catalog) written in a specific language into the master catalog. Using the monolingual category integration (MnCI) technique as a performance benchmark, our empirical evaluation results show that our proposed FR-PLCI technique achieves better integration accuracy than MnCI does in both English and Chinese category integration tasks.

Keywords: Poly-lingual Category Integration, Category Integration, Feature Reinforcement, Multilingual Document Management, Text Mining.

1 Introduction

With advances in information and networking technologies, organizations generate and maintain a tremendous amount of textual documents in organizational repositories. To facilitate management of and subsequent access to these documents, organizations generally use categories to organize this ever increasing volume of documents. Meanwhile, an organization constantly acquires relevant documents from various organizations (e.g., their suppliers or online sources). Because the categories used by an information provider to organize its documents generally are not identical to those employed by the acquiring organization, document-category integration (or

C. Weinhardt, S. Luckner, and J. Stößer (Eds.): WEB 2008, LNBIP 22, pp. 159–171, 2009.
© Springer-Verlag Berlin Heidelberg 2009

category integration for short) that integrate relevant categorized documents into the acquiring organization's existing categories becomes an important issue.

In a typical category integration scenario, one set of categories is designated as the master catalog M, and another set of categories assumes the role of the source catalog S. Category integration essentially is to integrate categorized documents in S into appropriate categories in M. Category integration is essential for integrating information along supply chains. For instance, a distributor maintains an online product catalog from which its customers can access and order. Imaginably, a distributor may have tens or even hundreds of suppliers, each of which has its own product categorization scheme. As a result, the distributor must integrate individual product catalogs from each of its suppliers [2, 6]. Effective category integration is also desperately needed in emerging e-commerce environments, because many websites are aggregators of information from various online sources. For example, Yahoo! News (news.yahoo.com) aggregates news stories from multiple news providers (e.g., Reuters, Forbes.com) into such categories as economy, stock markets, earning, personal finance, and industries commentary. In contrast, Forbes.com includes categories such as manufacturing, technology, commerce, and services. Confronted with the non-identical categories used by various news providers, Yahoo! News evidently requires a category integration mechanism to automatically and effectively integrate categorized news stories from news providers into its own categories [8].

Several category integration techniques have been proposed [2, 8, 13, 14, 15]. All of them focus only on monolingual document-category integration, i.e., the category sets of the master and source catalogs are both written in the same language. However, because of the trend of globalization, an organization often archives documents written in different languages. Assume that the languages involved in a repository include $L_1, L_2, ..., L_s$, where $s \geq 2$. That is, the set of ploy-lingual documents contains some documents in L_1, some in $L_2,...$, and some in L_s. Consider the following scenario: An organization may already have a catalog M, within which each category contains poly-lingual documents. If the organization receives a collection of poly-lingual documents also organized into a catalog S by the information provider, the acquiring organization faces the challenge of integrating the source catalog S into its current master catalog M, where both catalogs are in effect poly-lingual. This specific problem is referred to as the poly-lingual category integration (PLCI) problem. Evidently, existing category integration techniques are not designed to deal with the PLCI requirement.

PLCI can simply be approached as multiple, independent monolingual category integration problems. That is, this naïve approach only considers the documents of the same language in the master catalog M and the source catalog S to perform the monolingual category integration task of that language and ignores all documents of other languages. When the monolingual category integration is performed for each language appearing in both catalogs, we complete the target PLCI task. However, this naïve approach fails to utilize the opportunity offered by poly-lingual documents in the two catalogs, thus possibly limiting the effectiveness of category integration in the poly-lingual environment.

This study is motivated by the importance of providing PLCI support to organizations in the increasingly globalized and multilingual environment. Specifically, we propose a feature-reinforcement–based PLCI (FR-PLCI) technique that takes into account all master documents of all languages when performing a monolingual category integration task for a specific language. For the purposes of our intended feasibility assessment and illustration, this study concentrates on only two languages involved in poly-lingual documents and deals with single-category documents rather than multi-category documents. The remainder of this paper is organized as follows: In Section 2, we review literature relevant to this study. We depict the detailed development of our proposed FR-PLCI technique in Section 3, including the overall processes and specific designs. Section 4 details our data collection and evaluation design, followed by important evaluation results in Section 5. We conclude the paper in Section 6 with a summary and discussions of the study's results together with some important future research directions.

2 Literature Review

As mentioned, the category integration problem is to assign each categorized document in the source catalog S into the most appropriate category in the master catalog M or into a new category if the document cannot be properly assigned to any predefined category in M [2]. Agrawal and Srikant [2] considered that if two documents belong to the same category in S, they are more likely to belong to the same category in M. Accordingly, they developed an Enhanced Naïve Bayes (ENB) technique for improving the accuracy of category integration by taking into consideration the implicit categorization information of S. After ENB was proposed, several different category integration techniques, including Cluster Shrinkage [13, 14], Co-Bootstrapping [13, 15], and Clustering-based Category Integration [8], have been proposed in the literature. However, all of the existing techniques focus only on monolingual category integration, i.e., the category sets of the master and source catalogs are both written in the same language. Because ENB is a prevalent category integration technique and is often used as performance benchmarks in previous studies, we provide a brief review of ENB and its underlying algorithm (i.e., Naïve Bayes classifier).

The Naive Bayes classifier uses the joint probabilities of words and categories to estimate the probabilities of categories given a document. It is based on the assumption that the conditional probability of a word given a category is independent from the conditional probabilities of other words given that category. The Naive-Bayes classifier estimates the posterior probability of the category C_i given a document d (i.e., $p(C_i|d)$) via Bayes rule as:

$$p(C_i|d) = \frac{p(d|C_i) \times p(C_i)}{p(d)} \tag{1}$$

where $p(C_i)$ is the probability that C_i occurs, $p(d)$ is the probability that d occurs, and $p(d|C_i)$ is the conditional probability that d occurs given C_i.

$p(C_i)$ can be estimated by the number of documents in C_i divided by the total number of documents in the dataset. $p(d)$ can be ignored when estimating $p(C_i|d)$ since it is identical for all categories and the relative probability of the categories can be used to determine d's category assignment. Due to the word independence assumption,

$p(d|C_i)$ can be derived as $p(d|C_i) = \prod_{f \in d} p(f|C_i)$, where f represents a word in d. The maximum likelihood estimate, smoothed by Lidstone's law of succession [1], is typically employed for estimating $p(f|C_i)$ as:

$$p(f|C_i) = \frac{freq(C_i, f) + \lambda}{freq(C_i) + \lambda |V|} \tag{2}$$

where $freq(C_i, f)$ is the number of occurrences of f in all documents in C_i, $freq(C_i) = \sum_{f \in C_i} freq(C_i, f)$ refers to the total number of words (counting multiple occurrences) in C_i, $|V|$ is the number of distinct words in all documents across categories, and $\lambda \geq 0$.

To improve accuracy of category integration, Agrawal and Srikant [2] extended the described Bayes rule based on the rationale that if two documents belong to the same source category, they are more likely to belong to the same master category. Accordingly, to determine the category assignment for a document d in S, the Enhanced Naïve Bayes (ENB) technique employs the posterior probability of the category C_i in M given d belonging to the category S_j in S as:

$$p(C_i|d, S_j) = \frac{p(d|C_i) \times p(C_i|S_j)}{p(d|S_j)} \tag{3}$$

$p(d|S_j)$ can be ignored when estimating $p(C_i|d, S_j)$ since $p(d|S_j)$ is the same for all C_i. To estimate $p(C_i|S_j)$, the documents in S_j are first classified using the standard Naïve Bayes classifier. Subsequently, using the majority principle, $p(C_i|S_j)$ will be increased if the majority of documents in S_j is predicted to be in C_i. Correspondingly, the estimate for $p(\underline{C_i}|S_j)$ is revised as:

$$p(C_i|S_j) = \frac{|C_i| \times (\text{number of documents in } S_j \text{ predicted to be in } C_i)^w}{\sum_{k=1}^{n} (|C_k| \times (\text{number of documents in } S_j \text{ predicted to be in } C_k)^w)} \tag{4}$$

where $w \geq 0$ and $|C_i|$ is the number of documents in the master category C_i.

PLCI is relevant to poly-lingual text categorization (PLTC). PLTC aims to construct text categorization models automatically from a set of training documents written in a mix of languages, and then classify unclassified documents in any of those languages [9]. Wei et al. [9] proposed a feature-reinforcement–based PLTC (FR-PLTC) technique that considers the training documents of all languages when constructing a monolingual classifier for a specific language. They argued that if the training documents of the target language (e.g., L_i) contain features (i.e., terms) that are non-semantic-bearing for the predefined categories, the inclusion of those noisy features into the induced classifier degrades its effectiveness. However, terms in other language (e.g., L_j) that linguistically correspond to the noisy features in L_i may not appear in the training documents of L_j. Therefore, a cross-check of features occurring in the training documents of different languages would help remove the noisy features of individual languages. In this study, we take the same approach as the FR-PLTC technique does for poly-lingual text categorization and propose the FR-PLCI technique for poly-lingual category integration.

3 Poly-Lingual Category Integration (PLCI) with Feature-Reinforcement

As mentioned previously, PLCI can be approached simply as multiple, independent monolingual category integration problems. However, when performing a monolingual category integration task for a specific language, this naïve integration approach does not exploit the documents of another language in the master catalog to improve the integration effectiveness. In this study, we propose the FR-PLCI technique with the support of a statistical-based bilingual thesaurus to address the potential limitation of the naïve integration approach.

Figure 1 shows the overall design of our proposed FR-PLCI technique, which consists of three main tasks: 1) *bilingual thesaurus construction* to build a statistical bilingual thesaurus (in this study, English and Chinese) from a parallel corpus, 2) *feature reinforcement and selection for master catalog (for L_i)* to select representative features (in L_i) by considering the documents of all the languages in the master catalog, and 3) *monolingual category integration (for L_i)* to integrate each source document (in L_i) into an appropriate master category.

3.1 Bilingual Thesaurus Construction

This task automatically constructs a statistical-based bilingual thesaurus using the co-occurrence analysis technique [5, 10], which is commonly employed in cross-lingual information retrieval research. Given a parallel corpus, the thesaurus construction process starts with term extraction and selection. In this study, we deal with only English and Chinese documents. Accordingly, we use the rule-based part-of-speech tagger developed by Brill [3, 4] to tag each word in the English documents in the parallel corpus. Subsequently, we implement the approach proposed by Voutilainen [7] to extract noun phrases from the syntactically tagged English documents. For the Chinese documents in the parallel corpus, we employ a hybrid approach that combines dictionary-based and statistical approaches (specifically, mutual information measure) [10, 11].

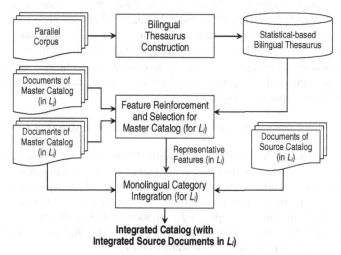

Fig. 1. Overall Process of the FR-PLCI Technique (for L_i)

After term extraction, the term selection step selects representative terms in both languages for each parallel document. We adopt the TF×IDF selection metric proposed by Yang and Luk [10], which measures the weight tw_{ij} of a term f_j (English or Chinese) in a parallel document d_i as:

$$tw_{ij} = tf_{ij} \times \log\left(\frac{N_P}{n_j} \times l_j\right) \tag{5}$$

where tf_{ij} is the term frequency of f_j in d_i, N_P is the total number of parallel documents in the corpus, n_j is the number of parallel documents in which f_j appears, and l_j is the length of f_j (where l_j denotes the number of English words if f_j is an English term or the number of Chinese characters if f_j is a Chinese term).

For each parallel document, the top k_{clt} English and k_{clt} Chinese terms with the highest TFIDF values (i.e., tw_{ij}) that simultaneously occur in more than δ_{DF} documents are selected for each parallel document. On the basis of the concept that relevant terms often co-occur in the same parallel documents, the co-occurrence analysis first measures the co-importance weight cw_{ijh} between terms f_j and f_h in the parallel document d_i as follows [10]:

$$cw_{ijh} = tf_{ijh} \times \log\left(\frac{N_P}{n_{jh}}\right) \tag{6}$$

where tf_{ijh} is the minimum of tf_{ij} and tf_{ih} in d_i, and n_{jh} is the number of parallel documents in which both f_j and f_h occur.

Finally, the relevance weights between f_j and f_h are computed asymmetrically as [10]:

$$rw_{jh} = \frac{\sum_{i=1}^{N_P} cw_{ijh}}{\sum_{i=1}^{N_P} tw_{ij}} \text{ and } rw_{hj} = \frac{\sum_{i=1}^{N_P} cw_{ijh}}{\sum_{i=1}^{N_P} tw_{ih}} \tag{7}$$

where rw_{jh} (or rw_{hj}) denotes the relevance weight from f_j to f_h (or from f_h to f_j).

After we estimate all directional statistical strengths between each pair of English and Chinese terms selected by the term extraction and selection step, we prune insignificant strengths. Specifically, if the statistical strength from a term in one language to a term in another language is less than a relevance threshold δ_{rw}, we remove the link. Upon completion of link pruning, we construct a statistical-based bilingual thesaurus from the input parallel corpus.

3.2 Feature Reinforcement and Selection for Master Catalog (for L_i)

This task is the core of the FR-PLCI technique. As we show in Figure 2, before performing a monolingual integration task for language L_i, the feature reinforcement and selection task (for the documents of L_i in the master catalog) selects representative features (in L_i) by taking into account not only the master documents in L_i but also the master documents in another language L_j, as well as the statistical-based bilingual thesaurus. Specifically, this task involves two major steps: feature extraction (for L_i and L_j) and feature reinforcement and selection (for L_i).

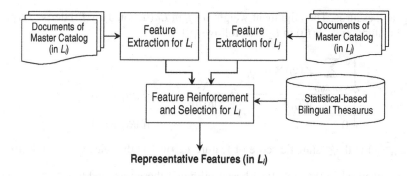

Fig. 2. Process of Feature Reinforcement and Selection (for L_i)

Feature Extraction: In this step, we extract features from the master documents in each language. As in the bilingual thesaurus construction task, we use the rule-based part-of-speech tagger [3, 4] and the noun phrase parser [7] to extract nouns and noun phrases as features from English documents of the master catalog. For the Chinese documents, we employ a hybrid of dictionary-based and statistical-based approach to extract Chinese terms from the master catalog [10, 11].

Feature Reinforcement and Selection: Following feature extraction, we assess the discriminating power of each feature in the master catalog (in L_i). In this study, we employ the χ^2 statistic metric for the target assessment purpose. We first derive the χ^2 statistic of the feature f_j relevant to each category C_i in the master catalog M and then calculate the overall χ^2 statistic of f_j for all categories in M according to the weighted average scheme [12]. That is,

$$\chi^2(f_j) = \sum_{C_i \in M} p(C_i) \times \chi^2(f_j, C_i) \tag{8}$$

where $p(C_i)$ is the number of documents in C_i divided by n (the total number of documents in M).

After the χ^2 statistic scores for all features in both languages are obtained, we reassess the discriminating power of a feature in one language by considering the discriminating power of its related features in another language. The reason for such cross-checking between two languages is that if a feature in one language and its related features in another language possess high χ^2 statistic scores, it is likely that the feature has greater discriminatory power. However, inconsistent assessments between two languages (i.e., χ^2 statistic score of a feature f_j is high in one language but the χ^2 statistic scores of f_j's related features are low in another language) result in lower confidence in the discriminatory power of the feature. In this study, we refer this cross-checking process as feature reinforcement.

Assume a total of N_1 features in language L_1 are extracted from the master documents in L_1 and N_2 features in L_2 are extracted from the master documents in L_2. Given a feature f_i in L_1, let $R(f_i)$ be the set of features in L_2 that have direct cross-lingual associations to f_i according to the previously constructed statistical-based bilingual thesaurus. The alignment weight for f_i in L_1 (denoted $aw(f_i)$) derived from its related features (i.e., $R(f_i)$) in L_2 is as follows [9]:

$$aw(f_i) = \begin{cases} \dfrac{\displaystyle\sum_{\forall g_j \in R(f_i)} \chi^2(g_j) \times rw_{g_j f_i}}{|R(f_i)|} \times \log\dfrac{N_2}{|R(f_i)|} & \text{if } |R(f_i)| \neq 0 \\ 0 & \text{if } |R(f_i)| = 0 \end{cases} \qquad (9)$$

where $\chi^2(g_j)$ is the χ^2 statistic score of feature g_j, $rw_{g_j f_i}$ is the relevance weight from g_j to f_i, as specified in the statistical-based bilingual thesaurus, and $\log\dfrac{N_2}{|R(f_i)|}$ is referred to as the inverse term frequency (ITF).

Subsequently, we use the following formula to arrive at the overall weight of a feature f_i by combining the weights of f_i derived from the master documents in both languages [9]:

$$w(f_i) = \alpha \times \chi^2(f_i) + (1-\alpha) \times aw(f_i) \qquad (10)$$

where α denotes the trade-off between the χ^2 statistic score of f_i in its original language and the alignment weight of f_i derived from the other language (where $0 \leq \alpha \leq 1$).

When $\alpha = 1$, the overall weight of a feature completely relies on the original language. In contrast, when $\alpha = 0$, the assessment of a feature depends completely on related features in another language. After the overall weights of all features for both languages are derived, we perform feature selection. For each language (L_i or L_j), we select the k features with the highest overall weights as the features to represent each master document of the respective language.

3.3 Monolingual Category Integration

Among the existing monolingual category integration techniques, ENB [2] is the most prevalent monolingual category integration technique. Therefore, in this study, we adopt ENB as the underlying algorithm in our FR-PLCI technique for mononlingual category integration. For each language L_i, we use the feature set selected in the feature reinforcement and selection task for the respective language as the basis for representing both the master documents (in L_i) and the source documents (in L_i), using the TFxIDF representation scheme. Subsequently, we apply the ENB algorithm to integrate the source documents (in L_i) into the master catalog (in L_i). This monolingual category integration process is repeated for both languages and the result forms an integrated catalog.

4 Data Collection and Evaluation Design

In this section, we describe our data collection and evaluation design, together with the metrics used to evaluate the effectiveness of the proposed FR-PLTC technique.

4.1 Data Collection

As mentioned previously, the construction of a statistical-based bilingual thesaurus requires parallel documents in two languages. News releases from Government Information Center, Hong Kong Special Administrative Region of The People's Republic of China (accessible at http://www.info.gov.hk/), were collected to construct a statistical-based bilingual thesaurus. Specifically, the parallel corpus collected for our experimental purpose contains 2,074 pairs of Chinese and English news presses.

Two additional monolingual document corpora also were collected to evaluate the effectiveness of the proposed FR-PLTC technique. These English and Chinese corpora also include news releases collected from the Government Information Center, Hong Kong. Both the English and Chinese corpora consist of 278 news releases related to eight categories (i.e., Commerce & Economy, Communication & IT, Culture & Leisure, Education, Health & Environment, Housing & Land, Security, and Transportation & Traffic). We merge these two monolingual corpora into a poly-lingual corpus for our evaluation purpose.

4.2 Performance Benchmark and Evaluation Design

As mentioned, the naïve approach to the PLCI problem is to divide this problem into several independent monolingual category integration problems. That is, given two poly-lingual catalogs, we perform a monolingual category integration task for each language based on the source documents and master documents of the respective language (i.e., not performing feature reinforcement). We adopt this naïve integration approach as our benchmark technique and refer it as the MnCI technique in this study.

This evaluation study focuses on investigating the effectiveness of FR-PLCI and MnCI under different categorization homogeneities between two catalogs to be integrated. Specifically, we simulate three scenarios, namely homogeneous, comparable and heterogeneous. To create a synthetic dataset for a particular scenario, the original eight categories in the Chinese and English corpus are considered as the "true" categories and serve as the foundation for synthetically generating the dataset that consists of a master and a source catalog. Specific organization of the master and source catalogs are then determined according to the scenario of choice. The organization of the catalogs for each scenario is described as follows:

1. *Homogeneous* scenario: To generate a synthetic data set whose master and source catalogs have homogeneous categorization schemes, we randomly select 50% of documents in the true categories of each monolingual corpus (English and Chinese) and assign them to the master catalog, and place the other 50% of documents in the true categories of each monolingual corpus into the source catalog..
2. *Comparable* scenario: To generate a synthetic dataset with comparable catalogs, the master and source catalogs initially are created in the same manner as that described for the homogeneous scenario. To simulate comparable categorization schemes, we randomly select some documents from a source category and re-assigned them to other source categories. Following Guassian-4 distribution, we first decompose each source category into a dominant subset and three minor subsets, which contain 68.2%, 27.2%, 4.3% and 0.3% of the documents in the original source category, respectively. All dominant subsets remain in their respective

(original) categories, while each minor subset is randomly merged with the dominant subset from another source category.

3. *Heterogeneous* scenario: In this scenario, the master and source catalogs are first generated as for the homogeneous scenario. Subsequently, the documents in the initial source catalog are randomly and evenly assigned to eight categories.

4.3 Evaluation Procedure and Criteria

To evaluate the effectiveness of FR-PLCI and MnCI, we randomly generate a synthetic data set for the integration scenario of choice. To avoid possible bias caused by random sampling and obtain a reliable evaluation performance estimate, we repeat the synthetic dataset generation and PLCI performance evaluation process 30 times for each integration scenario and evaluate the effectiveness of the PLCI techniques under investigation (i.e., FR-PLCI or its benchmark technique) by averaging the performance obtained from these 30 individual processes. We measure the effectiveness of PLCI on the basis of integration accuracy (*IA*), defined as the percentage of documents in the source catalog being correctly integrated into a master catalog.

5 Empirical Evaluation Results

In this section, we first describe the results of various parameter tuning experiments, and then discuss some important evaluation results.

5.1 Parameter-Tuning Results

We conduct a series of tuning experiments to determine the appropriate values for the parameters involved in the evaluation experiment. Our tuning experimental results show that setting the document frequency threshold δ_{DF} as 3, k_{clt} as 30, and the relevance threshold δ_{rw} as 0.15 is appropriate. Moreover, for the feature reinforcement and selection task involved in FR-PLCI, we set the tradeoff factor (i.e., α) as 0.1 when estimating the overall weight of each feature. Subsequently, we set the number of features for category integration, k, as 1000, for the FR-PLCI technique and its benchmark technique (i.e., MnCI).

Because ENB is the underlying algorithm of FR-PLCI as well as MnCI, we need to determine appropriate values for the parameter, w, of ENB for each integration scenario and each language. According to parameter tuning procedure used in [2, 8], we experimentally evaluate the performance of ENB with w in the range of {0, 1, 3, 10, 30, 100, 300, and 1000}. The results of parameter tuning for w for Chinese category integration in the various homogeneity scenarios are shown in Figure 3. As shown, the higher w is, the better performance the MnCI technique achieves. MnCI achieves the highest accuracy (i.e., 92.13%) when w is set as 1000 in the homogenous scenario. On the other hand, the higher w is, the better MnCI performs when w is less than 100. MnCI achieves the best performance (i.e., 70.75%) when w reaches 100 in the comparable scenario. Finally, in the heterogeneous scenario, the performance of MnCI is degenerating as w increases. Specifically, in this scenario, MnCI achieves the highest accuracy (i.e., 62.34%) when w is set as 0.

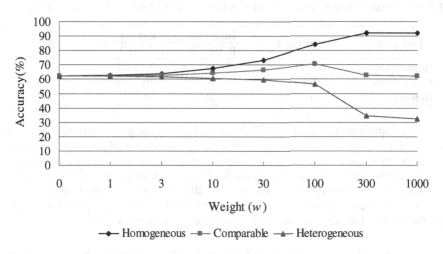

Fig. 3. Effects of *w* for MnCI (Chinese)

The parameter tuning results of English category integration resemble those of Chinese category integration in three different homogeneity scenarios. MnCI performs better as *w* increases and it reaches the best performance (i.e., 91.18%) when *w* is 1000 in the homogenous scenario. In the comparable scenario, the performance of MnCI improves as *w* increases from 0 to 100 and degrades as *w* further increases. In this specific integration scenario, MnCI reaches its best performance (i.e., 71.45%) when *w* is set as 100. Moreover, in the heterogeneous scenario, MnCI arrives at its best performance (i.e., 64.54%) when *w* is 0. According to our parameter tuning results depicted above, we summarize the appropriate settings for w for each language and each homogeneity scenario in Table 1.

5.2 Comparative Evaluation Results

Using the parameter values selected (shown in Table 1), we evaluate the MnCI and FR-PLCI techniques for each language (English and Chinese) in the three different scenarios (i.e., homogeneous, comparable and heterogeneous). The performance comparisons of MnCI and FR-PLCI for Chinese category integration are shown in Table 2. As shown, in all homogeneity scenarios, the integration accuracy achieved by FR-PLCI is higher than that attained by MnCI. Compared to MnCI, FR-PLCI improves the integration accuracy by 0.07% for the homogeneous scenario, 0.34% for the comparable scenario, and 0.51% for the heterogeneous scenario.

Table 1. Summary of Tuning Results for Weight *w* in Different Homogeneity Scenarios

Language	Homogeneity Scenario		
	Homogeneous	Comparable	Heterogeneous
Chinese	1000	100	0
English	1000	100	0

Table 2. Comparison of Effectiveness of MnCI and FR-PLCI for Chinese Category Integration

| Homogeneity | Weight (w) | Integration Accuracy | | Δ |
		FR-PLCI	MnCI	
Homogeneous	1000	92.20%	92.13%	0.07%
Comparable	100	71.09%	70.75%	0.34%
Heterogeneous	0	62.85%	62.34%	0.51%

The comparisons of MnCI and FR-PLCI for English category integration are shown in Table 3. FR-PLCI also achieves better performance than MnCI does for English category integration in all scenarios. Moreover, for each scenario, the performance differential between FR-PLCI and MnCI for English category integration is larger than that for Chinese category integration. Specifically, for English category integration, the difference between the two techniques is 2.59% for the homogeneous scenario, 3.31% for the comparable scenario, and 2.05% for the heterogeneous scenario.

Table 3. Comparison of Effectiveness of MnCI and FR-PLCI for English Category Integration

| Homogeneity | Weight (w) | Integration Accuracy | | Δ |
		FR-PLCI	MnCI	
Homogeneous	1000	93.77%	91.18%	2.59%
Comparable	100	74.76%	71.45%	3.31%
Heterogeneous	0	66.59%	64.54%	2.05%

Overall, our evaluation results suggest that our proposed FR-PLCI technique is more effective than the benchmark technique (i.e., MnCI) for both Chinese and English category integration, across different homogeneity scenarios investigated.

6   Conclusion and Future Research Directions

Because of the trend of globalization, the requirement for category integration has been extended from monolingual to poly-lingual settings. PLCI aims to integrate two catalogs, each of which consists of documents written in a mix of languages. In this study, we propose the FR-PLCI technique that takes into account the master documents of all languages when integrating source documents (in the source catalog) written in a specific language into the master catalog. Using the MnCI technique as a performance benchmark, our empirical evaluation results show that our proposed FR-PLCI technique outperforms MnCI in both English and Chinese integration tasks.

Some future research works related to this study include the following. First, in this study, we only adopt ENB as our underlying monolingual category integration algorithm of the proposed FR-PLCI technique. It will be interesting to extend our proposed FR-PLCI technique, using other monolingual category integration techniques (e.g., Cluster Shrinkage [13, 14], Co-Bootstrapping [13, 15], and Clustering-based Category Integration [8]) as its underlying algorithm. Second, the documents included in this study are only written in Chinese and English. It will be interesting to use documents written in other languages for evaluation purposes. In addition, it is also important to evaluate the effectiveness of our proposed technique in other application domains (e.g., using patent documents or web pages). Finally, we assume in this study that each document in either catalog belongs to one category only. However, in real-world situations, documents may belong to multiple categories simultaneously. Thus, it would be desirable to extend our proposed technique to deal with poly-lingual category integration involving multi-category documents.

Acknowledgement. This work was supported by the National Science Council of the Republic of China under the grant NSC 96-2416-H-218-010.

References

1. Agrawal, R., Bayardo, R., Srikant, R.: Athena: Mining-based Interactive Management of Text Databases. In: Zaniolo, C., Grust, T., Scholl, M.H., Lockemann, P.C. (eds.) EDBT 2000. LNCS, vol. 1777, pp. 365–379. Springer, Heidelberg (2000)
2. Agrawal, R., Srikant, R.: On Integrating Catalogs. In: Proceedings of the Tenth International Conference on World Wide Web, pp. 603–612. ACM Press, Hong Kong (2001)
3. Brill, E.: A Simple Rule-based Part of Speech Tagger. In: Proceedings of the Third Conference on Applied Natural Language Processing, pp. 152–155. Association for Computational Linguistics, Trento (1992)
4. Brill, E.: Some Advances in Rule-Based Part of Speech Tagging. In: Proceedings of the 12th National Conference on Artificial Intelligence (AAAI 1994), Seattle, WA, pp. 722–727 (1994)
5. Jing, Y., Croft, W.B.: An Association Thesaurus for Information Retrieval. Technical Report, Department of Computer Science, University of Massachusetts at Amherst (1994)
6. Stonebraker, M., Hellerstein, J.M.: Content Integration for E-business. In: Proceedings of the 2001 ACM SIGMOD International Conference on Management of Data, pp. 552–560. ACM Press, Santa Barbara (2001)
7. Voutilainen, A.: Nptool: A Detector of English Noun Phrases. In: Proceedings of Workshop on Very Large Corpora, Ohio, pp. 48–57 (1993)
8. Wei, C., Cheng, T.: A Clustering-Based Approach for Supporting Document-category Integration. In: Proceedings of 7th Pacific Asia Conference on Information Systems (PACIS), Adelaide, South Australia, pp. 1314–1326 (2003)
9. Wei, C., Shi, H., Yang, C.C.: Feature Reinforcement Approach to Poly-Lingual Text Categorization. In: Proceedings of International Conference on Asia Digital Library (2007)
10. Yang, C.C., Luk, J.: Automatic Generation of English/Chinese Thesaurus Based on a Parallel Corpus in Laws. Journal of the American Society for Information Science and Technology 54(7), 671–682 (2003)
11. Yang, C.C., Luk, J., Yung, S., Yen, J.: Combination and Boundary Detection Approach for Chinese Indexing. Journal of the American Society for Information Science 51(4), 340–351 (2000)
12. Yang, Y., Pedersen, J.O.: A Comparative Study on Feature Selection in Text Categorization. In: Proceedings of 14th International Conference on Machine Learning, pp. 412–420 (1997)
13. Zhang, D., Lee, W.S.: Learning to Integrate Web Taxonomies. Journal of Web Semantics 2(2), 131–151 (2004)
14. Zhang, D., Lee, W.S.: Web Taxonomy Integrating using Support Vector Machines. In: Proceedings of 13th International Conference on World Wide Web (WWW), New York, pp. 472–481 (2004)
15. Zhang, D., Lee, W.S.: Web Taxonomy Integration through Co-Bootstrapping. In: Proceedings of the 27th Annual International ACM SIGIR Conference on Research and Development in Information Retrieval, Sheffield, United Kingdom, pp. 410–417 (2004)

On Logic and Standards for Structuring Documents

David M. Eyers[1], Andrew J.I. Jones[2], and Steven O. Kimbrough[3]

[1] University of Cambridge,
Cambridge, United Kingdom
dme26@cl.cam.ac.uk
[2] King's College London,
London, United Kingdom
andrewji.jones@kcl.ac.uk
[3] University of Pennsylvania,
Philadelphia, Pennsylvania, USA
kimbrough@wharton.upenn.edu

Abstract. The advent of XML has been widely seized upon as an opportunity to develop document representation standards that lend themselves to automated processing. This is a welcome development and much good has come of it. That said, present standardization efforts may be criticized on a number of counts. We explore two issues associated with document XML standardization efforts. We label them (i) the dynamic point and (ii) the logical point. Our dynamic point is that in many cases experience has shown that the search for a final, or even reasonably permanent, document representation standard is futile. The case is especially strong for electronic data interchange (EDI). Our logical point is that formalization into symbolic logic is materially helpful for understanding and designing dynamic document standards.

Keywords: EDI, messaging, messaging standards, XML, logic.

1   Introduction

Structure affords automation. In large part for this reason, the advent of XML has been widely seized upon as an opportunity to develop document representation standards that lend themselves to automated processing. It is widely hoped that for commercial, legal, and regulatory purposes, representation of important documents in XML will reduce transaction costs, delay in decision making, and errors, while at the same time improve information discovery. We share this hope and agree it is substantially warranted. This is not to say that current XML-based document standardization efforts proceed having solved all pertinent problems. Just because there is very much to be gained from well-considered document standardization and structuring ventures, it is well to consider how the standardization is undertaken.

When done seriously, document XML standardization efforts have proven to be slow and costly, and to consume large amounts of time from experts who have

C. Weinhardt, S. Luckner, and J. Stößer (Eds.): WEB 2008, LNBIP 22, pp. 172–186, 2009.

ample scope for other applications of their knowledge. For this reason there is a strong impetus to "get it right, once and for all." Developing standards and changing standards for document representation are so expensive and slow that it seems imperative to make the initial investment that will suffice for establishing a permanent, or at least long-lasting, standard. This in turn encourages standards-developers to try to foresee all possible future needs for representation, which only increases the development costs.

In what follows we briefly explore (given space limitations) two issues associated with document XML standardization efforts. We label them (i) the dynamic point and (ii) the logical point. In a nutshell, our dynamic point is that in many cases experience has shown that the search for a final, or even reasonably permanent, document representation standard is futile. The case is especially strong for electronic data interchange (EDI). In consequence, the main example we use in what follows is the ISO 20022 standards (www.iso20022.org) which embody the best of current practice in XML representation of documents. Given that requirements will change, what is the best strategy for promulgating document representation standards?

Our logical point is to demonstrate a useful and very general technique for logical (in the sense of formal logic) representation of the sorts of documents now being represented in XML. There are a number of benefits to having such a logical representation. Among them is support for dynamically evolving document representation standards. The logical point complements the dynamic point.

2   Example: EDI Messages

SWIFT (Society for Worldwide Interbank Financial Telecommunication, www.swift.com) is a not-for-profit corporation owned by a consortium of international banks. Its primary business is to provide EDI (electronic data interchange) messaging services for international (and to some extent domestic) transactions and to serve as a trusted third party in these transactions.

> SWIFT is the industry-owned co-operative supplying secure, standardised messaging services and interface software to nearly 8,000 financial institutions in 206 countries and territories. SWIFT members include banks, broker-dealers and investment managers. The broader SWIFT community also encompasses corporates as well as market infrastructures in payments, securities, treasury and trade. [http://www.swift.com/index.cfm?item_id=43232]

As such, SWIFT owns and operates a worldwide telecommunications network and takes responsibility for specifying the messaging protocols for its network. SWIFT has moved to make its new generation of messaging protocols part of the ISO standardization process, in particular the ISO 20022, "UNIversal Financial Industry message scheme (UNIFI)," series (http://www.iso20022.org/). In this process, SWIFT has taken a leading role among peer participants. The current catalogue of UNIFI messages may be found at http://www.iso20022.org/

(accessed 2008-9-8). We focus (for convenience and without significant loss of generality) on the FIToFICustomerCreditTransferV01 message `http://www.iso20022.org/UNIFI_payments_messages.page` (accessed 2008-9-8). The purpose of the FIToFICustomerCreditTransferV01 message is described as follows:

> The FinancialInstitutionToFinancialInstitutionCustomerCreditTransfer message is sent by the debtor agent to the creditor agent, directly or through other agents and/or a payment clearing and settlement system. It is used to move funds from a debtor account to a creditor. [1, page 42]

The FIToFICustomerCreditTransfer message is composed of 2 building blocks [1, page 42]:

A. Group Header
This building block is mandatory and present once. It contains elements such as MessageIdentification, CreationDateAndTime.
B. Credit Transfer Transaction Information
This building block is mandatory and repetitive. It contains elements related to the debit and credit side of the transaction such as Creditor, CreditorAgent, Debtor, DebtorAgent.

```
<pacs.008.001.01>
<GrpHdr>
<MsgId>BBBB/061109-CBJ056</MsgId>
<CreDtTm>2006-11-09T10:13:00</CreDtTm>
<NbOfTxs>1</NbOfTxs>
<SttlmInf>
<SttlmMtd>CLRG</SttlmMtd>
<ClrSys>
<ClrSysId>CBJ</ClrSysId>
</ClrSys>
</SttlmInf>
<InstgAgt>
<FinInstnId>
<BIC>BBBBIE2D</BIC>
</FinInstnId>
</InstgAgt>
<InstdAgt>
<FinInstnId>
<BIC>CCCCIE2D</BIC>
</FinInstnId>
</InstdAgt>
</GrpHdr>
<CdtTrfTxInf>
```

Fig. 1. Header portion, followed by the beginning of the body, of an example FIToFICustomerCreditTransfer message

Each of the two building blocks are composed of *message elements*, specified by the standard. This structure applies to all of the ISO 20022 messages. The messages differ with respect to which message elements are present in the *header* (building block A) and the *body* (building block B). The FIToFICustomerCreditTransfer message standard identifies 31 message items in the header, 95 in the body.

The XML fragment in Figure 1 is from the header of an example FIToFICustomerCreditTransfer message [1, page 110]. The kind of structure evident in the figure is also present in the body of the FIToFICustomerCreditTransfer

message, and indeed of all the ISO 20022 messages. We focus on the fragment
in Figure 1 without essential loss of generality.

Message items, either in the header or in
the body, are fundamentally propositional.
Some are simple, others are complex; some
are required, others are optional. At bottom
an ISO 20022 message is a list of message
items, each of which has a propositional interpretation. Let us see how the representation can be made using logic. We illustrate
with an entirely typical example, Settlement-
Method. See Figure 3 from [1, page 49].

```
<SttlmInf>
<SttlmMtd>CLRG</SttlmMtd>
<ClrSys>
<ClrSysId>CBJ</ClrSysId>
</ClrSys>
</SttlmInf>
```

Fig. 2.   SettlementInformation
XML example

Propositionally, we can interpret Figure 3
[1, page 49] as specifying required use of a
proposition, SettlementInformation, having one required argument, Settlement-
Method, and 8 optional arguments, SettlementAccount, ClearingSystem, and so
on. The example in Figure 1 includes only one optional element, ClearingSystem,
as extracted in Figure 2. Unpacking this further, Figure 5 defines the standard
for SettlementMethod. The standard as we see identifies exactly four permitted
codes, each of which is interpreted as a proposition, described in the "Definition"
column of the table in Figure 5 [1, page 50].

Finally, Figure 6 [1, pages 50–1] constitutes the specification for the ClearingSystem element. Immediately following this we find the specification for
ClearingSystemIdentification. It begins with the passage in Figure 4 which is
followed by a table three pages long, where we learn that CBJ is the standardized code for the clearing system in Ireland.

In the notation of first-order logic, then, the XML fragment in Figure 2 might
be represented as *SttlmInf(CLRG, CBJ)*, it being understood that the first argument is for the required SettlementMethod, and the second is for the optional
ClearingSystem. This representation, however, is problematic. How are we to

Index	Or	Message Item	\<XML Tag>	Mult.
1.9		SettlementMethod	\<SttlmMtd>	[1..1]
1.10		SettlementAccount	\<SttlmAcct>	[0..1]
1.11		ClearingSystem	\<ClrSys>	[0..1]
1.14		InstructingReimbursementAgent	\<InstgRmbrsmntAgt>	[0..1]
1.15		InstructingReimbursementAgentAccount	\<InstgRmbrsmntAgtAcct>	[0..1]
1.16		InstructedReimbursementAgent	\<InstdRmbrsmntAgt>	[0..1]
1.17		InstructedReimbursementAgentAccount	\<InstdRmbrsmntAgtAcct>	[0..1]
1.18		ThirdReimbursementAgent	\<ThrdRmbrsmntAgt>	[0..1]
1.19		ThirdReimbursementAgentAccount	\<ThrdRmbrsmntAgtAcct>	[0..1]

Fig. 3. 1.8 SettlementInformation \<SttlmInf> Presence: [1..1] Definition: Specifies the
details on how the settlement of the transaction(s) between the instructing agent and
the instructed agent is completed. Type: This message item is composed of the above
SettlementInformation1 element(s).

handle optional arguments? One alternative would be to give our predicate an arity of 11 and allow nulls for the optional arguments. This is a possibility, albeit an unattractive one because adding new arguments over time (or removing them), changing the arity of the predicate, will be disruptive in any implementation.

With the well-known *binary representation* for predicates, we can re-represent any arity n predicate with $n+1$ binary (arity 2) predicates [2, pages 33–7]. For the case in point, SettlementInformation, we can generate $12 = 11+1$ binary predicates for representing settlement information. Eleven of these come directly from the ISO specification, Figure 3:

1.9. $SttlmMtd(\langle ID \rangle, \langle SttlmMtd \rangle)$

"The SettlementMethod of message $\langle ID \rangle$ is $\langle SttlmMtd \rangle$." $\langle ID \rangle$ is the message ID and $\langle SttlmMtd \rangle$ names the settlement method with permitted names specified as in Figure 5.

1.10. $SttlmAcct(\langle ID \rangle, \langle SttlmAcct \rangle)$

"The SettlementAccount of message $\langle ID \rangle$ is $\langle SttlmAcct \rangle$." $\langle SttlmAcct \rangle$ names the settlement account, whose specification is paragraph 1.10 of [1, page 50].

1.11. $ClrSys(\langle ID \rangle, \langle ClrSys \rangle)$

"The ClearingSystem of message $\langle ID \rangle$ is $\langle ClrSys \rangle$."

$\langle ClrSys \rangle$ names the clearing system, specification given in Figure 6.

And so on. The remaining predicate, number $n+1$, identifies the message and its type:

$$Message(\langle ID \rangle, FIToFICustomerCreditTransfer) \tag{1}$$

"Message $\langle ID \rangle$ is a *FIToFICustomerCreditTransfer* message." This information is, as it must be, already captured in the XML specification. For the example in Figure 1 we can see from `<MsgId>BBBB/061109-CBJ056</MsgId>` that the message ID is BBBB/061109-CBJ056 and from the standard [1, pages 43, 48] we see that `<MsgID>` is a required tag. Further, the standard specifies that the body (part B) of every FIToFI-CustomerCreditTransfer message contain at least one `<CdtTrfTxInf>...</CdtTrfTxInf>`, or CreditTrnsferTransactionInformation, block. It is this block or tag set that unambiguously identifies the XML message as a FIToFI-CustomerCreditTransfer. In consequence, *Message*($\langle ID \rangle$, *FIToFICustomerCreditTransfer*) can do double duty as predicate number $n+1$ for predicates in the body of the message.

1.12   ClearingSystemIdentification
 <ClrSysId> Presence: [1..1]
This message item is part of
choice 1.11 ClearingSystem.
Definition: Infrastructure through
which the payment instruction is
processed. Data Type: Code
One of the following
CashClearingSystem3Code
values must be used:

Fig. 4. ClearingSystemIdentification

Code	Name	Definition
CLRG	ClearingSystem	Settlement is done through a payment clearing system.
COVE	CoverMethod	Settlement is done through a cover payment.
INDA	InstructedAgent	Settlement is done by the agent instructed to execute a payment instruction.
INGA	InstructingAgent	Settlement is done by the agent instructing and forwarding the payment to the next party in the payment chain.

Fig. 5. 1.9 SettlementMethod `<SttlmMtd>` Presence: [1..1] Definition: Method used to settle the (batch of) payment instructions. Data Type: Code One of the above SettlementMethod1Code values must be used.

The move to binary predicates for representing the propositional structure of the XML specifications is very neat and works generally. There is, however, a complication, which can be illustrated through the SettlementInformation example. Our binary representation, above, of 1.10, SettlementAccount, was:

1.10. $SttlmAcct(\langle ID \rangle, \langle SttlmAcct \rangle)$

   "The SettlementAccount of message $\langle ID \rangle$ is $\langle SttlmAcct \rangle$." $\langle SttlmAcct \rangle$ names the settlement account, whose specification is paragraph 1.10 of [1, page 50].

The complication is that, unlike SettlementMethod and ClearingSystem which are specified as simple lists, SettlementAccount, like other items, is specified in the standard as a complex entity. It contains four message items, one of which is required. See Figure 7. What are we to do? The move to binary predicates works again. We can think of SettlementAccount as prima facie a predicate with arity 4. So, we re-represent it with $4+1 = 5$ binary predicates. First, we require that $\langle SttlmAcct \rangle$ in 1.10 be a new, uniquely defined, arbitrary ID, in the same way that the message ID is. Then our $n = 4$ *structural* predicates are created as before, but now using Figure 7.

1. $Identification(\langle SttlmAcct \rangle, \langle Id \rangle)$

   "The Identification of entity $\langle SttlmAcct \rangle$ is $\langle Id \rangle$." $\langle SttlmAcct \rangle$ is an Entity ID and $\langle Id \rangle$ names the identification as specified as in Figure 7.

And similarly for the other three message items of Figure 7. Our fifth, or *typing*, predicate here is then:

− $Entity(\langle SttlmAcct \rangle, FIToFICustomerCreditTransfer)$ "Entity with ID $\langle SttlmAcct \rangle$ is a *SettlementAccount*."

Arbitrarily complex XML standards for documents may be re-expressed in binary predicate form.

We are now in position to discuss the dynamic problem, the problem of change, for document representation. We do so under three headings—(i) fixing reference, (ii) propositional structure, and (iii) constraints—and in the context of our particular examples, now laid out. We will, for the most part, focus on the ISO 20022 FIToFICustomerCreditTransfer message. The points we make will generalize.

Index	Or	Message Item	`<XML Tag>`	Mult.	Represent./ Type
1.12	{ Or	ClearingSystemIdentification	`<ClrSysId>`	[1..1]	Code
1.13	Or}	Proprietary	`<Prtry>`	[1..1]	Text

Fig. 6. 1.11 ClearingSystem `<ClrSys>` Presence: [0..1] Definition: Specification of a pre-agreed offering between clearing agents or the channel through which the payment instruction is processed. Type: This message item is composed of one of the above ClearingSystemIdentification1Choice element(s).

Or	Message Item	`<XML Tag>`	Mult.	Represent./ Type
	Identification	`<Id>`	[1..1]	
	Type	`<Tp>`	[0..1]	
	Currency	`<Ccy>`	[0..1]	Code
	Name	`<Nm>`	[0..1]	Text

Fig. 7. 1.10 SettlementAccount `<SttlmAcct>` Presence: [0..1] Definition: A specific purpose account used to post debit and credit entries as a result of the transaction. Type: This message item is composed of the above CashAccount7 elements.

3   Fixing Reference

FIToFICustomerCreditTransfer messages must, as must messages generally, refer to various things, including financial institutions, accounts, dates, currencies, and so on. The message definition report [1] devotes pages 445–500 to the task of identifying referring expressions and providing instructions for how they are composed and what they mean. This is under the heading "Message Item Types." We focus on just a few examples, which are representative.

Figure 8 (after [1, page 463]) provides instructions for identifying (naming or referring to) a financial institution. A financial institution identifier must be one of five types of expression. First is BIC (Bank Identifier Code, "as described in the latest version of the standard ISO 9362"). Note that this device affords changes in the list of permitted BICs. If ISO 9362 changes the list, then ISO 20022 automatically incorporates the changes. This is *not* to say that there is any automated support for accommodating changes in the list of BICs. It is up to the maintainers of message processing application software to keep it current with ISO 9362. (See paragraph 2.1.3, [1, page 463].)

The second way Figure 8 gives of referring to a financial institution is via a ClearingSystemMemberIdentification (see paragraph 2.1.4, pages 463–4). The instructions are basically to use valid identifiers defined by the accepted clearing system members, but there is no authority given for who is an accepted clearing system member. What if the list changes? The third possibility for referring to a financial institution is to give its name and address (see paragraph 2.1.7, page 464). This device will certainly allow a message sender to refer to an otherwise unnamed financial institution. The problem is that the message receiver will

Ref	Or	Message Item	<XML Tag>	Mult.	Represent./Type
2.1.3	{Or	BIC	<BIC>	[1..1]	Identifier
2.1.4	Or	ClearingSystemMemberIdentification	<ClrSysMmbId>	[1..1]	
2.1.7	Or	NameAndAddress	<NmAndAdr>	[1..1]	
2.1.18	Or	ProprietaryIdentification	<PrtryId>	[1..1]	
2.1.21	Or}	CombinedIdentification	<CmbndId>	[1..1]	

Fig. 8. 2.1.2 FinancialInstitutionIdentification <FinInstnId> Presence: [1..1] Definition: Unique and unambiguous identifier of a financial institution, as assigned under an internationally recognised or proprietary identification scheme. Type: This message item is composed of one of the [above] FinancialInstitutionIdentification5Choice element(s).

normally (or at least often) have to resort to manual processing in order to validate the named institution. What if the named institution is one that is on a list of prohibited entities, say for legal or policy reasons? The fourth possibility is for the sender and receiver to agree on naming an otherwise unnamed institution and to use that convention. If only the sender and receiver are interested in referring to this new institution, perhaps this device is efficient. However, a series of bilateral agreements is quite an inefficient way to introduce a commonly used name. Finally, the fifth possibility is to use a combination of the above. Its drawbacks are also a combination of the those for the above.

Consider now a sixth possibility. At the time of promulgation of the ISO 20022 standard (and indeed nearly any standard) it is impossible to know all the referring expressions that will be needed by users of the standard. ISO 20022 recognizes this partially, with its incorporation of standards maintained by other bodies, e.g., the BICs. This, however, merely displaces the problem of standards revision. Further, as we have seen, there remains a recognized need to introduce names not covered by the BICs (or other standards-based lists, e.g., Figure 5). The sixth possibility is to move the ISO 20022 standard to a higher level of abstraction and to introduce a procedure for adding new names. Constraints on any such procedure are that it identify the referents of new names sufficiently clearly that participants will be willing to use them in a legally binding way, that automated introduction (or removal) of the names is facilitated, and that any disputes arising can be unproblematically resolved.

Here in outline is one way to do this. The standard itself could describe a procedure for adding and removing names (or other referring expressions) not explicitly included in the standard. Such a procedure might rely on a trusted third party to publish on the Web names and necessary descriptive information (What does the name actually refer to?), subject to a basic review for adequacy. Once published, a name and its descriptive information would have unique URIs (Uniform Resource Identifiers). The sender of a message invoking a new name would—as required by the standard—use the name in conjunction with its URI.

The receiver of such a message could monitor the posted names and validate them as they are posted. So informed the receiving application software could in many cases proceed to complete the processing without raising an exception. In other cases, the software could raise an exception and in doing so report on the name's information posted by the trusted third party. Further details are needed, of course, and many variants are possible. Our point is that procedures of this sort can plausibly be devised to meet the problem of automated support for referring to a changing list of entities. We note that the namespace conventions of XML and the URI mechanism of the Web are well suited to support the kind of procedure we have just outlined.

4   Propositional Structure

It will be helpful to work with a simplified, abstract model of an ISO 20022 message. Again, but without loss of generality, we will use the FIToFICustomer-Credit Transfer message as a running example. Recall that the message is composed of "message items" and that these are of two kinds: those in the group header, of which there are 31 types, and those in the body of the message (the "Credit Transfer Transaction Information" section), of which are there 95 types. We abstract from this and represent a message as follows:

$$\langle (H_1, H_2, \ldots, H_m), (B_1, B_2, \ldots, B_n) \rangle \tag{2}$$

InstructedAgentRule
If GroupHeader/InstructedAgent is present, then
CreditTransferTransactionInformation/InstructedAgent
is not allowed.

InstructingAgentRule
If GroupHeader/InstructingAgent is present, then
CreditTransferTransactionInformation/InstructingAgent
is not allowed.

TotalInterbankSettlementAmount1Rule
If GroupHeader/TotalInterbankSettlementAmount is present, then all occurrences of
CreditTransferTransactionInformation/Interbank-SettlementAmount must have the same currency as the currency of
GroupHeader/TotalInterbankSettlementAmount.

TotalInterbankSettlementAmount2Rule
If GroupHeader/TotalInterbankSettlementAmount is present,
then it must equal the sum of all occurrences of
CreditTransferTransactionInformation/Interbank-SettlementAmount.

Fig. 9.   FIToFICustomerCreditTransferV01   example constraints spanning header and body

Let us call expression (2) the ISO very-high-level format. The 31 header message items in a FIToFICustomer-CreditTransfer message are represented by the H_is and the 95 body message items (for a single transfer; we are simplifying) are represented by the B_js.

Articulating this format, we can consider each message item as a logical proposition with arguments, all of which resolve to names. Each proposition has a fixed (but here unspecified) number of arguments, which we indicate with vector notation: $\boldsymbol{h}_i$ for header element H_i and $\boldsymbol{b}_j$ for body element B_j. This leads to expression (3), the ISO high-level format:

$$\langle(H_1(\boldsymbol{h}_1),\ldots,H_m(\boldsymbol{h}_m)),(B_1(\boldsymbol{b}_1),B_2(\boldsymbol{b}_2),\ldots,B_n(\boldsymbol{b}_n))\rangle \qquad (3)$$

Articulating further, let us assume that each predicate element has been re-expressed in binary form. Call this the *ISO binary-high-level format*:

$$\langle(H_1(h_{1,1},h_{1,2}),\ldots,H_{m_b}(h_{m_b,1},h_{m_b,2})), \qquad (4)$$

$$(B_1(b_{1,1},b_{1,2}),\ldots,B_{n_b}(b_{n_b,1},b_{n_b,2}))\rangle \qquad (5)$$

This merely formalizes and makes explicit points in the examples given above.

All three formats, very-high-level, high-level and binary-high-level, are structures that collect propositional expressions, as indicated. They are not *logical* formats unless we specify the nature of the structured collection. Just what is a list of propositions? It happens that the FIToFICustomerCreditTransfer message can be understood as a conjunction of its constituent (propositional) message items. So far as we are aware, this also holds for all of the other messages in ISO 20022.[1] This leads to the ISO *binary-high-level logical format*—

$$(H_1(h_{1,1},h_{1,2}) \wedge \ldots \wedge H_{m_b}(h_{m_b,1},h_{m_b,2})) \wedge \qquad (6)$$

$$(B_1(b_{1,1},b_{1,2}) \wedge \ldots \wedge B_{n_b}(b_{n_b,1},b_{n_b,2})) \qquad (7)$$

which is indeed quite a simple structure. A message is representable as a conjunction of propositions, each constituent proposition is a binary predicate for which name constants have been supplied.

We are now in position to address a resolution of our dynamic point, the need to have a systematic approach to accommodating change. Suppose first, as before, that we wish to be able to add names to the permitted list of ClearingSystemIdentifications (or to the list of 4 SettlementMethods). One way this could be done would be to designate *in the protocol* a mechanism for adding names. At a syntactic level the XML that ISO 20022 uses for its messages would easily support such mechanisms; all XML tags can be made globally unambigous by pairing them with an XML namespace Universal Resource Indicator[2] (URI).

The mechanism for adding ClearingSystemIdentifications names, could specify a trusted third party (perhaps SWIFT in this case) whose responsibility it is to

---

[1] For present purposes we are ignoring issues having to do with sentence complexity, speech acts, and intensionality. These can, we believe, be satisfactorily addressed [3,4], but to do so would divert us from our main points. Also, the ISO 20022 standards permit repetition of items in the message body. One credit transfer header will, for example, cover multiple credit transfer transactions, all in one message. Because this is not material to our points, we simplify.

[2] This is actually only true in this case because all ISO 20022 messages will be validated against a schema, and thus will include the XML namespace definition required to pair XML tags with the namespace URI.

maintain a Web site in which permitted names can be listed and their definitions and other characteristics stated. Any recognized member of the community (here, e.g., a member of SWIFT) could post a new name and associated metadata. The trusted third party would be responsible for basic validation (completeness, non-duplication, etc.). Two communicants wishing to use a new name now simply need to augment the argument of `<ClrSys>` with the new name defined by URI, such that the new name (along with version information) falls within the set of names owned by the trusted third party[3].

InstructedReimbursementAgentAccountRule
If InstructedReimbursementAgent is not present, then InstructedReimbursementAgentAccount is not allowed.

InstructingReimbursementAgentAccountRule
If InstructingReimbursementAgent is not present, then InstructingReimbursementAgentAccount is not allowed.

SettlementMethod1Rule
If SettlementMethod is equal to INDA or INGA then:
- SettlementAccount may be present;
- ReimbursementAgent(s) is(are) not allowed;
- ClearingSystem is not allowed.

SettlementMethod2Rule
If SettlementMethod is equal to COVE then:
- SettlementAccount is not allowed;
- Reimbursement agent(s) must be present;
- ClearingSystem is not allowed.

SettlementMethod3Rule
If SettlementMethod is equal to CLRG then:
- SettlementAccount is not allowed;
- Reimbursement agent(s) is(are) not allowed;
- ClearingSystem must be present.

Fig. 10. FIToFICustomerCreditTransferV01 SettlementInformation example constraints

The mechanism, just outlined again, for adding new names can also be used for adding new predicates. As in the case of names, each predicate could be expressed as a URI, a trusted third party could host and maintain a Web site for these URIs, and rules governing the use of this mechanism could be specified as part of a higher-level protocol.

We note that there are important advantages in publicly (at least for the relevant community) posting new names and predicates, along with their metadata. In virtue of being public other members of the community may critique the entry and make suggestions, and may use the entry if so desired. Further, a message sender might use a new entry in a message without notifying the recipient. Being unprepared to process the new name or predicate, the recipient's software may easily be designed to flag an exception and report on the nature of the unfamiliar entry by following the namespace indicator.

5 Message Constraints

The ISO 20022 standards are explicit and clear in articulating constraints for the messages governed by these standards. For example, the rule "Within an

---

[3] Here ownership of a name is taken as synonymous with ownership of the URI's domain name.

ChargesInformationGuideline
The repetitive ChargesInformation should contain all separate information on charges amount and which party has taken the charges for all agents along the payment chain.
UltimateCreditorGuideline
UltimateCreditor may only be present if different from Creditor.
UltimateDebtorGuideline
UltimateDebtor may only be present if different from Debtor.

Fig. 11. FIToFICustomerCreditTransferV01 Credit-TransferTransactionInformation guidelines

order message, the requested delivery date shall be a future date" is given as an example in a document overviewing the standards [5, page 9]. Officially, message constraint rules are presented in the standards as part of the narrative, which we have been discussing, that also describes the message items. Again, we advert to the FIToFICustomerCreditTransferV01 message for illustration, and do so without loss of generality vis-à-vis the ISO 20022 standards. Three examples follow. First, as noted above, a FIToFICustomerCreditTransferV01 message has two parts: the header, identified by the GroupHeader or `<GrpHdr>` XML tag; and the body, identified by the CreditTransferTransactionInformation or `<CdtTrfTxInf>` tag. See Figure 1. The specified constraints spanning both the header and the body are shown in Figure 9 [1, pages 42–3]. As our second example we return to the SettlementInformation message item, Figure 3. Associated with it are the constraints shown in Figure 10 [1, pages 49–50].

These examples (Figures 9 and 10) are examples of what ISO 20022 calls *rules*. They are constraints that must be satisfied. The FIToFICustomerCredit-TransferV01 standard also lists a number of *guidelines*.

These are constraints that it is recommended be satisfied. Figure 11 displays some examples [1, page 62]. Together, Figures 9–11 constitute a comprehensive illustration of constraint features in ISO 20022. The subject of constraints for handling documents—notably legal documents, contract documents (such as EDI messages), and regulatory documents (such as environmental or financial reporting documents)—is large and complex. Prior work on database constraints, e.g., [6], is directly relevant and provides a payoff for logical representation of document structures and constraints, as we have advocated. We limit our comments to three points and even these, for reasons of space and focus, can only be adumbrated.

(1) The Dynamic Point. We have observed that permitted names and predicates ("message items" in ISO 20022; typically tag pairs in XML) inevitably change over time, and have concluded that in such cases document representation standards (or instructions) need to be designed to accommodate this fact. Further in the case of names and predicates, we have argued that effective higher-order standards (instructions) can be designed, in conjunction with XML's namespace conventions, that go far to meet the demand for dynamic specification of document representation. This mechanism, we believe, can also be made to work in meeting the need for dynamic specification of constraints.

(2) The Logical Point. Our logical point with respect to documents proper has been that document structuring protocols now in use (e.g., by ISO 20022) lend themselves straightforwardly to representation in formal logic. Such representation has a number of uses including conceptual clarity and facilitation of dynamic standards. We make the same point with regard to constraints: they are naturally represented in formal logic; such representation is useful for a number of purposes, including facilitation of dynamic standards, testing for consistency, and for drawing upon prior work on the logic of database constraints.

(3) The Scope Point. Constraints and constraint processing are very broadly useful, yet the scope of specified constraints is generally fairly narrow. The ISO 20022 constraints are entirely representative in this regard (although it represents in our opinion the best of current practice). Our scope point with respect to constraints is two faceted. First, the distinction (in ISO 20022) between rules and guidelines is a good one, but can be abstracted and generalized for broader application. Second, the scope of useful application of constraints pertaining to structured documents is much broader than realized in existing standards, e.g. ISO 20022. We will now briefly elaborate on the logical point and the scope point.

On the logical point, we observe that the example rules in ISO 20022, Figures 9 and 10, can be represented rather straightforwardly in first-order logic. Consider the InstructedAgentRule (top of Figure 9). Let $InstructedAgent^H$ ($InstructedAgent^B$) be a binary predicate belonging to the header (body) in the *binary-high-level logical format*, and $Message(\langle ID \rangle, FIToFICustomerCreditTransfer)$ be an identifying constituent for any FIToFICustomerCreditTransfer message (see expression (1) above). Then a simple way to represent the InstructedAgentRule is as follows.

$$\forall x \forall y \{ (Message(x, FIToFICustomerCreditTransfer) \wedge \tag{8}$$

$$InstructedAgent^H(x, y)) \rightarrow \neg \exists z\, InstructedAgent^B(x, z) \} \tag{9}$$

Rendered into (stilted) English we have, "For any FIToFICustomerCreditTransfer message, x, if there is any y that is the *Instructed-Agent^H* of x, then there is no z that is the *InstructedAgent^B* of x." The pattern in evidence here can be made to apply to all of the examples in Figures 9 and 10.[4] We note that expression (9) embodies one of several alternatives for representing the constraint formally. For present purposes one representation is enough. The salient point about the InstructedAgentRule (and indeed all rule constraints in ISO 20022), taken as a systems specification rule, is that it is aimed at preventing messages from being in certain states. It is, in the terminology of [7], a *regimentation* approach to constraints, in distinction to what we might call a *repair* approach.

---

[4] A real world implementation may require inclusion of the closed-world assumption. This and many other matters must be deferred for lack of space.

Under regimentation, appropriate for hard constraints, the system (here the message) is absolutely prohibited from violating the constraint. Refusal of database systems to add records with keys duplicating existing records is an example of regimentation. Expression (9) does *not* have a logical form appropriate for soft constraints. For these, regimentation is (normally) not the right policy to enforce. Instead, soft constraints are understood as violable, with violations typically calling for invocation of a response policy. The system may be in violation of a soft constraint, but if so some sort of repair is called for.

The ISO 20022 guidelines, Figure 11, are naturally modeled as soft constraints, constraints whose violation is possible (unlike hard constraints) but nonetheless undesirable (see [6] for an exploration of this concept in the context of database constraints). One issue this raises, both for theory and practice, is the complicating problem of what to do in the event of violation of soft constraints. ISO 20022 has little to say on the matter. In practice there may well be cascaded or otherwise related soft constraints that come into play. This raises the vexing theoretical problem known as contrary-to-duty obligations. See [8] for a review and an original treatment of the problem. Interpreting the documents and their constraints logically yields the prospect of drawing upon and applying to practice the very considerable body of work in this area.

Regarding the scope point, as we have noted the ISO 20022 rules are examples of, or special cases of, what are known as *hard* (or *inviolable*) constraints. Similarly, guidelines are naturally thought of as instances of *soft* (or *violable*) constraints. So generalized, hard and soft constraints have applications and uses for structured document processing that go well beyond what is delineated in, for example, the ISO 20022 standards. These constraints are understandably directed at guaranteeing internally valid messages; they are not aimed at supporting business rules or processing policies. Nor are they aimed at guaranteeing valid sequences of messages. They are, in the terminology of [6], *static* constraints in distinction to *transition* constraints. Constraints are useful, even essential, for many purposes. Providing a synoptic account of and approach to constraint representation and processing is an important agenda item for future research.

6   Conclusion

We conclude with a very brief summary, followed by remarks on the larger significance of the points we are making. In summary, there is a permanent need to structure business documents so that they can be communicated as messages that are fully machine processable. EDI is a but one example of this fact. The structuring and formal specification of EDI (and other) documents has proved to be an expensive and time-consuming venture, whose results have rarely been fully satisfactory. The recent efforts to use XML as a representation framework for structured business documents does represent a technical advance, even if it has failed to address the underlying difficulties. All of these points are, we assume, widely known and largely uncontroversial.

We have focused on the dynamic problem, the problem of managing change in document structuring standards, as a key to treating the outstanding problems.

If dynamic standards could be accommodated, then many of the recognized problems, and costs, could be ameliorated. In turn, we think that well-designed *logical* representation of business documents facilitates change management in the standards. We have illustrated our reasons for thinking so by examining in some detail (albeit shortened by space limitations) an ISO EDI standard that represents, in our view, the best of current practice. We believe the illustration generalizes. If indeed it does, then we have succeeded in giving (an outline of) how standards for business documents may be expressed in formal logic.

Now two larger points. First, we have said little about implementation. That is not the subject of this paper. While logical representation of standards may be very useful, implementing the standards in a logical representation programming language is hardly required. Nothing we have said militates against using XML. We also note that RDF maps closely to the basis in binary predicates we have advocated. This will facilitate real-world implementation. Second, the job of carefully articulating logical representations of business documents is very appropriately done by IS *academics.* Herein lies important work.

References

1. ISO 20022, Payments standards – clearing and settlement (October 2006), http://www.iso20022.org/index.cfm?item_id=60053 (accessed 2007-1-7). File: Payments_Standards-Clearing_and_Settlement_updated.pdf
2. Kowalski, R.: Logic for problem solving. Artificial Intelligence Series, vol. 7. North Holland, New York (1979)
3. Kimbrough, S.O.: Reasoning about the objects of attitudes and operators: Towards a disquotation theory for representation of propositional content. In: Proceedings of ICAIL 2001, International Conference on Artificial Intelligence and Law (2001)
4. Kimbrough, S.O.: A note on interpretations for federated languages and the use of disquotation. In: Gardner, A. (ed.) Proceedings of the Tenth International Conference on Artificial Intelligence and Law (ICAIL 2005), Bologna, Italy, In cooperation with ACM SIGART and The American Association for Artificial Intelligence, June 6–11, 2005, pp. 10–19 (2005)
5. ISO 20022, Financial services — UNIversal Financial Industry message scheme — part 1: Overall methodology and format specifications for inputs to and outputs from the iso 20022 repository (December 2004), http://www.iso20022.org/index.cfm?item_id=42953 (accessed 2007-1-10). Reference number ISO 20022-1:2004(E)
6. Carmo, J., Jones, A.J.I.: Deontic database constraints, violation and recovery. Studia Logica 57, 139–165 (1996)
7. Jones, A.J.I., Sergot, M.J.: On the characterization of law and computer systems: The normative systems perspective. In: Meyer, J.-J.C., Wieringa, R.J. (eds.) Deontic Logic in Computer Science: Normative System Specification, pp. 275–307. John Wiley & Sons, Chichester (1993)
8. Carmo, J., Jones, A.J.I.: Deontic logic and contrary-to-duties. In: Gabbay, D., Guenthner, F. (eds.) Handbook of Philosophical Logic, vol. 8, pp. 265–343. Kluwer Academic Publishers, Dordrecht (2002)

Patent Analysis for Supporting Merger and Acquisition (M&A) Prediction: A Data Mining Approach

Chih-Ping Wei[1], Yu-Syun Jiang[2], and Chin-Sheng Yang[3]

[1] Inst. of Service Science, National Tsing Hua University, Hsinchu, Taiwan, R.O.C.
[2] Inst. of Technology Management, National Tsing Hua University, Hsinchu, Taiwan, R.O.C.
[3] Dept. of Information Management, Yuan-Ze University, Chung-Li, Taiwan, R.O.C.
cpwei@mx.nthu.edu.tw, aloha6131@gmail.com,
csyang@saturn.yzu.edu.tw

Abstract. M&A plays an increasingly important role in the contemporary business environment. Companies usually conduct M&A to pursue complementarity from other companies for preserving and/or extending their competitive advantages. For the given bidder company, a critical first step to the success of M&A activities is the appropriate selection of target companies. However, existing studies on M&A prediction incur several limitations, such as the exclusion of technological variables in M&A prediction models and the omission of the profile of the respective bidder company and its compatibility with candidate target companies. In response to these limitations, we propose an M&A prediction technique which not only encompasses technological variables derived from patent analysis as prediction indictors but also takes into account the profiles of both bidder and candidate target companies when building an M&A prediction model. We collect a set of real-world M&A cases to evaluate the proposed technique. The evaluation results are encouraging and will serve as a basis for future studies.

Keywords: Merger and Acquisition (M&A), M&A Prediction, Patent Analysis, Data Mining, Ensemble Learning.

1 Introduction

Merger and Acquisition (M&A) refers to the process of merging or acquiring all or parts of other companies' property rights under certain conditions in order to have the controlling rights [17], and is a critical business behavior to pursue complementarity between companies from different dimensions such as resource, channel, brand, and technology [2], [9], [19], [20]. Proper M&A behavior has the benefit of changing the market structure and increasing market power, generating economies of scale and other synergies, having tax advantage, or serving managerial ambitions [6]. M&A plays an increasingly important role in the highly competitive business environment and is a major tool that companies adopt to sustain or even extend their competitive advantages. According to the report conducted by Thomson Financial[1], the volume of

---

[1] http://www.tfsd.com/marketing/banker_r2/HomeWelcome.asp

C. Weinhardt, S. Luckner, and J. Stößer (Eds.): WEB 2008, LNBIP 22, pp. 187–200, 2009.

worldwide announced M&As during 2007 reached US$4.5 trillion, a 24.2% increase over the previous record set in 2006. Even the volume of completed M&As reached a 23.9% increase from US$3.0 trillion to US$3.8 trillion between 2006 and 2007.

The motivation of M&A can be diverse but the goals are similar, i.e., to assist companies to strengthen their weaknesses and to consolidate their strengths. However, in contrast with the intended goals, M&A frequently results in market-share losses, skimpier profits, and in long term, loss money for shareholders [20]. For example, according to a study of 150 mergers with values greater than US$500 million in the 1990s by Mercer Management, 50% of M&A cases were failures judged by their effect on stockholders wealth after three years. Another study by Sirower [16] found that of 168 deals analyzed, roughly two-thirds of M&As destroyed value for shareholders [16]. To increase the success of M&A activities, the critical first step for a bidder company is to identify suitable target companies that have resources complementary to those of the bidder company.

Given a bidder company, M&A prediction deals with the selection of target companies that have resources complementary to those of the bidder company. As mentioned, it is the critical first step of an M&A activity because an inappropriate selection likely leads to the failure of this M&A activity. M&A prediction is also important from the perspective of possible target companies (i.e., those companies that are possible to be acquired or merged by bidder companies). For example, M&A prediction can help startup companies assess their possibility of being acquired or merged and who are the possible bidder companies. Such assessment will facilitate startup companies to develop appropriate strategies for improving their possibility of being acquired or merged and/or increasing economic benefits to the shareholders of the startup companies obtained from future M&A activities. In addition, M&A prediction can also be valuable for venture capitals to hunt for investment targets. For venture capitals, the first-rate investment targets are those who have the potential for growing rapidly in the very near future. An important indicator for evaluating the growing potential of a company is the probability of being merged or acquired, because M&A targets are generally those that have unique resources or superior solutions for emerging techniques.

M&A prediction has received much research attention [1], [6], [10], [13], [15], [17]. Most of prior studies mainly employ financial and managerial variables as indicators on constructing their M&A prediction models. However, prior studies incur some limitations. First, the absence of including technological variables may limit the scenarios where M&A prediction can be applied. M&A activities are especially critical for those high-tech industries, because they often use M&As to acquire state-of-the-art technologies or rapidly expand their R&D capabilities. Thus, most of the existing M&A prediction studies may not effectively be applied to high-tech industries in which the technological-oriented competitive strategy prevails. Second, most of existing studies concentrate on identifying candidate M&A targets without considering the profile of the bidder company under discussion [7]. Such M&A prediction can support the assessment of the probability of a company being acquired or merged, but who are likely to be bidder companies is not a concern in the assessment. Consequently, M&A prediction models developed by prior studies may not be effective because the profile of the respective bidder company and its compatibility with a candidate target company are not taken into consideration.

In response to the aforementioned limitations of existing M&A prediction studies, we propose an M&A prediction technique that not only incorporates technological variables as prediction indicators but also takes into account the profiles of two companies (where one being the possible bidder company and another being the candidate target company) and their compatibility. Specifically, in this study, we employ patent analysis to derive technological variables for M&A prediction. Due to the properties of novelty and exclusion of patents, we believe that patents are an excellent source for evaluating the technological capability of a company. The remainder of the paper is organized as follows. Section 2 reviews literature relevant to this study. In Section 3, we depict the detailed design of our proposed patent-based M&A prediction technique. Subsequently, we describe our experimental design and discuss important evaluation results in Section 4. Finally, we conclude in Section 5 with a summary and some future research directions.

2 Literature Review

In this section, we review existing studies on M&A prediction. Several prior studies have concentrated on M&A prediction and most of them adopt financial and managerial variables as indicators for M&A prediction. Common financial variables employed include firm size [1], [6], [10], [13], [17], market to book value ratio (or Tobin's Q) [6], [10], [15], [17], cash flow [1], [6], [15], [17], debt to equity ratio [6], [15], [17], and price to earning ratio [10], [17]. Other financial variables, such as cost to income ratio [13], net loans to total asset ratio [13], capital expenditures to total asset ratio [15], growth [13], outperformance [6], return on average asset [13], and tax shield effect [17], are also used in some prior studies. Besides the financial variables, managerial variables, such as management inefficiency [1], [10], resource richness [10], industry variations [10], and relevance degree of the business boundaries [17], represent another category of indicators adopted by existing M&A prediction studies.

As for the analysis methods applied to learn an M&A prediction model, logistic regression is the most common one [1], [6], [10], [13], [15]. Discriminant analysis and rule induction can also be found in some prior studies [15].

The results of existing M&A prediction studies are promising and beneficial for M&A research and practices. However, there are some limitations that may degrade the effectiveness or restrict the applicability of the prior studies. First, most of existing M&A prediction studies consider only financial and/or managerial variables. Given the growing importance of technology and innovation to strategic competitiveness, it is essential for bidder companies to pay attention to technological issues in their M&A decision making [9]. Appropriate assessment of the technological capabilities of bidder and target companies in an M&A activity not only helps to avoid costly errors and reduce the failure rate but also helps the bidder company to better realize the value of the technological assets acquired [9]. Although few studies utilizing technological information to perform the M&A prediction (e.g., [1]) employ patent information of target companies to help select M&A candidates for a bidder company, only very limited technological information (e.g., whether a firm has any granted or applied patents and the number of granted or applied patents) is employed. The exclusion or limited use of technological variables for M&A prediction limits the scenarios where M&A prediction can be applied. M&A activities are especially critical for those high-tech industries (e.g., information and communication technology, electronics, bio-technology, pharmaceutical), because they often use M&As to acquire state-of-the-art technologies or rapidly expand their R&D capabilities. Thus, most of the existing M&A prediction studies may not effectively be applied to high-tech industries in which the technological-oriented competitive strategy prevails. As a result, there is a pressing need to develop an alternative approach that employs comprehensive technological variables for M&A prediction.

Second, most of existing studies induce the M&A prediction model depending solely on the information of candidate target companies (i.e., without considering the profile of the bidder company under discussion). Such M&A prediction can support the assessment of the probability of a company being acquired or merged, but who are likely to be bidder companies is not a concern in this assessment. Accordingly, most of prior studies are not practicable in some important application scenarios. For example, for venture capitals, the described M&A prediction provides insufficient information for hunting investment targets because the growth potential of a company that is likely to be acquired or merged depends on who the potential bidder company is (e.g., whether the potential bidder company is the industry leader). In addition, prior studies may not produce effective M&A prediction models because the profile of the respective bidder company and its compatibility with a candidate target company are not taken into consideration.

3   Patent Analysis for M&A Prediction

In this study, we formulate the M&A prediction problem as follows: given a bidder company and a candidate target company, M&A prediction is to predict whether the candidate target company will be acquired or merged by the bidder company. That is, we consider M&A prediction as a classification problem with two possible decision categories: M&A (i.e., the candidate target company will be acquired or merged by the bidder company) and non-M&A (i.e., the candidate target company will not be acquired or merged by the bidder company). In this section, we first define and describe the technological variables (derived from patent analysis) employed in our proposed M&A prediction technique. Subsequently, we depict the ensemble learning algorithm developed for our proposed technique.

3.1   Variables for M&A Prediction

A patent is a collection of exclusive rights that protect an inventor's new machine, process, article, or any new improvement theory for a fixed period of time. Due to its properties of novelty and exclusion, patent is an excellent source for evaluating the capability of technology or innovation of a company. Patent analysis has been widely applied to many application domains, such as the estimation of stock performance [5], M&A analysis [1], [3], [4], evaluation of R&D collaboration [18], and analysis of corporate strategy [12]. Patent analysis is mainly based on the statistic and citation information of patents. For example, a commonly adopted statistic variable for patent analysis is the number of patents [1], [3], [4], [5], [12]. When citation information is considered, variables, such as impact of patent [3], [5], technology strength [3], [4],

[8], [12], [14], science link [3], [4], [5], [8], technology cycle time [3], [4], [5], [12], [14], and concentration rate [12], [18], are usually employed. The idea behind patent citation analysis is that patents cited by many later patents tend to contain important ideas upon which many later inventions are built [3]. As a result, a company with a large number of frequently cited patents is likely to possess technological and competitive advantages in that specific domain.

According to the review of the existing patent analysis studies, we summarize and develop five categories of variables, namely *technological quantity*, *technological quality*, *technological innovation*, *technological diversity*, and *technological compatibility*, for building the patent-based M&A prediction model. Specifically, thirteen variables, which cover the first four categories of technological variables, are estimated to measure individual technological capability of the given bidder company (f_b) and the given candidate target company (f_c), respectively. In addition, seventeen variables are included to measure the technological compatibility between f_b and f_c. As a result, a total of forty-three variables are employed for M&A prediction in this study.

For each company involved in the target M&A prediction (i.e., f_b or f_c), we measure the company's ***technological quantity*** as follows:

- Number of Patents (*NP*): *NP* measures the number of patents granted to a company under discussion and is an indicator of the technological capability of the company [3], [5], [14]. If a company has a higher number of patents, the company is likely to have better technological capability. For a company i (f_b or f_c), $NP_i = |P_i|$ where P_i is the set of patents granted to company i.

- Number of Recent Patents (*NRP*): *NP* measures the overall technological capability of a company from its establishment. However, for a company with a long history, *NP* may not be an effective measure of the company's technological capability because its patents may be granted long time ago. Thus, we adopt another measure *NRP* to estimate the recent technological capability of the company [3]. Specifically, *NRP* considers the patents granted within three years only. For a company i (f_b or f_c), $NRP_i = \displaystyle\operatorname*{count}_{j \in P_i \text{ and } age(j) \leq 3} (j)$, where $age(j)$ returns the number of years between the year when the patent j was granted and the current year (or more specifically, the year when the target M&A is concerned).

For each company (i.e., f_b or f_c), we measure its ***technological quality*** as follows:

- Impact of Patents (*IP*): *IP* measures the impact of patents of a company based on the number of forward citations to these patents [8]. However, it is common that earlier patents tend to have higher number of forward citations. To avoid this possible bias due to the ages of patents, we employ the *novel citation index* (*NCI*) to estimate the *IP* of a company. The NCI of a patent j (i.e., NCI_j) is calculated as: $NCI_j = \alpha \times (Y_c - Y_j + 1)^\sigma \times C_j$, where Y_c is the current year, Y_j is the published year of the patent j, C_j is the number of forward citations received by patent j, and α and σ are constant variables to adjust the weight. Accordingly, the impact of patents of a company i (f_b or f_c) is then estimated by averaging the *NCIs* across all patents of the company. Specifically, $IP_i = \dfrac{\sum\limits_{j \in P_i} NCI_j}{|P_i|}$.

- Technology Strength (_TS_): _TS_ is another measure of the impact of a company's patents and is typically estimated by the average current impact index (_CII_) of a company's patents within a specific technological field [3], [14]. The _CII_ of a company i in technological field d is defined as: $CII_{id} = \dfrac{C_{id}/K_{id}}{C_d/K_d}$, where C_{id} is the total number of forward citations received by the patents of company i in technological field d in the current year, K_{id} is the number of patents of company i in technological field d, C_d is the total number of forward citations received in the current year by all patents in technological field d, and K_d is the number of patents in technological field d. Accordingly, the overall technology strength of a company i (f_b or f_c) is then estimated by averaging the _CII_ values across all the technological fields covered by the company. That is, $TS_i = \dfrac{\sum\limits_{d \in F_i} CII_{id}}{|F_i|}$, where F_i is the set of technological fields covered by company i.

  In this study, the technological field of a patent is determined by the patent classification system (i.e., IPC classification system [21]). An IPC class of a patent can be specified at four levels: section, class, subclass, and subgroup. For example, given a patent with an IPC class as A01B/01, its technological field at section, class, subclass, and subgroup levels are 'A', 'A01', 'A01B', and 'A01B/01' respectively. To consider the impacts of different classification levels when estimating _TS_ of a company, we further differentiate _TS_ into four variables according to their classification levels. That is, for the bidder company f_b, _TS-S$_b$_ (for the section level), _TS-C$_b$_ (for the class level), _TS-SC$_b$_ (for the subclass level), and _TS-G$_b$_ (for the subgroup level) are used for M&A prediction. Likewise, four variables are developed for the candidate target company f_c: _TS-S$_c$_, _TS-C$_c$_, _TS-SC$_c$_, and _TS-G$_c$_.

For each company (i.e., f_b or f_c), we measure its **technological innovation** as follows:

- Link to Science (_LS_): The link between patents and scientific articles reveals the extent to which a company is building on scientific research and is often used to measure the degree of technological innovation of a company [4], [8], [12]. Let ls_j be the number of links to scientific articles in patent j. Accordingly, the link to science of company i (f_b or f_c) is calculated as the average link to scientific articles across all patents of the company: $LS_i = \dfrac{\sum\limits_{j \in P_i} ls_j}{|P_i|}$.

- Technology Cycle Time (_TCT_): _TCT_ measures the average median year of the patents cited by the patents of a company [4], [12], [14]. Companies whose patents cite relatively recent patents are likely to be innovating faster than those whose patents cite older patents. Given a patent j with k citations and the ordered published years of references cited by patent j (i.e., $<y_1, y_2, \ldots, y_k>$, where $y_h \leq y_{h+1}$ for all h where $1 \leq h < k$). We determine the technology cycle time of a patent j as: $tct_j = y_{(k+1)/2}$ if k is an odd number and $tct_j = \dfrac{y_{k/2} + y_{(k/2)+1}}{2}$ if k is an even number. Subsequently, the TCT of company i (f_b or f_c) is then computed as:

$$TCT_i = \frac{\sum\limits_{j \in P_i} tct_j}{|P_i|}.$$

For each company (i.e., f_b or f_c), we measure its **technological diversity** as follows:

- Concentration Rate (_CR_): CR measures the concentration of patents of a company across all technological fields covered by the patents of the company [18].

  Accordingly, for a company i (f_b or f_c), $CR_i = \dfrac{\sum\limits_{d \in F_i} \left(\dfrac{K_{id}}{K_i} \times \log_2 \dfrac{K_{id}}{K_i} \right)}{\log_2 |F_i|}$. Evidently, if a

  company concentrates only in one technological field, its respective CR value will be 0 (i.e., no diversity). However, if a company's patents are evenly distributed across different technological fields, its CR value will approach to 1.

  As with technology strength, the technological field of a patent is determined by the IPC classification system. Correspondingly, when estimating CR for a company, we differentiate CR into four variables by considering the impacts of different classification levels. That is, $CR\text{-}S_b$ (for the section level), $CR\text{-}C_b$ (for the class level), $CR\text{-}SC_b$ (for the subclass level), and $CR\text{-}G_b$ (for the subgroup level) are included to measure the concentration rate of f_b. Similarly, $CR\text{-}S_c$, $CR\text{-}C_c$, $CR\text{-}SC_c$, and $CR\text{-}G_c$ are employed for f_c.

Subsequently, we describe the seventeen variables employed to measure the **technological compatibility** between the bidder company (f_b) and the candidate target company (f_c).

- Compatibility of Technological Fields (_CTF_): CTF measures the cosine similarity of percentages of patents of f_b and f_c across all technological fields covered by the

  two companies. Specifically, $CTF_{bc} = \dfrac{\sum\limits_{d \in F_{bc}} R_{bd} \times R_{cd}}{\sqrt{\sum\limits_{d \in F_{bc}} R_{bd}} \times \sqrt{\sum\limits_{d \in F_{bc}} R_{cd}}}$, where R_{id} is

  the percentage of patents of company i in technological field d (i.e., $R_{id} = \frac{K_{id}}{|P_i|}$) and F_{bc} is the union of the technological fields covered by f_b and those covered by f_c.

  According to the IPC classification system, we also consider four possible levels of technological fields and use four variables to measure the CTF between f_b and f_c. That is, $CTF\text{-}S_{bc}$ (at the section level), $CTF\text{-}C_{bc}$ (at the class level), $CTF\text{-}SC_{bc}$ (at the subclass level), and $CTF\text{-}G_{bc}$ (at the subgroup level) are included.

- Relative Strength of Technological Quantity: The relative strength of technological quantity calculates the ratio of each of the two technological quantity measures defined previously (i.e., number of patents and number of recent patents) between f_b and f_c. Specifically, the relative strength in number of patents (NP) is defined as: $RNP_{bc} = \dfrac{NP_b}{NP_c}$, and the relative strength in number of recent patents (NRP) is $RNRP_{bc} = \dfrac{NRP_b + 0.5}{NRP_c + 0.5}$. The constant 0.5 is added to avoid the situation when the denominator is zero.

- Relative Strength of Technological Quality: The relative strength of technological quality calculates the ratio of each of the two technological quality measures defined previously (i.e., impact of patents and technology strength) between f_b and f_c. Specifically, the relative strength in impact of patents (IP) is measured as: $RIP_{bc} = \dfrac{IP_b + 0.5}{IP_c + 0.5}$. For the technology strength (TS), four variables are defined for different IPC classification levels: $RTS\text{-}S_{bc} = \dfrac{TS\text{-}S_b + 0.5}{TS\text{-}S_c + 0.5}$ (for the section level), $RTS\text{-}C_{bc} = \dfrac{TS\text{-}C_b + 0.5}{TS\text{-}C_c + 0.5}$ (for the class level), $RTS\text{-}SC_{bc} = \dfrac{TS\text{-}SC_b + 0.5}{TS\text{-}SC_c + 0.5}$ (for the subclass level), and $RTS\text{-}G_{bc} = \dfrac{TS\text{-}G_b + 0.5}{TS\text{-}G_c + 0.5}$ (for the subgroup level).

- Relative Strength of Technological Innovation: The relative strength of technological innovation calculates the ratio of each of the two technological innovation measures defined previously (i.e., link to science and technology cycle time) between f_b and f_c. Specifically, the relative strength in link to science (LS) is measured as: $RLS_{bc} = \dfrac{LS_b + 0.5}{LS_c + 0.5}$, and the relative strength in technology cycle time (TCT) is defined as: $RTCT_{bc} = \dfrac{TCT_b}{TCT_c}$.

- Relative Strength of Technological Diversity: The relative strength of technological diversity calculates the ratio of concentration rate (CR) between f_b and f_c. Specifically, four variables are defined according to the IPC classification levels: $RCR\text{-}S_{bc} = \dfrac{CR\text{-}S_b + 0.5}{CR\text{-}S_c + 0.5}$ (for the section level), $RCR\text{-}C_{bc} = \dfrac{CR\text{-}C_b + 0.5}{CR\text{-}C_c + 0.5}$ (for the class level), $RCR\text{-}SC_{bc} = \dfrac{CR\text{-}SC_b + 0.5}{CR\text{-}SC_c + 0.5}$ (for the subclass level), and $RCR\text{-}G_{bc} = \dfrac{CR\text{-}G_b + 0.5}{CR\text{-}G_c + 0.5}$ (for the subgroup level).

3.2 Ensemble Learning Algorithm

As mentioned, we formulate M&A prediction as a classification problem with two possible decision categories: M&A and non-M&A. To learn an M&A prediction model, we need to prepare a set of training examples of the two categories. Because it is easier to obtain non-M&A cases than M&A cases, a set of training examples tends to be highly asymmetric or skewed in the two categories. To deal with such skewness in a training set, we develop an ensemble approach for learning. Given a training set, the basic idea of our ensemble learning algorithm is that we sample k training subsets from the training set for training k base classifiers. Assume that we have n M&A cases and m non-M&A cases (where $n < m$) in the training set. Each training subset will comprise all of the n M&A cases and $\alpha \times n$ randomly sampled non-M&A cases, where α is used to adjust the ratio of non-M&A and M&A cases in a training subset. Subsequently, an induction learning algorithm (specifically, Naïve Bayes classifier [11] in this study) is applied to build a base classifier for each training subset.

To predict a new (unseen) case (i.e., a pair of a bidder company and a candidate target company), each base classifier will produce the probability that the case belongs to the M&A category. We can employ the average method by averaging the probability predicted by each base classier to arrive at the overall probability. Consequently, if the overall probability is equal to or greater than 0.5, the case will be predicted as in the M&A category; otherwise, the non-M&A category. Alternatively, we can adopt the weighted average method to obtain an overall probability, where the weight of a base classifier depends on its prediction accuracy on the training set.

4 Empirical Evaluation

In this section, we describe our data collection and evaluation design, and then discuss some important evaluation results of the proposed patent-based M&A prediction technique.

4.1 Data Collection

The M&A cases from January 1, 1997 to May 27, 2008 are collected from the SDC Platinum database[2] for our evaluation purpose. We limit the M&A cases to companies in certain industries in Japan. The procedure of data collection and filtering is illustrated in Fig. 1. We apply four filtering rules to form the M&A cases in our dataset. We first search each M&A case in which both the bidder and the target are from the same country (i.e., Japan) from the SDC Platinum database. The bidders and targets in SDC Platinum Database could be companies or departments of companies. It is possible that the bidder and target are different departments in the same company or the bidder and target are departments from different companies. Because the analysis unit of this study is at the company level, the first filtering rule filters out those M&A cases retrieved from the SDC Platinum database that the bidder or target is a department rather than a company.

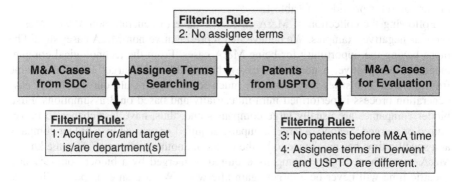

Fig. 1. Procedure of Data Collection and Filtering

---

[2] http://www.thomsonreuters.com/products_services/financial/sdc

Table 1. Summary of M&A Cases in Japan Dataset

Industry	Original[#]	After[†]	Industry	Original	After
Electronics	592	38	Machinery	548	6
Communication	83	4	Prepackaged Software	571	3
Computer Equipment	106	5	Chemical	494	5
Total Number of Usable M&A cases: 61 out of 2394 original cases					

#: Number of M&A cases retrieved from the SDC Platinum database.
†: Number of M&A cases retained after the filtering process.

Subsequently, we submit the name of each company that passes through the first filtering rule to the Derwent Innovation Index database[3] to search for their assignee terms in the USPTO database[4]. The purpose of assignee term search is to find alternative names of a company and allow us to search for all the patents granted to this specific company. For example, the company name of the "Taiwan Semiconductor Manufacturing Company Ltd." in the SDC Platinum database is "Taiwan Semiconductor Mnfr Co." It has three possible assignee terms according to the Derwent Innovation Index database, namely "Taiwan Semiconductor Mfg Co Ltd," "Taiwan Semiconductor Mfg Co," and "Taiwan Semiconductor Mfg Corp Ltd." After finding all alternative names for each company appearing in our dataset, the second filtering rule is then applied to eliminate those cases without having any assignee terms. A company without any assignee terms implies that it does not have any issued patents and thus should be removed from our dataset.

Subsequently, M&A cases with corresponding assignees terms are employed to search for patent documents from the USPTO database, which will then be used to derive the values for the forty-three variables depicted in Section 3.1. In this stage, the third filtering rule is applied to remove these cases that do not have any issued patents before the year of the corresponding M&A case. In addition, the fourth filtering rule, which filters out cases whose assignee terms in the Derwent Innovation Index database are different from those in the USPTO database, is executed forthwith. The remaining M&A cases are then used for our empirical evaluation purposes. After the data filtering process, 61 useable M&A cases are retained our dataset. The summary of our dataset is provided in Table 1.

Following the collection of M&A cases, we have to generate non-M&A cases to serve as negative examples. We believe that representative non-M&A cases should be those having the opportunity for being M&A cases. From the technological complementarity perspective, a non-M&A case whose bidder and target companies come from different industries may not make much sense. As a result, our non-M&A case generation process is performed intra-industrially and based on 3 assumptions. First, bidder companies are usually large companies and, thus, have less chance to be acquired or merged. Second, a target company acquired or merged by a bidder company at a specific time has no chance to be the target of another company before the known M&A case. Third, a target company acquired or merged by a bidder company at a specific time will never be a target again afterward. We use an example to illustrate our non-M&A case generation process. Assume that there are three M&A cases in the

---

[3] http://scientific.thomsonreuters.com/products/dii/
[4] http://www.uspto.gov/main/patents.htm

same industry: A acquired B on time t_1, C acquired D on time t_2, and E acquired F on time t_3. Moreover, assume that t_1 is earlier than t_2 and t_2 is earlier than t_3. Consequently, we can generate three non-M&A cases including A did not acquire D and A did not acquire F on time t_1, and C did not acquire F on time t_2. Following this non-M&A case generation process, we create 523 non-M&A cases from the 61 M&A cases for our Japan dataset.

4.2 Evaluation Design

To evaluate the effectiveness of the proposed patent-based M&A prediction technique, we design two evaluation experiments. The first experiment is to evaluate the prediction power of the proposed technique. The second experiment examines the effect of different decision combination methods (i.e., average and weighted average) in our ensemble learning algorithm.

In all experiments, a tenfold cross-validation strategy is employed to estimate the learning effectiveness. That is, given a dataset, we divide all cases in the dataset randomly into ten mutually exclusive subsets of approximately equal size. In turn, we designate each subset as the testing examples while the others serve as training examples. To minimize the potential sampling biases, we perform the tenfold cross-validation process three times and the overall effectiveness is estimated by averaging the performance estimates obtained from the 30 individual trials. In addition, we set the number of base classifiers (k) in our ensemble learning algorithm as 30.

4.3 Effectiveness of the Proposed M&A Prediction Technique

In this experiment, we employ the average method for decision combination in our ensemble learning algorithm and investigate the effectiveness of the proposed M&A prediction technique across different values for α (the ratio of non-M&A cases and M&A cases in a training set), ranging from 1 to 3 in increment of 1. As Table 2 shows, an increase of α improves prediction accuracy, precision rate for the M&A category, and recall rate for the non-M&A category. Because the increase of α means the inclusion of more non-M&A cases into each training set. As a result, the M&A prediction model induced with more non-M&A cases will favor the majority category (i.e., having the tendency of predicting the non-M&A category); thus, decreasing recall rate for the M&A category and precision rate for the non-M&A category. Overall, a smaller value for α is more desired, because it improves recall rate for the M&A category, which is the major concern of this study. Specifically, when setting α as 1,

Table 2. M&A Prediction Results in the Japan Dataset

α	Accuracy	M&A Category		Non-M&A Category	
		Recall	Precision	Recall	Precision
1	88.16%	46.43%	42.93%	92.97%	93.83%
2	88.43%	45.90%	44.00%	93.27%	93.80%
3	88.78%	44.30%	45.30%	93.87%	93.60%

Table 3. M&A Prediction Results with Different Weighting Methods in the Japan Dataset

Decision Combination Method	Accuracy	M&A Category		Non-M&A Category	
		Recall	Precision	Recall	Precision
Average	88.16%	46.43%	42.93%	92.97%	93.83%
Weighted Average	87.94%	45.37%	41.97%	92.80%	93.67%

the recall and precision rates for the M&A category are 46.43% and 42.93%, respectively. Given the complexity of M&A decision, the prediction effectiveness attained by our M&A prediction technique is considered satisfactory. We believe that the expansion of the size of the dataset should further improve the effectiveness of the proposed technique.

4.4   Effects of Decision Combination Methods

As mentioned, we propose two different decision combination methods (i.e., average and weighted average) in the ensemble learning algorithm. We conduct this experiment to empirically investigate their effects on the effectiveness of the proposed M&A prediction technique. According to the evaluation result suggested by the previous experiment, we set α as 1. As Table 3 illustrates, the average method outperforms the weighted average one in all measures examined. Especially, the performance differentials of recall and precision for the M&A category (i.e., 1.06% and 0.96%, respectively) are greater than those of recall and precision for the non-M&A category (i.e., 0.17% and 0.16%, respectively). This result suggests that the weighted average method (weighted by the accuracy of each base classifier) appears to favor the prediction of the non-M&A category and thus sacrifice the recall and precision for the M&A category.

5   Conclusion and Future Research Direction

M&A plays an increasingly important role in the modern business environment. Companies usually conduct M&A to pursue complementarity from other companies for preserving and/or extending their competitive advantages. Appropriate selection (prediction) of M&A targets for a given bidder company is a critical first step to the success of the M&A activity. However, most of existing studies apply only financial and managerial as indicators on constructing M&A prediction model and select candidate target companies without considering the profile of the respective bidder company and its compatibility with candidate target companies. These limitations greatly limit the applicability of the prior studies. To overcome these limitations, we propose an M&A prediction technique that not only encompasses technological variables as prediction indictors but also takes into account the profiles of both bidder and candidate target companies when building an M&A prediction model. Forty-three technological variables are derived from patent analysis and an ensemble learning algorithm is developed for our proposed patent-based M&A prediction technique. We collect a set of real-world M&A cases to evaluate the proposed technique. The evaluation results are encouraging and will serve as a basis for future studies.

Some ongoing and future research directions are summarized as follows. First, in this study, we only examine the effectiveness of the proposed technique in one dataset (i.e., Japan). It is essential to collect additional datasets to empirically evaluate the proposed M&A prediction technique. Second, this study only includes technological variables in the M&A prediction model. Incorporating other types of variables (e.g., financial and managerial) into the M&A prediction model is desirable and should further improve the prediction effectiveness reported in this study. Last but not least, there is still room for improving the effectiveness (especially recall and precision rates for the M&A category) of our proposed technique. One direction is to include additional technological measures and the other is to further extend the ensemble learning algorithm proposed in this study.

Acknowledgement

This work was supported by the National Science Council of the Republic of China under the grants NSC96-3114-P-007-002-Y and NSC97-2410-H-155-052.

References

1. Ali-Yrkkö, J., Hyytinen, A., Pajarinen, M.: Does Patenting Increase the Probability of Being Acquired? Evidence from Cross-border and Domestic Acquisitions. Applied Financial Economics 14(1), 1007–1017 (2005)
2. An, S., He, Y., Zhao, Z., Sun, J.: Measurement of Merger and Acquisition Performance Based on Artificial Neural Network. In: 5th IEEE International Conference on Cognitive Informatics, pp. 502–506. IEEE Press, New York (2006)
3. Breitzman, A., Thomas, P.: Using Patent Citation Analysis to Target/Value M&A Candidates. Research-Technology Management 45(5), 28–36 (2002)
4. Breitzman, A., Thomas, P., Cheney, M.: Technological Powerhouse or Diluted Competence: Techniques for Assessing Mergers via Patent Analysis. R&D Management 32(1), 1–10 (2002)
5. Deng, Z., Lev, B., Narin, F.: Science and Technology as Predictors of Stock Performance. Financial Analysts Journal 55(3), 20–32 (1999)
6. Gugler, K., Konrad, K.A.: Merger Target Selection and Financial Structure (July 2002), http://homepage.univie.ac.at/klaus.gugler/public/rio.pdf
7. Gupta, D., Gerchak, Y.: Quantifying Operational Synergies in a Merger/Acquisition. Management Science 48(4), 517–533 (2002)
8. Harhoff, D., Scherer, F.M., Vopel, K.: Citations, Family Size, Opposition and the Value of Patent Rights. Research Policy 32(8), 1343–1363 (2003)
9. James, A.D., Georghiou, L., Metcalfe, J.S.: Integrating Technology into Merger and Acquisition Decision Making. Technovation 18(8), 563–573 (1998)
10. Meador, A.L., Church, P.H., Rayburn, L.G.: Development of Prediction Models for Horizontal and Vertical Mergers. Journal of Financial and Strategic Decisions 9(1), 11–23 (1996)
11. Mitchell, T.: Machine Learning. McGraw Hill, New York (1997)
12. Narin, F.: Technology Indicators and Corporate Strategy. Review of Business 14(3), 19–23 (1993)

13. Pasiouras, F., Gaganis, C.: Financial Characteristics of Banks Involved in Acquisitions: Evidence from Asia. Applied Financial Economics 17(4), 329–341 (2007)
14. Pegels, C.C., Thirumuthy, M.V.: The Impact of Technology Strategy on Firm Performance. IEEE Transactions on Engineering Management 43(3), 246–249 (1996)
15. Ragothaman, S., Naik, B., Ramakrishnan, K.: Predicting Corporate Acquisitions: An Application of Uncertain Reasoning Rule Induction. Information Systems Frontiers 5(4), 401–412 (2003)
16. Sirower, M.L.: The Synergy Trap. Free Press, New York (1997)
17. Song, X., Chu, Y.: A Study on Financial Strategy for Determining the Target Enterprise of Merger and Acquisition. Journal of Modern Accounting and Auditing 2(4), 55–60 (2006)
18. Teichert, T., Ernst, H.: Assessment for R&D Collaboration by Patent Data. In: Portland International Conference on Technology and Innovation Management, pp. 420–428. IEEE Press, New York (1999)
19. Trautwein, F.: Merger Motives and Merger Prescription. Strategic Management Journal 11, 283–295 (1990)
20. Webber, J.A., Dholakia, U.M.: Including Marketing Synergy in Acquisition Analysis: A Step-Wise Approach. Industrial Marketing Management 29(2), 157–177 (2000)
21. World Intellectual Property Organization, International Patent Classification (8th ed.) (2006), http://www.wipo.int/export/sites/www/classifications/ipc/en/guide/guide_ipc8.pdf

Use of Ontology to Support Concept-Based Text Categorization

Yen-Hsien Lee[1], Wan-Jung Tsao[1], and Tsai-Hsin Chu[2,*]

[1] Department of Management Information Systems, National Chiayi University, Chiayi, Taiwan
{yhlee, s0951317}@mail.ncyu.edu.tw
[2] Department of E-learning Design and Management, National Chiayi University, Chiayi, Taiwan
Tel.: +886-5-226-3411x1826; fax: +886-5-206-2328
thchu@mail.ncyu.edu.tw

Abstract. Huge volumes of worldwide accessible information have led to the tool necessity for better handling of massive information to overcome the conventional manual method. Thus, automated text categorization technique serves to support a more effective document organization management. Fundamentally, conventional text categorization techniques concentrate on the analysis of document contents and measure the similarity based on the overlap among the features of unlabeled documents and that of pre-classified documents. However, such feature-based approach will be confront with the problems of word mismatch and word ambiguity. To lessen these problems, this study proposes an ontology-based text categorization technique. It employs the specific domain ontology to enable documents to be classified in accordance to their range of relevant concepts. The effectiveness of the proposed technique is measured and compared with its benchmark techniques. The evaluation results suggest our proposed technique is more effective than the benchmarks.

Keywords: Document-category management, Concept-based text categorization, Ontology, k-nearest neighbors.

1 Introduction

Volumes of knowledge are created and accumulated in the daily operations of organizations. Such knowledge is commonly in the form of textual documents to facilitate their storage, dissemination, and sharing within and across organizations. Organizing documents into various document-categories based on their types or contents has been one of the most popular approaches to archive documents. In the past, documents are usually organized manually; however, classification predominated by the subjectivity of management staff has resulted in the difficulties in accessing documents by other users. The report from Delphi Group surveyed in 2002 indicates that most of respondents are not satisfied with the management of document-category

---

* Corresponding author.

C. Weinhardt, S. Luckner, and J. Stößer (Eds.): WEB 2008, LNBIP 22, pp. 201–213, 2009.
© Springer-Verlag Berlin Heidelberg 2009

of their organizations. More than 60% agree that it is difficult to access the information necessary to their performing jobs [9]. On the other hand, the rapid development of information technology and huge volumes of Internet utilization enable the making and availability of wide range and worldwide accessible information. This also makes the manual approach impracticable to categorizing documents. In a word, current organizations are facing the issue of enhancing method to better manage their working knowledge, particularly those of disorder text.

Previous research has proposed various automated text categorization approaches to support organizations their needs of effective document management. Text categorization technique uses the automated learning technique in artificial intelligence (AI) to induce the rules from the pre-classified document collection, and applies these induced rules to classify unlabeled documents into the appropriate predefined document-categories. A Review of relevant research on text categorization suggests their uses of document content analysis. That's, the classifier decides the belonging category of an unlabeled document on the basis of the similarity between the features representing the category and the unlabeled document. Nevertheless, based on the similarity of representing features to classify documents has caused text categorization technique facing the problems of word mismatch and word ambiguity. For example, the feature-based approach may mismatch the terms, like "classification" and "categorization," which refer to the same connotation. On the contrary, it is unable to recognize whether the term "apple" refers to as a fruit or the computer company.

Prior research has proposed Latent Semantic Indexing (LSI), a statistical method to overcome the word mismatch problem by analyzing the term correlation structure existed in the document corpus. It employs Singular Value Decomposition (SVD) to construct a new semantic space for a set of documents and re-represent them within the space. Though LSI has shown its effectiveness in addressing the word mismatch problem, it is inefficient and impractical when the size of document set is unstable. Any modification to the original set of documents will require reconstruction of the semantic space, since it is constructed for the particular set of documents. In addition, the semantic space merely represents the term-document relationships, using which as a basis to categorize documents won't be able to reveal the connection between document and its assigning category.

In this study, we focus on the word mismatch and ambiguity problems relevant to the feature-based text categorization technique. Typically, a domain-specific ontology is composed of a set of related concepts, relations, and axioms (e.g., constraints) [18] and provides a shared, common comprehension of a domain easily communicated between or among humans and application systems [13]. We, therefore, propose an Ontology-based Text Categorization (OTC) technique to support classifying documents at the conceptual rather than lexical level. This paper is organized as follows: relevant research on text categorization, Latent Semantic Indexing, and an overview of ontology will be in sequence provided in section 2. In section 3, we detail the proposed Ontology-based Text Categorization (OTC) technique, followed by the discussion on evaluation design and results in section 4. Finally, we will conclude in section 5 our research finding.

2 Literature Review

2.1 The Feature-Based Text Categorization Technique

Text categorization is a process to construct a document classification model from a set of well-classified documents (training corpus) and accordingly to assign unlabeled documents into appropriate categories. In general, text categorization techniques establish relationships between predefined categories and their respective documents by analyzing document contents, and typically consist of three phases including feature extraction and selection, document representation, and classifier construction.

Feature extraction and selection phase initials with document parsing to generate a set of features (e.g., nouns and noun phrases), and excludes pre-specified non-semantic-bearing words, i.e., stopwords. Representative features are then selected to reduce the number of the extracted features and to avoid the possible biases existing in them [12, 32]. Specifically, the weight (discrimination power) of each extracted feature is first measured by a feature selection metric, and the top-k features with the highest weights are selected as the representative feature set. Common feature selection metrics include document frequency (DF), term frequency and inverse document frequency (TF×IDF), information gain, mutual information, odd ratios, term strength, and χ^2-statistic [17, 34, 42].

In the document representation phase, each document (in the training corpus) is represented as a feature vector and is jointly defined by the top-k features. A review of previous research suggests several salient feature representation methods, including binary (i.e., presence versus absence of a feature in a document), within-document TF, and the feature weighting (i.e., The values of TF×IDF or χ^2-statistic) [17, 42].

In the classifier construction phase, text categorization technique employs a classification analysis technique to construct the classification model for establishing relationships between classes and feature weights from the training corpus. Depending on the learning strategy adopted as well as the type of classification model induced, classification techniques can be classified into the following types, including decision tree induction (such as ID3 [30], C4.5 [31], CART [4], and CHAID [19], decision rule induction (such as CN2 [5, 7]), neural network (such as back-propagation neural network [33]), Bayesian classification [15, 22, 25, 27, 38], the nearest neighbor classification [6, 10], and etc.

A review of the extant text categorization literature suggests the prevalent use of document content analysis. Traditional text categorization techniques make decision on the basis of the similarity between the features used in unlabeled documents and in each category of training corpus. Such feature-based approach, which compares the unlabeled documents with existing categories at the lexical level, will be confronted by the problems of word mismatch and ambiguity. Thus, in this study, we intend to address the problems inherent to the feature-based text categorization techniques by exploiting a domain-specific ontology to support classifying document at the conceptual level.

2.2 Latent Semantic Indexing in Text Categorization

Latent Semantic Indexing (LSI) was proposed by [11] to alleviate the problems of word mismatch and ambiguity in information retrieval system [3, 11]. LSI analyzes the term correlation structure to automatically cope with synonymies by observing the usage patterns of terms in documents. It employs Singular Value Decomposition (SVD) to the term-document matrix to build a new semantic space (i.e., the LSI space) [11]. Both terms and documents, which are closely associated will be re-represented in the same semantic space. Specifically, a $m \times n$ dimension feature-document matrix X is decomposed by SVD into three parts including a $m \times r$ dimension matrix T, $r \times r$ dimension matrix S, and $r \times n$ dimension matrix D^T. The rows of matrix T are the basic positions of features and that of matrix D are the basic positions of documents in the r-dimensional semantic space. S is a diagonal matrix to rescale the axes of the LSI dimensions, and the rows of the matrices $T \times S$ and $D \times S$ are the exact positions of terms and documents in the semantic space, respectively.

LSI, in the application of text categorization, is generally applied to reduce the dimension of feature vectors [8, 43]. In general, LSI-based text categorization techniques apply LSI method to derive the semantic space from the training document set. Keeping the first k columns of T and D, and pruning S as a $k \times k$ matrix, the derived semantic space is then reduced to k dimensions to represent important associations among terms and documents. As completed, each training document is, at the same time, represented in the reduced space. On the other hand, the testing (unlabeled) document set will then be mapped into the constructed semantic space. They are first represented, using the terms that appear in both sets of training and testing documents, as the term-document matrix X_p. The position of each unlabeled document in the reduced LSI space is available by multiplying the transpose matrix of X_p and the matrix T_k, which is the dimension-reduced matrix of T. The document similarity between the training documents and the testing documents will be able to be measured when both of them are mapped into the same semantic space. Finally, a text categorization approach can be applied to the training document set to derive the classification rules and use which to classify each of the unlabeled documents into appropriate categories. In addition to the kNN (i.e., feature-baed kNN), we implement the LSI-based kNN in this study for the comparative evaluation purpose. The performance achieved by these two techniques will be adopted as our evaluation benchmarks.

2.3 Ontology and Ontology Enrichment Technique

Computationally, ontology defines a common set of vocabularies to represent knowledge formally and to facilitate the sharing and reuse of knowledge. In this connection, ontology describes the specification of a representational vocabulary for a shared domain of interest [14]. Generally, an ontology is composed of concepts, relations, instances, and axioms formally represented in a machine readable format [18]. Concepts represent a set or class of entities in a domain, and are divided into two types as primitive concept and defined concept. Relations are the definitions about the interactions between concepts or the properties of concept. An axiom constrains the value of a class or an instance, and hence, the properties of a relation are usually take as axioms.

Recently, ontology has been used to support knowledge sharing and reuse in various domains, such likes information integration [20, 39], knowledge based systems [29], and text indexing and querying [21]. Ontology has shown its promising value in various application domains; however, the time-consuming and knowledge-intensive engineering process of ontology has prohibited its widespread use [28]. To expedite the construction of ontology and improve its maintenance overt time, previous research has suggested various supervised learning techniques to extract concepts or to discover important relations, taxonomic or associations of an ontology from a set of document concerning a particular domain [24, 28, 26, 35, 36, 40].

In this study, ontology is defined as a set of concepts of interesting domain organized as a hierarchical (or heterarchical) structure, and each of the concepts is described by a set of descriptors [16]. Many professional associations have created their own concept hierarchies, but the concept descriptors are almost not readily available. For example, the Computing Classification System (CCS)[1] built by the Association for Computing Machinery (ACM) is primarily used as an indexing scheme for organizing articles published in ACM periodicals and therefore the concept descriptors are not defined in the classification system. [23] proposed an ontology enrichment (OE) approach to extract the concept descriptors for a given concept hierarchy from a set of well-classified documents of relevance [23]. OE adopted a feature weighting function to measure the discrimination power for the feature of a concept to its sibling concepts. To measure the weight of a feature f_i in concept o_j, it considers the term frequency of feature f_i in concept o_j, the percentage of the documents that contain feature f_i in concept o_j, and the distribution of feature f_i across all siblings of concept o_j. OE selects top-k_{cd} features as the descriptors for a target concept at level one and select $(k_{cd} + (n-1) \times \delta_{cd})$ descriptors for a concept at the level n, on the basis of the weights of features in respective concept. Finally, a pre-determined commonality threshold α_p was applied to exclude the features while it appears in over α_p percent of the concepts in the hierarchy. In this study, we adopt OE approach to discover the concept descriptors to construct the domain ontology needed in the empirical evaluation.

3   Design of Ontology-Based Text Categorization (OTC) Technique

We detail the design of our proposed Ontology-based Text Categorization (OTC) technique in this section. OTC technique employs a domain-specific ontology to address the limitations inherent to the lexicon-based text categorization techniques (i.e., the word mismatch and word ambiguity problems). It first maps each document onto the concept space of the domain-specific ontology and represents which as a vector of concepts using the document-concept similarity. Subsequently, a set of top-k concepts is selected as the representative concepts on the basis of their discrimination power to document categories existing in the training document corpus. Once selected, all documents in the training and testing corpora (the unlabeled documents) are represented using the selected representative concepts. Finally, a classification analysis technique (i.e., kNN) is adopted to assign all unlabeled documents into their appropriate categories. As shown in Figure 1, the overall process of OTC technique can be divided into three phases, including the document-concept transformation, document representation, and document categorization.

3.1 Document-Concept Transformation

The purpose of document-concept transformation phase is to transform the feature-represented documents into concept-represented ones. As shown in Figure 1, this

---

[1] http://www.acm.org/class/1998/

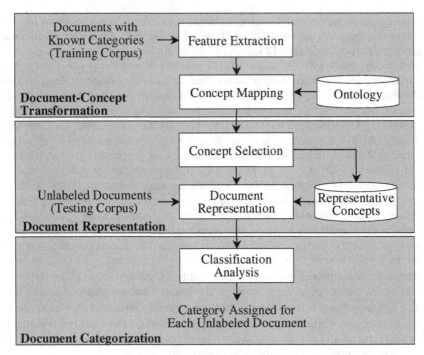

Fig. 1. Overall Process of Ontology-based Text Categorization (OTC) Technique

phase that consists of two steps, including *feature extraction* and *concept mapping* are detailed as follows:

Feature Extraction. The task of feature extraction is to extract features from the document corpus. Firstly, the rule-based part of speech tagger implemented by [1, 2] is applied to tag each word in documents. Subsequently, the approach suggested by [37] is followed to develop a noun phrase parser for extracting the nouns and noun phrases from each syntactically tagged document.

Concept Mapping. The task of concept mapping is to measure the similarity between a document d_i and each concept o_j in the domain-specific ontology, and converts the feature-represented documents into concept-represented ones. With the availability of a domain-specific ontology, the degree of relevance is measured between a document and each concept in it. We define the weighting function of relevance degree between document d_i and concept o_j as $w_m(d_i, o_j) = \sum_{f_k \in o_j} (w_c(f_k, o_j) \times TF(f_k, d_i)) \times pf_{ij}$, where f_k is the concept descriptor derived by the ontology enrichment approach that belongs to concept o_j, $w_c(f_k, o_j)$ is the weight of f_k in o_j, $TF(f_k, d_i)$ is the within-document term frequency of f_k in document d_i, and pf_{ij} is the percentage of concept descriptors that belongs to concept o_j and appears in document d_i. Our underlying assumption is that the more concept descriptors of a concept appear in a document, the greater the document embraces that concept. The relevance degree is then adjusted by multiplying pf_{ij} to avoid the domination of frequent concept descriptors. Once the concept mapping completed, each document will be represented as a set of concepts with their respective relevance degrees.

3.2 Document Representation

The purpose of document representation phase is to select the representative concepts from the documents with known categories and use the selected concepts to re-represent the documents with known categories as well as the unlabeled documents. This phase that consists of *concept selection* and *document representation* steps are detailed as follows:

Concept selection. After transforming the documents into the concept space of the domain-specific ontology, the step of concept selection is performed to select a set of representative concepts for the concept-based document representation. To measure the importance, the discrimination power, of a concept in relation to the whole document corpus with known categories, a weighing average χ^2-statistic measure is adopted. We calculate the weighting average χ^2-statistic as $\chi^2_{avg}(o_j) = \sum_{C_i \in M} (p(C_i) \times \chi^2(C_i, o_j))$, where $p(C_i)$ is the number of documents in C_i divided by total number of documents. Accordingly, the top-k concepts with the highest average χ^2-statistic score are selected and included in the set of representative concepts.

Document representation. OTC technique uses the selected set of representative concepts to represent each of the training documents and the unlabeled documents as a concept vector with particular weights. Three weighting schemes are considered in this study including the binary (i.e., presence versus absence of a concept in a document), within-document concept frequency (i.e., the frequency of a concept appears in a document), and weighting schemes.

3.3 Document Categorization

Once the training document corpus and unlabeled documents are all represented, OTC classifies the unlabeled documents into their appropriate categories based on the adopted categorization algorithm. As suggested by prior research, k-Nearest-Neighbor (kNN) classifier has been one of the top-performers among various text categorization methods [41]. In addition, the algorithm of kNN classifier is quite simple and efficient. Given an unlabeled document, cosine similarity is used to measure the document similarity of the unlabeled document along with all training documents. Then, the k training documents closest to the unlabeled document are selected; the decision category for the unlabeled document is assigned as the majority decision category in k closest neighbors. In this study, we therefore adopt the kNN classifier as the categorization algorithm for the OTC technique.

4 Evaluation Design and Results

In this section, we used the document corpus collected from the real-world environment to empirically evaluate our proposed Ontology-based Text Categorization (OTC) technique. In addition, the feature-based as well as the LSI-based text categorization techniques were developed and adopted as performance benchmarks for the purpose of comparative evaluation. In the following section, we first describe the evaluation design, including the data collection, and evaluation procedure. Subsequently, we elaborate the parameter-tuning experiments for all evaluation techniques, followed by the discussion of our comparative analysis results.

4.1 Evaluation Design

Data Collection. As mentioned, we adopted the ontology enrichment approach for the automated construction of domain-specific ontology needed in this study [23]. For the purpose of concept descriptor learning, source documents are obtained from ACM and used the ACM CCS classification structure as the concept hierarchy for learning concept descriptors. During the evaluation, the first two level-one nodes are removed, A (i.e., General Literature) and B (i.e., Hardware), and their child nodes from the concept hierarchy because of their irrelevance to the documents used during the evaluation experiment. Furthermore, the general and miscellaneous nodes at level-two and level-three do not depict concrete concepts and therefore were excluded from the hierarchy used in the evaluation. To discover important concept descriptors, a total of 14,729 abstracts of research articles are randomly selected from the ACM digital library. Each article is indexed by one or more designations to indicate its subject areas within the CCS classification structure. These nodes in which had only one abstract are removed from the hierarchy, because the number of documents is not sufficient for generating descriptors representative of such nodes. The nodes, which do not have siblings, were also removed from the hierarchy, because the relative importance of the features was unable to be measured by the concept descriptor weighting function. As a result, a total of 1,032 nodes were retained in the hierarchy, including 9 nodes at level one, 49 at level two, 263 at level three, and 711 at level four.

For the evaluation purpose, the abstract of 433 research articles in information systems and technology are collected from a digital library website (i.e., http://citeseer.ist.psu.edu) that specializes in the computer science literature. Choice of the document corpus is appropriate because most standard document sets (e.g., Reuters 21578) do not support the use of an established ontology, a distinct focus of the evaluation used for this study. Because the collected document corpus relates to information systems, we recruited the subjects who major in management information systems to manually organized the randomly ordered documents into a set of categories. A total of 29 subjects accomplished the manual organization of the documents. For each subject's classification, we excluded the category that has less than 10 documents in it to maintain a comparable number of documents in each category. We provide in Table 1 the summary of the number of categories created by the 29 subjects and the number of documents existed after pruning the inappropriate categories.

Table 1. Summary of Evaluation Document Set After Pruning Category

	Maximum	Minimum	Average
Number of Categories	14	9	11.7
Number of Documents	433	307	383.68

Evaluation Procedure. We employed categorization accuracy to measure the effectiveness of our proposed OTC technique and its performance benchmarks. The accuracy is defined as

$$Accuracy = \frac{\text{Correctly Assigned Documents}}{\text{Total Candidate Documents}} \qquad (1)$$

"Correctly Assigned Documents" is the number of documents correctly assigned to the belonging categories, and "Total Candidate Documents" is number of documents to be assigned.

We run the experiments separately for each individual subject and evaluate the effectiveness of each investigated technique using its average accuracy across the 29 subjects' classifications. For each document, we consider the category specified by respective subject to be accurate; i.e., true category. 30% of the documents are randomly selected from each true category of particular subject to form his/her testing document set. Each document in the testing corpus will then be classified by OTC technique as well as its benchmark techniques; i.e., Feature-based kNN and LSI-based kNN. To expand the number of trials and avoid the possible biases, the random selection-and-classification process is repeated 10 times. The effectiveness of the investigated techniques on particular subject's classification will be measured by averaging its performances across the 10 random trials.

4.2 Evaluation Results

Prior to our comparative evaluation, we take a computational approach to tune parameters critical to the OE technique, which is employed to discover the concept descriptors in our study, as well as the investigated techniques; i.e., OTC, feature-based kNN, and LSI-based kNN techniques. Three parameters need to be determined their appropriate values in the OE technique, including the number of descriptors for each concept at level one (k_{cd}), the increment of descriptors for each concept at the next level (δ_{cd}), and a pre-specified commonality threshold required in concept refinement (α_p). On the other hand, for the OTC, feature-based kNN, and LSI-based kNN techniques, we have to tune the number of concepts (k_c), the number of representative features (k_f), and the number of spaces (k_s), respectively. In additional, the document representation schemes for OTC and feature-based kNN have to be determined as well. We randomly selected 10 subjects and used their classifications to determine the appropriate parameter values for each technique investigated. Based on our experimental tuning results, we set k_{cd} at 20, δ_{cd} at 10, α_p at 6%, k_c at 300, k_f at 4000, and k_s at 200, and adopt the term frequency and weighting method as the document representation schemes respectively for feature-based kNN and OTC in the subsequent comparative evaluation experiments.

Using the parameter values selected based on our parameter-tuning experiments, we compare the effectiveness of OTC, feature-based kNN, and LSI-based kNN achieved. We examine the effects of number of neighbors, ranging from 1 to 65 in increments of 5, on the classification accuracy of all techniques investigated. As shown in Figure 2, the effectiveness of OTC and LSI-based kNN noticeably outperforms that of feature-based kNN. OTC technique maintains its accuracy above 0.6 and advantageous over LSI-based kNN across all levels of number of neighbors. In addition, we further statistically test the difference between the best performances achieved by the investigated techniques using the two-tailed *t*-test. OTC, LSI-based *k*NN, and feature-based *k*NN arrive at the best performance, i.e., 0.662, 0.644, and 0.526, when setting the number of neighbors as 25, 15, and 10, respectively. The statistical test result shows that OTC technique is significantly advantageous over LSI-based and Feature-based *k*NN at the *p*-value less than 0.01. Overall, our proposed ontology-based text categorization technique outperforms its benchmarks, the LSI-based and Feature-based text categorization techniques.

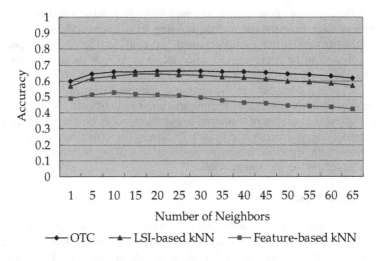

Fig. 2. Comparative Evaluation Results

5   Conclusion and Future Research Directions

Text categorization technique has shown its effectiveness and robustness in supporting the automated management of vast amounts of textual documents. Most traditional document categorization techniques are on the basis of content analysis to discover the classification patterns and assign unlabeled documents into appropriate document-categories. Such approach may cause the text categorization techniques inevitably facing the problems of word mismatch and ambiguity. To address the problem, we advance traditional document management approach and propose an ontology-based text categorization (OTC) technique to classify document on the basis of its containing concepts. Our empirical evaluation results reveal that the effectiveness of OTC outperforms its benchmark (i.e., the feature-based and LSI-based text categorization techniques).

The research contributions of this study are twofold. First, we have contributed to text categorization research by advancing the analysis of classification on the basis of document concepts to addressing the problems of word mismatch and ambiguity faced by feature-based text categorization techniques. Second, the proposed ontology-based approach also contributes to document management research. The evaluation results suggest that the performance of our proposed OTC is advantageous over the feature-based and LSI-based ones. Thus, the process of OTC technique can provide an illustration for ontology-based document management.

Three possible directions for further extension of this study are discussed as follows. First, we suggest the collection of more document corpora to evaluate our proposed OTC technique to avoid the possible evaluation bias. In addition, the adaptability of OTC to the domains, other than computer science, should be further examined as well. Second, this study focuses on assigning documents into a flat set of document category. However, document categories are usually organized as hierarchy rather than a flat set of categories in real-world situations. The ability to handle the hierarchical structure of and relations between document categories is necessary for the text categorization techniques. Finally, the proposed OTC technique provides a basis for continued ontology-based document management research. The development and evaluation of advanced ontology-based techniques for text categorization represent interesting and essential future research directions.

Acknowledgements. This work was supported by National Science Council of the Republic of China under the grant NSC97-2410-H-415-016.

References

1. Brill, E.: A Simple Rule-based Part of Speech Tagger. In: Third Conference on Applied Natural Language Processing, pp. 152–155. Association for Computational Linguistics, Trento (1992)
2. Brill, E.: Some Advances in Rule-based Part of Speech Tagging. In: 12th International Conference on Artificial Intelligence, pp. 722–727. AAAI Press, Seattle (1994)
3. Berry, M.W., Dumais, S.T., O'Brien, G.W.: Using Linear Algebra for Intelligent Information Retrieval. SIAM Review 37(4), 573–595 (1995)
4. Breiman, L., Friedman, J., Olshen, R., Stone, C.: Classification and Regression Trees. Wadsworth, Pacific Grove (1984)
5. Clark, P., Boswell, R.: Rule Induction with CN2: Some Recent Improvements. In: Fifth European Working Session on Learning, Porto, Portugal, pp. 151–163 (1991)
6. Cover, T.M., Hart, P.E.: Nearest Neighbor Pattern Classification. IEEE Transactions on Information Theory 13(1), 21–27 (1967)
7. Clark, P., Niblett, T.: The CN2 Induction Algorithm. Machine Learning 3(4), 261–283 (1989)
8. Cardoso-Cachopo, A., Oliveira, A.: An Empirical Comparison of Text Categorization Methods. In: Nascimento, M.A., de Moura, E.S., Oliveira, A.L. (eds.) SPIRE 2003. LNCS, vol. 2857, pp. 183–196. Springer, Heidelberg (2003)
9. Delphi Group: Taxonomy and Content Classification: Market Milestone Report. A Delphi Group White Paper (2002)
10. Dasarathy, B.V.: Nearest Neighbor (NN) Norms: NN Pattern Classification Techniques. McGraw-Hill Computer Science Series. IEEE Computer Society Press, Las Alamitos (1991)
11. Deerwester, S., Dumais, S.T., Furnas, G.W., Landauer, T.K., Harshman, R.A.: Indexing by Latent Semantic Analysis. Journal of the American Society for Information Science 41(6), 391–407 (1990)

12. Dumais, S., Platt, J., Heckerman, D., Sahami, M.: Inductive Learning Algorithms and Representations for Text Categorization. In: Seventh ACM International Conference on Information and Knowledge Management, pp. 148–155 (1998)
13. Fensel, D.: Ontologies: Silver Bullet for Knowledge Management and Electronic Commerce. Springer, Berlin (2000)
14. Gruber, T.R.: A Translation Approach to Portable Ontology Specifications. Knowledge Acquisition 5(2), 199–220 (1993)
15. Heckerman, D.: Bayesian Networks for Data Mining. Data Mining and Knowledge Discovery 1(1), 79–119 (1997)
16. Hotho, A., Maedche, A., Staab, S.: Ontology-Based Text Clustering. In: IJCAI 2001 Workshop on Text Learning: Beyond Supervision, Seattle (2001)
17. Ikonomakis, M., Kotsiantis, S., Tampakas, V.: Text Classification Using Machine Learning Techniques. WSEAS Transactions on Computers 4(8), 966–974 (2005)
18. Keet, C.M.: Aspects of Ontology Integration. The PhD Proposal, School of Computing, Napier University, Scotland (2004)
19. Kass, G.V.: An Exploratory Technique for Investigating Large Quantities of Categorical Data. Applied Statistics 29, 119–127 (1980)
20. Kohler, J., Philippi, S., Lange, M.: SEMEDA: Ontology Based Semantic Integration of Biological Databases. Bioinformatics 19(18), 2420–2427 (2003)
21. Kohler, J., Philippi, S., Specht, M., Ruegg, A.: Ontology Based Text Indexing and Querying for the Semantic Web. Knowledge-Based Systems (19), 744–754 (2006)
22. Lewis, D.D., Ringuette, M.: A Comparison of Two Learning Algorithms for Text Categorization. In: Third Annual Symposium on Document Analysis and Information Retrieval, pp. 81–93 (1994)
23. Lee, Y.H., Wei, C.P., Hu, P.J.: Preserving User Preference in Document-Category Management: An Ontology-based Evolution Approach. In: Seventh Pacific-Asia Conference on Information Systems, New Zealand (2007)
24. Maedche, A.: Ontology Learning for the Semantic Web. Kluwer Academic Publishers, Dordrecht (2002)
25. Moulinier, I.: Is Learning Bias an Issue on The Text Categorization Problem? Technical report, LAFORIA-LIP6, University Paris VI (1997)
26. Morin, E.: Automatic Acquisition of Semantic Relations between Terms from Technical Corpora. In: Fifth International Congress on Terminology and Knowledge Engineering (1999)
27. McCallum, A., Nigam, K.: A Comparison of Event Models for Naive Bayes Text Classification. In: AAAI 1998 Workshop on Learning for Text Categorization (1998)
28. Maedche, A., Staab, S.: Semi-Automatic Engineering of Ontologies from Text. In: 12th International Conference on Software and Knowledge Engineering, Chicago (2000)
29. Perez, A.G., Benjamins, V.R.: Overview of Knowledge Sharing and Reuse Components: Ontologies and Problem-Solving Methods. In: IJCAI 1999 Workshop on Ontologies and Problem-Solving Methods. Stockholm, Sweden (1999)
30. Quinlan, J.R.: Induction of Decision Tree. Machine Learning (1), 81–106 (1986)
31. Quinlan, J.R.: C4.5: Programs for Machine Learning. Morgan Kaufmann, San Mateo (1993)
32. Roussinov, D., Chen, H.: Document Clustering for Electronic Meetings: An Experimental Comparison of Two Techniques. Decision Support Systems 27(1), 67–79 (1999)
33. Rumelhart, D.E., Hinton, G.E., Williams, R.J.: Learning Internal Representations by Error Propagation. In: Rumelhart, D.E., McClelland, J.L. (eds.) Parallel Distributed Processing Explorations in the Microstructures of Cognition, vol. 1, pp. 318–362. MIT Press, Cambridge (1986)

34. Sebastiani, F.: Machine Learning in Automated Text Categorization. ACM Computing Surveys 34(1), 1–47 (2002)
35. Szpakowicz, S.: Semi-automatic Acquisition of Conceptual Structure from Technical Texts. International Journal of Man-Machine Studies (33) (1990)
36. Suryanto, H., Compton, P.: Learning Classification Taxonomies from A Classification Knowledge Based System. In: Workshop on Ontology Learning, Berlin, Germany (2000)
37. Voutilainen, A.: NPtool: A Detector of English Noun Phrases. In: Workshop on Very Large Corpora, pp. 48–57 (1993)
38. Wei, C., Piramuthu, S., Shaw, M.J.: Knowledge Discovery and Data Mining. In: Holesapple, C. (ed.) Handbook of Knowledge Management (2002)
39. Wache, H., Vgele, T., Visser, U., Stuckenschmidt, H., Schuster, G., Neumann, H., Hbner, S.: Ontology-Based Integration of Information-A Survey of Existing Approaches. In: 17th International Joint Conference on Artificial Intelligence, Seattle, pp. 108–117 (2001)
40. Yamaguchi, T.: Acquiring Conceptual Relationships from Domain-specific Texts. In: Second Workshop on Ontology Learning, Seattle (2001)
41. Yang, Y.: An Evaluation of Statistical Approaches to Text Categorization. Information Retrieval 1(1), 69–90 (1999)
42. Yang, Y., Pedersen, J.: A Comparative Study on Feature Selection in Text Categorization. In: International Conference on Machine Learning, pp. 412–420 (1997)
43. Zelikovitz, S., Hirsh, H.: Using LSI for Text Classification in the Presence of Background Text. In: 10th ACM International Conference on Information and Knowledge Management (2001)

Author Index